A to Z
Guide to
White-tailed Deer
and
Deer Hunting

A to Z
Guide to
White-tailed Deer
and
Deer Hunting

Dr. Randall Gilbert

Front and back cover images: Ted Rose
A special thanks to Ted Rose for allowing us to use his images within the pages of
this book. Ted Rose is a respected wildlife photographer. His high quality images
have appeared in Outdoorsman's Edge, Woods N' Water, Buckmasters, Lyons Press,
Harris Publications and other noted outdoor publications. For a sample of his images,
he can be contacted at 219-982-6261.

All illustrations by Randall Gilbert/Buckhunter Associates.
Photos by: Ted Rose ii, 1, 7, 8, 13 top, 16, 21, 34, 36, 38, 45, 46, 48, 51, 53, 57, 63,
64, 65, 71, 73, 74, 78, 83, 92, 94, 95, 96, 98, 99, 102, 104, 108, 111, 122, 132, 133,
138, 139, 143, 154-156, 162, 164, 171, 174, 177, 178, 182, 187, 190, 192, 196 top,
198, 204, 205, 207, 208, 210, 211, 216, 220, 224, 226, 228, 231.
Fiduccia Enterprises: 13 bottom, 20, 23, 42, 61, 121, 130, 142, 160, 227.
Abbey Hetts/Buckhunter Associates: 76, 148, 215. Winchester Arms: 117.
Winchester-Olin: 31, 167. Pete Rickard, Inc.: 47, 68, 113. Georgia Boot: 67
Eastman's Outdoor World: 196. Thompson/Center Arms: 128.
Copper John: 159. Stoney Point Products, Inc.: 180. Leica: 116, 136.
Published by: Woods N' Water, Inc.
Peter and Kate Fiduccia
P.O. Box 65
Bellvale, NY 10912

Printed in the United States of America
10 9 8 7 6 5 4 3 2 1

ISBN: 0-9707493-9-2

A to Z
Guide to
White-tailed Deer
and
Deer Hunting

DEDICATION

From my youth I retain vivid memories of my father coming home late in the evening on a weekend in mid-November, but usually not alone. Most years he brought a white-tailed buck home with him, and I can remember avidly watching him skin out his deer. Beginning when I was twelve years old, I got up early in the morning and traveled the two hours with him in the dark to New York's Southern Tier and we hunted deer together. At first I watched and absorbed his woods and deer lore. Finally, when I was old enough, I, too, carried a shotgun. The smells of autumn were impregnated upon my memory. Of course, there was always the two-hour ride in the dark back home, again—sometimes not so alone. I owe the love of this sport to my father. Except for my very life itself, a greater gift he could have not given me, nor left me as his legacy!

I often replay in my mind the planning and preparation of the people I have hunted with, the strategies that we planned out and replanned, the deer I have taken and the deer that I have missed, and the lessons of the sport that I seem to learn and relearn over and over again. Each fall, as deer season approaches, I look forward to those long-ago imprinted odors that those first autumn deer left with me. These are the memories, the experiences, and the emotions that I treasure, and the ones that I build upon each season.

So, it is to my original deer hunting instructor and partner, my father, Russell F. Gilbert, that I dedicate my first deer hunting writing venture. He is responsible for my becoming what I am today—a buck hunter!

—Randall Gilbert

INTRODUCTION

This book is a treasure trove of white-tailed deer information, and is purposely written in "huntspeak" style; that is, the universally accepted language of the deer hunter. It is meant to be an all-inclusive work for both the archer and the firearms hunter. It is a compilation of personal trial and error; well-read (but *not* academically researched) and accumulated hard-earned knowledge from over thirty-five years of deer hunting. By paying the tuition and dues to the self-taught whitetail "school of hard knocks," a lifetime of sifting through magazines and books while reading about *Odocoileous virginianus*, engaging in purposeful and off-hand discussions with other hunters, and even absorbing some useful knowledge from hunting videos, several ideas sprang forth so that this work could help the seasoned veteran as well as the neophyte.

Although deer hunting is best experienced with hunting partners, when it comes right down to it, it is really a solitary sport. Most often, it is just you and your quarry going head to head, sense to scents, and maybe even eye to eye. That deer knows the lay of the land better than you ever will. You are in its bedroom, its living room, and its hallway as an uninvited guest. Deer have the advantages of total familiarity. What you as a hunter do there and how much you disturb that deer's home will influence your success.

I can remember having questions in the field or woods about some aspect of deer hunting and there was no immediate source to tap into. My dad or hunting partners were nowhere near and the magazine article that had the answer to my question was not with me. In essence, all I had with me was my memory that often said, "Yeah—I read about that somewhere, but what were the specifics? What should I do about it? What do I need to know so that I can effectively hunt this area now?" With these questions in mind, it would have been convenient to have pulled out a manual such as this and read a quick, yet concise answer to my question. That is the mission of this deer hunting book.

This book has been purposefully made as a resource arranged in alphabetical order. It can easily be a self-contained, armchair hunting trip in and of itself! There is no need for a table of contents, nor an index, as the manual is structured to be used as simply as possible. Think of a word that you have a question about; look it up alphabetically; cross-reference it (if so directed); go to that source and read about that topic. It has many commonly used terms included for cross referencing. But the crucial understandings, explanations, tips, and advice are concise, to-the-point, and above all answer your questions about a white-tailed deer topic.

ABOMASUM One of the four "stomachs" of a ruminant. Actually the fourth, or last, in order of digestion, this is often referred to as the "true stomach," where final absorption takes place. Here nutrients from food are broken down by the digestive juices and absorbed into the bloodstream for distribution to the body. **See Food/Nutrition/ Omasum/Reticulum/Rumen/Ruminant/Stomach.**

ACCESSORIES Any thing, item or helpful piece of hunting equipment that is of secondary importance. An object or device not essential to the hunt, but one that can add to the comfort of the hunter, the accuracy of the shot, or efficiency of the hunt. A list of all available deer hunting accessories would be endless. The variety of models available to the hunter is mind-boggling. Deer hunting equipment and accessories are discussed throughout this manual, rather than specifically listed or identified. Several new products on the market and organizations are exciting additions to the field of white-tailed deer hunting, so they may be specifically named. The choice of what accessories to use in hunting your deer is strictly up to you.

Many pieces of equipment and accessories are discussed throughout this book, as you take your journey through the cross-referenced items. **See All-Terrain Vehicle/ Backpack/Binoculars/Clothing/Equipment/Knife/Safety.**

ACCURACY Placing each shot where the shooter wishes it to go, accuracy depends upon many factors. For firearms, usually the first two to three shots can be predicted to hit where the firearm is aimed. However, after the gun barrel begins to heat up, shot placement creeps and accuracy is often lessened. **See Benchrest/Bipod/Grouping/ Kisser Button/Shooting Sticks/Shot Grouping/Shot Placement/Sighting In.**

ACORN The nut or seed-bearing fruit of the oak tree. White oak acorns are the preferred food source of the white-tailed deer, squirrels, and the turkey because they are high in carbohydrates (a source of energy and fat-building components). The red oak is slightly higher in tannic acid content, and thus more bitter in taste, but only slightly less preferable to wildlife. However, white oak acorns are not produced

New crop acorns.

every year. In lean winters without acorns, other mast crops, such as beechnuts, become the whitetails' favorite food. Deer have been known to abruptly abandon other food sources when the acorns start dropping. Wise hunters know where the oaks are located on the property that they hunt. They must be prepared to change their hunting strategies because once the acorns start falling, deer will find them. Fallen acorns rank at the top of the list as a preferred wintertime energy source for deer. The savvy hunter can use binoculars to check out the abundance of acorns while scouting for hunting hotspots. **See Beechnuts/Deciduous/Food/Hardwoods/Mast/Nuts/Oak/Preparation/ Scents/Scouting.**

ADRENAL GLANDS/ADRENALINE Glands located on each of a deer's kidneys are a primary source of adrenaline or epinephrine hormones. When a deer is frightened, part of these glands secrete this "fight or flight" hormone directly into the bloodstream, causing the heart to beat faster and the liver to release more glucose or blood sugars so that the body can respond appropriately to the newfound threat. The adrenal glands are also a secondary source of testosterone, often initiating the start of antler production in the springtime. However, they do not produce enough to finish the antler cycle of velvet shedding, antler hardening, and shed casting. A buck that inadvertently castrates itself while its antlers are still in velvet (for example, by becoming caught or hung up jumping a fence,) will probably see its resultant antlers form weird shapes, often called "cactus" antlers. **See Antlers/Cactus Buck/Cast/Castration/"Fight or Flight"/Hypogonadism/Injuries/Pedicle/Rut/Scent Marking/Shed/ Testes/Testosterone/Velvet.**

AERIAL PHOTOGRAPHS Also known as topographical photographs, these pictures of the land are taken by the Agricultural and/or Forestry Services of the U.S. government, the state, and sometimes by county extension offices (such as the Soil Conservation Service). Hunters can even hire private air services that will provide photographs of the area that they intend to hunt. By reviewing these maps, hunters can determine that some areas offer better habitat for deer than others. These aerial photographs allow hunters to get a feel for the "lay of the land" and identify funnels, ravines, creeks, rivers, and other water sources, changes in vegetation, power lines, potential hotspots, a buck's core area, and other topographical features. To order base maps and aerial photographs of land that you might hunt on, send your inquiries to

USGS   (United States Geological Service)
Washington, DC-ESIC (Earth Science Information and Sales Center)
U.S. Department of the Interior
1849 C Street, N.W., Room 2650
Washington, DC 20240
(202) 208-4047

See Aerial Survey/Balanced Herd/Bureau of Land Management/Compass/ Contours/Maps/Navigation/Orienteering/Orthophotoquad/Scouting/Soil Conservation Service/Terrain.

AERIAL SURVEY An estimate of the size of the deer herd in certain sections of a state or province made by flying over the prescribed section and actually counting the number of deer within it. This information, coupled with road-kill numbers, previous hunting take, and so on, allows the conservation departments to establish the number of whitetails to be harvested and thus the number of deer management permits to be issued. **See Aerial Photographs/Balance of Nature/Balanced Herd/ Biologist/Carrying Capacity/Census/Herd Size.**

AFTER THE SHOT A moment when it is important to keep your eye on the deer and observe it until it either falls down, lies down, or walks out of sight. Keep listening for a while and you might hear it collapse. Do not assume that you missed. You owe it to your quarry to follow up after every shot. **See Approaching Downed Deer/ Downed Deer/Follow-Up/Going Away Shot/Hair/Shot/Tracks/Wounded Game.**

AFTERBIRTH The placenta or maternal organs and tissues that provided sustenance to a mammal while it matured inside the mother. Soon after a fawn is born, does expel the afterbirth and typically eat it so as to leave no scent to attract predators. **See Amniotic Fluid/Birth/Fawn/Fetus/Nursing/Placenta/Twins.**

AGE OF BUCKS The stages of a deer's life. Fawns are the deer born in May or June of that year. By hunting season, most fawns will have lost their spots and can keep up running with their mother. A hunter can identify a fawn from older deer; in that a fawn is square-shaped, while an adult deer is rectangular. The majority of bucks are shot before they reach the age of three years.

> **A. Button buck (.5 year old)**—Most buck fawns only produce hair-covered knobs on their pedicles (where their antlers will grow) their first year of life. These are not readily identifiable by hunters except by feel if they have shot a button buck by mistake.
>
> **B. Yearling Buck (1.5 year old)**—The next year bucks usually produce a rack ranging from spikes to four or six points, depending upon genetics and the quality of the food source. Yearlings make up the bulk of number of bucks taken each year mainly because of their inexperience.
>
> **C. Buck (2.5-3.5 year old)**—Surviving bucks start producing increasingly better racks each year.
>
> **D. Buck (4.5-5.5 year old)**—This is usually the prime time for a dominant buck, when he is genetically at his best, reproductively viable, and displays his best rack.
>
> **E. Buck (6.5-7.5+ year old)**—At this age bucks are beginning to physiologically decline in body strength, antler size, and so on; accompanied by loss of dominance and breeding status.

The adult white-tailed deer has thirty teeth in its mouth. The most accurate way to properly age a deer is to pull one of those teeth, cross cut it, and count the rings, just like aging a tree trunk. That process must be performed by a professional, however, and is thus impractical in the field. **See Antlers/Biologist/Cementum/Fawn/ Graze/Incisors/Molars/Spike/Teeth/Yearling Buck.**

AGGRESSION Fight-like actions that can include charging, foot flailing, and so on. Both bucks and does can exhibit behavior that leads to actual physical contact with members of both sexes within their species and against other animals and threats of danger. **See Aggressive Snort/Agonistic Behavior/Bachelor Buck Groups/ Dominance/Fighting/Flail/Hierarchy/Sparring/ Testosterone.**

AGGRESSIVE SNORT This call consists of two to six blasts of sharply expelled air made in quick succession. They are often made when a buck deer feels like expressing his dominance or even fighting. **See Aggression/Agonistic Behavior/Alarm Snort/Deer Blow/Communication/Foot Stomp/Snort/Snort Wheeze/Sounds in the Deer Woods.**

AGING MEAT Hanging venison for several days (up to a week) after the deer has been field dressed and properly cleaned. This "aging process," whether in a meat hanger under controlled temperatures or outside at ambient temperatures just above freezing (thirty-four to thirty-eight degrees) supposedly allows for tenderization to occur through the natural breakdown of tissue structure. At higher temperatures (above forty degrees) spoilage, insects (flies laying eggs in/on the meat), and other forms of contamination are all of concern for the proper handling, future taste, and tenderness of the venison. **See Ambient Temperature/Buck Pole/Field Dressing/Gamey Taste/ Recipes/Skinning/Venison.**

AGONISTIC BEHAVIOR Aggressive behavior. A deer's nostrils are flared, its back hairs are erect, and it emits snorts and snort-wheezes. With its head lowered, it walks with a stiff-legged gait toward another buck. Get ready for a fight, as neither buck will be willing to give ground to the other. **See Aggression/Aggressive Snort/Alpha Buck/Bachelor Buck Groups/Dominance/Fighting/Flailing/Hierarchy/ Sparring/Testosterone.**

AIR CURRENTS Wind, or the flow of air, caused by the difference in temperatures between two areas of the earth's surface. Air currents generally move from a cold area to a warmer area. Cold air sinks, while warm air rises. **See Cross Wind/Downwind/ Exposure/Scent/Stand/Thermals/Upwind/Wind.**

ALARM POSTURE The "alert" mode that results when a deer has become fearful or alarmed over some perceived danger. A hunter can determine how alarmed the deer is by how high it is holding its head. At full alert the head is high, the eyes are focused, the ears are bent forward, and the tail is erect or at least flared. This indicates that the deer is ready to bolt or run away. **See Alert Snort/Blow/Communication/Ears/ Foot Stomp/Head Bob/Hearing/Snort/Snort Wheeze/Sounds in the Deer Woods/Vocalization.**

4

ALARM SNORT The loud sound of a deer blowing air forcefully through its nose or mouth that signals it has possibly discovered danger. Other deer hear this loud sound and go into an alerted state themselves. The "alarm snort" is the prevalent sound a hunter hears when he or she has been discovered and identified by the deer as a threat. **See Aggressive Snort/Alarm Posture/Alert Snort/Blow/ Communication/Ears/Snort/Snort Wheeze/Sounds in the Deer Woods/ Spooked/Vocalization.**

ALBINO(ISM) The absence of any pigment, which is usually controlled by the pituitary gland. An all-white deer features pink ears, lips, and eyes. True albino whitetails are extremely rare. A partially albino deer—called "piebald"—sports large white or dark spots on its hide. **See Melanistic/Pelage/Piebald/Pink-Eyed Deer/Pituitary Gland.**

ALERT SNORT A loud, nasal sound made by an alarmed deer, either standing still at alert or after it has sprinted a few yards to perceived safety. The deer is attempting to get the disturbance to identify itself in some way. A hunter who has disturbed a deer and hears this sound might try to "snort" back so as to indicate that he or she is another deer or utilize a turkey call. **See Alarm Posture/ Alarm Snort/Blow/Calls/Communication/Ears/Foot Stomp/ Head Bob/Hearing/Snort/Vocalization.**

ALFALFA A farm legume crop grown as silage and cattle feed. Alfalfa is extremely high in protein content and therefore is also a preferred food for whitetails. It is often planted by hunters to attract and keep deer on their own land. **See Crop Damage/Feeding Areas/ Field/Food Plot.**

ALLOMONE A chemical signal that gives the sender an advantage. (Skunk essence is a good example. Just the general odor about the skunk says that it would be unpleasant to attack or deal with, so "Leave me alone!") **See Communication/Kairomone/ Pheromone/Scent/Skunk.**

Buck on alert.

5

ALL-TERRAIN VEHICLE/ATV Any vehicle, usually with four or six wheels, and all-wheel drive, that allows hunters to gain greater access to their hunting camps and new hunting lands and to go further into the wilderness. **See Accessories/Snowmobile/ Equipment/Snowmobile.**

ALPHA BUCK The most dominant or "boss" buck. This buck is the top breeding buck and often the buck with the biggest rack of antlers. **See Agonistic Behavior/Bachelor Buck Groups/Boss Buck/Breeding/Fighting/Hierarchy/ Locking of Antlers/Mass/Mossyback/Rack/Sparring/Trophy.**

AMBIENT TEMPERATURE The outside temperature. **See Aging Meat/Temperature/Weather.**

AMMUNITION The projectile expelled from the barrel of a firearm, generally known as a bullet. These projectiles come in many sizes, shapes, or calibers. **See Ballistics/Bullet/Caliber/Factory Load/Firearms/Foot Pounds of Energy/ Gauge/Handgun/Handload/Kinetic Energy/Knock Down Power/Rifle.**

AMNIOTIC FLUID The protective cushion of water surrounding the fetus in the mother's womb. It is usually expelled first at the time of birth. It is followed by the newborn and then its afterbirth. **See Afterbirth/Birth/Fetus/Placenta.**

ANCHOR POINT A definite spot on the face, neck, chin, lips, ear, and so on that archers consistently touches when bringing their bow back to full draw. This consistency contributes to the hunters' accuracy of arrow placement. **See Bow and Arrow/ Draw/Finger Shooter/Kisser Button/Mechanical Release/Nock.**

ANTHRAX An extremely infectious disease, fatal to humans. Its bacteria and spores occur naturally in the soil, particularly in cattle country. Occasionally, due to over-population, white-tailed deer have been known to contract anthrax. **See Diseases/ Hunting Maladies/Parasites.**

ANTHROPOMORPHIC The attribution of human senses, feelings, and characteristics to animals, plants, or inanimate objects, such as in cartoons involving cute animals. **See Anti- Hunters/"Bambi" Syndrome/Disneyfication/Ethics/Sportsmanship.**

ANTI-HUNTERS A segment of the non hunting population that uses unethical methods and disseminates false information about hunting and hunters with the express purpose of denying this sport to those who do hunt. Anti-hunters often operate with little or no knowledge about conservation, overcrowding of the land, loss of habitat and die-off. Hunters are not going to change the antihunters' viewpoint except by being totally ethical and law-abiding. They should not flaunt or show off their quarry, thus giving antihunters no opportunity to criticize hunting. **See Anthropomorphic/ Bambi Syndrome/Disneyfication/Ethics/Sportsmanship.**

ANTLERS/ANTLER CYCLE   Hard head projections formed from mineral deposits similar to skeletal bones, are grown new annually, are used for adornment, sparring (fighting), and breeding dominance before and during the rut. They are grown new annually and shed each year after the breeding season. Deer antlers are not horns. Horns, as in mountain goat or sheep, are permanent, continually growing, and are made of a tough protein material similar to a cow's hoof.

Antlers are the fastest growing (up to one-half inch per day) animal organ known to science. Antler growth is hormonally activated in the springtime as the hours of sunlight lengthen (known as photoperiodism). The amount of light entering through the buck's eye causes the pineal gland in the buck's brain to secrete hormones, which in turn initiate the production of testosterone (the male sex hormone) in the testes. Testosterone causes antlers to grow from the two pedicles on top of the buck's head. The budding antlers are covered in a soft, velvety material that is warm to the touch and easily damaged. This living tissue is full of nerves and blood vessels and takes calcium and other minerals directly from the buck's skeleton.

Production of testosterone reaches its peak just before the rut. By then, the buck's antlers have reached their peak growth and become fully hardened under the velvet. He then begins to rub off the velvet covering and probably eats it for its mineral content. This hardening of the antlers and maximum rack size are timed perfectly for the buck's breeding season. Likewise, when the peak of the rut is over, testosterone production in the buck's testes decreases (in response to decreasing periods of sunlight) and the buck's aggressive attitude and behavior changes. He becomes more docile and less aggressive toward other deer. By January or February, the base of the buck's antlers have become weakened enough that they will begin to fall off. The pedicle area heals over, the buck goes into a winter survival mode. The whole process will start up again in a few weeks, when the

Antlers

Broken antler

increasing length of sunlight will trigger the growth of a new set of antlers.

Besides superior nutrition requirements and years (3.5-6.5) of maturity, for a buck to grow a "trophy" set of antlers, good genetic stock is also required. Huge-antlered bucks tend to produce the same genetic trait in their offspring. A yearling spike buck is generally considered genetically inferior and more than likely will not produce a trophy rack in later years. There is some consideration that poor mineral (calcium, phosphorous) supply in the soil or poor food quality will hold back a buck's antler development. A buck's best rack will occur at five and a half to seven and a half years of age if he lives that long. Thereafter, his rack dimensions start to deteriorate. Sometimes, an older buck will develop "drop tines," or downward facing points on his rack.

Before signs of the rut begin (prerut), hunters should only rattle antlers in a light fashion. Once rut signs appear, bucks are actively fighting for dominance and breeding rights. Rattling antlers together, raking them through the leaves or against bushes, using grunts, and so on during this phase simulates two bucks fighting and can serve to call in a buck, who wants to see who the combatants are, and if there is a "hot" doe (one coming into estrus) that he can steal from them. **See Beam/Bifurcate/Browtine/Drop Tine/Forkhorn/Genetics/Keratin/Mass/Non-typical/Ossification/Pedicle/Spread/Testosterone/Typical/Velvet.**

ANUS The posterior end of the alimentary canal; the exit place of the rectum where the whitetail eliminates its fecal droppings (solid waste). **See Droppings/Fecal Droppings/Field Dressing/Internal Organs/Rectum.**

APPLES/APPLE TREES One of the whitetail's favorite fall foods. Deer have been known to travel miles from their core area (home range) when apples start falling from the trees. Deer readily gorge themselves on apples and stay in the area until most have been consumed. Farmers and hunters have both reported incidences of deer eating so many apples and so often that they became intoxicated (drunk), start to stumble around and bump into objects. Deer are also fond of pears, persimmon, and other available fruit. **See Crab Apple/Crop Damage/Food/Fruit/Hygiene/Orchards/ Pears/Permission to Hunt/Persimmons/Soft Mast.**

APPROACHING DOWNED DEER An action that should be taken with caution Never run up to a downed deer and grab its antlers to examine them. Campfire stories abound of neophyte hunters who placed their gun or bow in their first buck's antlers and backed off for a picture, only to see the deer awaken, get up, and run off—hunter's weapon and all. Always approach a downed deer from behind, being extremely aware that it may just be stunned. If it senses that you are close, it will lash out with its hooves or antlers. Look at the deer's eyes; if they are glazed over, the deer is probably dead. Touch the deer's open eye with a stick or an arrow: No reaction from any part of the body indicates that the deer is dead. **See After the Shot/Downed Deer/ Ethics/Follow-Up/Hair/Tracks/Wounded Game.**

APPROACHING DOWNED DEER

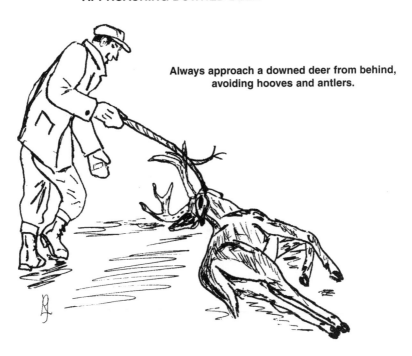

Always approach a downed deer from behind, avoiding hooves and antlers.

Touching a live deer in the eye with a stick will cause it to react, necessitating a follow-up shot.

AQUATIC VEGETATION Plants growing in water and along the banks of a creek, river, or lake. White-tailed deer have been observed eating aquatic plants **See Creek Bottom/Food/ Swamp/Water.**

ARCHERY A generalized term used to refer to the art, practice, or skill in using a bow and arrow to shoot at paper targets, 3-D animals targets, or in the sport of bowhunting. **See Arrowhead/Arrow Speed/Arrow Weight/Bow and Arrow/Bowhunting/ Feathers/Kisser Button/Nocking Loop/Nocking Point/Release.**

AROMATIC A strongly scented tree or bush such as cedar or pine, that imparts a strong smell or odor when bruised or broken, such as when a whitetail rubs the bark off with its antlers. Hunters also use these strong odors to cover up or mask their own human scent, in hopes that the deer will come near them. **See Antler/Cover Scent/ Rub/Scent/Signpost/Velvet.**

ARROWHEAD The sharp point or tip of a hunting arrow used to penetrate the hide, muscle, vital organs and sometimes bone of the white-tailed deer. Examples are
    A. Fixed broadhead. A tip with two or more flat cutting blades that can cause the arrow to plane or curve at the shot.
    B. Mechanical broadhead. A hunting tip built to fly like a field/practice point. These tips open up upon contact with the deer's body, exposing razor-sharp cutting edges, thus causing much bleeding.
    C. Field point/practice point. A tip used to tune your bow, improve your accuracy, and be used over and over again, without damaging or dulling your actual hunting points. Field points are best matched to the actual weight of your hunting point. Be sure to practice shooting with the type and tip of hunting arrows that you will actually use in the field.
    D. Judo point. A practice tip used for shooting at stumps, clumps of grass, and so on. The wire side projections usually catch onto something and flip the arrow up, making it easily recoverable.
    E. Blunt. A hard rubber tip or a pistol bullet casing that fits the arrow shaft and is used for small-game hunting in the field.
    See Archery/Broadheads/Equipment/Hemorrhage/Mechanical Broadheads.

ARROW SPEED The speed of an arrow leaving the bow. The faster the arrow, the flatter its trajectory. No matter how fast an arrow is, however, gravity will still pull it down at a constant rate, but because of its increased speed, the arrow will travel further. **See Archery/Arrow Head/Arrow Weight/Draw Weight.**

ARROW WEIGHT Lighter arrows are generally faster than heavier arrows but they have less penetration energy. Too light an arrow (low spine) will not absorb enough of the recoil of the bow's energy and could cause vibrations that adversely affect the bow, possibly causing damage. **See Archery/Arrow Head/Arrow Speed/ Draw Weight.**

ARTHROPOD Invertebrate animals that have articulated or jointed bodies or limbs, such as insects (ticks), arachnids (spiders), crustaceans (crabs, crawfish, or lobsters). **See Health/Hunting Maladies/Ixodes Tick/Lyme Disease/Parasites/Ticks.**

ARTIFICIAL INSEMINATION The nonnatural act of manually breeding a doe using a buck's semen but not his "delivery system," or genitalia. This breeding system is used by game farms, high-fence hunting operations, and others for propagating and selectively advancing the highly desirable characteristics of whitetails that hunter seek. **See Breeding/Contraception/Copulation/Ejaculation.**

ARTIODACTYLA Even toed. White-tailed deer have four toes or metacarpals on each leg: two main hooves and two "dewclaws" located higher up the leg. **See Cloven Hooves/Dewclaws/Hooves/Metacarpals/Splay/Toes/Tracks.**

ATROPHY The withering or diminishing of a muscle or organ through non-use or injury. **See Hunting Maladies/Injury/Parasites.**

ATTITUDE An important factor in hunters' success. A positive, optimistic outlook and belief that they will ultimately tag a deer and allows hunters to remain on stand longer, be patient, and be there when the deer comes by. **See Ethics/Poaching/Sportsmanship.**

ATTRACTANT SCENT This refers to commercially made or homegrown lures that are designed to "lure" or bring whitetails within bow or gun range. Lures can be a food such as acorn, apple, or corn; sex such as estrus or doe-in-heat, doe urine, or buck scrape; or the nebulously termed "curiosity" lures. All are designed to be wafted upon the breezes and draw the whitetail to a shooting lane. **See Allomone/Estrus/Kairomone/Lures/Repellent/Scent.**

ATV See All-Terrain Vehicle.

AUTOLOADER/AUTO-RIFLE/AUTO-SHOTGUN A type of mechanical action of a firearm. Once it has been cocked, pulling the trigger will activate the firing mechanism, automatically eject the spent cartridge, and inject a live load, so that the trigger is ready to be pulled again. This type of firearm is not to be confused with a truly automatic firearm that repeatedly fires ammunition when the trigger is held back. **See Bolt Action/Lever Action/Pump Action.**

AUTOMOBILE-DEER ACCIDENTS Deer hit by automobiles. The number of accidents takes a drastic upswing in the fall of the year. One can easily correlate this increase to the breeding season. During this time bucks greatly expand their range, casting caution to the wind, and seek out does who are emitting estrous pheromones. **See Blood Trailing Dogs/Chase Phase/Pheromones/Prerut/Rut/Wounded Deer.**

AUTUMN The season between summer and winter; also called fall because all the nuts and leaves seem to "fall" or drop off the trees at the same time each year, sometime after the first hard frost. During autumn deciduous trees turn color in some parts of the country and farmers usually harvest their crops. Whitetail hunting season usually begins in autumn. **See Autumnal Equinox/Chlorophyll/Harvest Moon/ Leaf Drop/Photosynthesis/Seasons.**

AUTUMNAL EQUINOX Usually occurs about September 23 of each year, when the length of daylight hours equals the length of nighttime hours. Deer are sensitive to the decreasing amount of sunlight as this helps trigger the onset of the breeding season or rut. **See Autumn/Harvest Moon/Hunter's Moon/Moon/Solstice/Vernal Equinox.**

BABY TEETH The first set of teeth that a mammal baby has, also referred to as "milk teeth." They are usually replaced with a permanent set later as the baby's diet changes from milk to solid food. **See Age of Deer/Colostrum/Fawn/Nursing/Teeth.**

BACHELOR BUCK GROUPS Small groups of bucks of the same age class who travel together for much of the year. They generally are not aggressive toward each other at this time, which is just prior to the "false rut" in early October. Although they can physically breed once their velvet comes off, bucks are still primarily interested in

food. But once those special feelings that come about when an increase of testosterone occurs in their bodies, each buck begins to change into a solitary "breeding machine." He then is on the lookout for does in heat (estrus) and does not want any competition from other bucks. The bachelor groups break up into individual breeders, only to reform again after the rutting

Bachelor Buck Groups

season is over. **See Aggression/Agonistic Behavior/Core Area/Dominance/Hierarchy/Home Range/ Rut/Sparring.**

BACK COVER Natural material such as limbs. leaves, tree trunks, and so on used to break up a hunter's silhouette. If none exists, it is relatively easy to make your own back cover. Just cut branches or brush, and tie them to the back and sides of the tree, thus breaking up your outline. **See Camouflage(Hunter)/Silhouette/Skyline.**

Backpack

BACKPACK A carrier for items brought into the field that are usually too big to fit in a fanny pack, such as an extra sweatshirt or binoculars. A backpack can also be used to pack out meat, antlers, and so on. **See Accessories/Equipment/Fanny Pack/First Aid/Flashlight/ Safety/Survival.**

BACKSTOP What is directly in back of a target. If another hunter could possibly be in back of your target, it is better to pass or wait on it until a better, safer shot opportunity is offered. **See Safety(Hunter)/Shot Placement.**

BACK STRAP The long muscles located adjacent to the spinal column on the outside of a whitetail's back. These muscles are considered second only to the tenderloins in delicacy. Similar muscles are located internally along the spine on the whitetail. Other venison cuts include roasts, chops, steaks, shanks, sausage, venison burger, and stew meat. **See Field Dressing/Gamey Taste/Jerky/Recipes/Tenderloins/Venison.**

BACKTRACKING An effective method to discover the bedding area of deer by following their trails from the feeding areas back up a hillside or into thick cover. Often staging areas, rub lines, scrapes, and daytime bedding areas will be discovered. **See Backtrail/Beds/Doubling Back/Rub Line/Scrapes/Staging Area/Tracks.**

BACK-TRAIL The line of travel from one area to another leading from where the deer currently is to where it came from. A white-tailed deer often moves so that it can look back at its own trail just to see if it is being followed by a predator, a buck in search of an estrous doe, and so on. Deer will even bed down in a preferred location (a bench or a slope on a hillside, for example) that will let them observe their own incoming trail. **See Back Tracking/Beds/Cover/Doubling Back/Escape Route/Vision.**

BAITING/BAIT HUNTING Hunting over a pile of corn, sugar beets, alfalfa pellets, apples, or a salt block purposely set out to lure deer. This practice is legal in about half of the states that have deer hunting. Be sure that you know the game laws regarding this hunting technique for your area. **See Controlled Hunt/Dogs/Ethics/Fair Chase/High Fence Hunting/Managed Hunt/Outfitters/Poaching/Saltlick.**

BALANCE OF NATURE An often misused phrase that refers to the equilibrium or "balanced" state of all living creatures that supposedly would exist in the wild if nature was left alone. In truth, this so-called balance is in a constant state of flux and adjustment. For example, as predators increase in numbers due to an adequate supply of prey animals, those very prey animals must increase their production in order for their species to be sustained. If their numbers are decreased to below their species survival rate, the predator animal also starves and dies off if it cannot find an alternative source of prey. **See Aerial Survey/Antihunters/Biologist/Buck-Doe Ratio/ Carrying Capacity/Census/Die-Off/Herd Size/Winterkill.**

BALANCED HERD A herd with the proper ratio of bucks to does. Biologists tell us that the ideal ratio is one to one. A more realistic figure for a deer population in balance with its environment is three does per buck. In a well-balanced whitetail population, most does are bred by the prime or dominant buck. **See Aerial Survey/Buck-Doe Ratio/ Carrying Capacity/Conservation Department/Die-Off/Doe Harvest/Habitat/Herd Size/Quality Deer Management/Skewed Ratio/ Winterkill.**

BALLISTICS The statistical charting of the effects that bullet weight, amount of powder or propellant behind the bullet, muzzle velocity, barrel rifling, and so on, have after the bullet leaves the barrel of the firearm. These effects include bullet speed, downrange distance, height above and below the aimpoint. **See Ammunition/Bullets/Firearms/ Foot Pounds of Energy/Muzzle Velocity/Pistol/ Rifle/Rifled Slug/Shotgun.**

BAMBI SYNDROME The idea that animals share human traits and characteristics. The name comes from an early Walt Disney animated movie that depicts a young deer's mother being shot by "man." Deer hunters are often referred to by the anti-hunting world as "Bambi killers." In fact, hunting is the best deer conservation method. **See Anthropomorphic/Antihunters/Disneyfication/Ethics/Poaching.**

BAROMETER/BAROMETRIC PRESSURE A device that measures atmospheric pressure. A hunter should be aware of changes in barometric pressure. White-tailed deer sense pressure changes long before hunters experience an actual change in the weather. Deer movement always seems to increase with a change in the barometric reading. A constant wind in the evening, lasting into nightfall, is a good indication that the barometric pressure is going to change (that is a front is coming in). A rising barometer indicates fair or good weather is on the way. A falling barometer signals the approach of worsening weather. **See Crepuscular Activity/Diurnal Activities/ Fronts/Lunar Influence/Moon/Movement/Nocturnal/Pressure/Storms/ Weather/Wind.**

BASAL METABOLIC RATE Calculated with an organism at rest, this basic food consumption figure is determined by the amount of energy or calories needed to maintain an organism's functioning. White-tailed deer burn up calories from their body fat reserves during the winter, when food is scarce. To assist them in their survival, their metabolism rate is slowed down. **See Food/Metabolism/Nutrition/Winter Feeding.**

BAWL See Blat.

BEAD A small metal or fluorescent knob located on a firearm's barrel used as a front sight. **See Accuracy/Laser/Line of Sight.**

BEAM/ANTLER BEAM The main stem of a whitetail buck's antlers from which branch other points or tines. Biologists use a yearling buck's antler beam diameter as an index to a deer's physical condition and the quality of its range. **See Antlers/Drop tine/G-1/G-2/Main Beam/Point/Rack/Spread/Tine.**

BEAR A predator of whitetail fawns. Bear are aggressive and opportunistic carnivores and are at the top of the food chain, with no enemies, except man. **See Food Chain/Predator/Prey.**

BEAR, FRED An early and successful bowhunter who became famous for his instinctive shooting skills and use of traditional bowhunting equipment. Inspired by the archery exploits of Saxton Pope and Art Young in 1925, Bear jumped headlong into a fifty year career in archery. He traveled the world seeking to improve the equipment used in the sport of bowhunting and the techniques of wildlife management. He founded Bear Archery, a bow and bowyer equipment manufacturer. Fred Bear died in 1988, but not before inpiring bowhunters around the world and leaving a proud legacy of appreciation for bowhunting. **See Archery/Boone and Crockett Club/Bow and Arrow/Pope & Young.**

BED/BEDDING AREA Places where deer have lain down to rest and possibly continue their digestion process ("chewing their cud"). Finding several beds together, accompanied by multiple droppings scattered about and numerous tracks is a good indication of a bedding area. This is where the deer spend the majority of their day.

Mid-Day Bed

Deer usually bed down with their noses facing the prevailing wind or air currents so as to detect predators. A bedding area will often be used over again if it affords the deer good visibility of predators approaching and ease of access to escape cover. Beds are oval impressions in grass, snow, or leaves, where the vegetation has been matted down or even cleared away. Beds found in open cover near feeding areas are typically nighttime beds, while those found in heavier cover, usually on a ridge or hillside, are daytime beds.

By midmorning, deer are usually in their beds. Except for a brief mid-day feeding close by, that is where they will stay for most of the day, if undisturbed, chewing their cud, resting, and occasionally getting up to stretch. Daytime bedding areas are usually located in thick, brushy areas as well as on the top of wooded ridges. Bucks often like to lie down next to a blown-down tree, facing downhill for a visual perspective of what is below it and taking advantage of rising thermals for scenting any danger. Numerous rubs close together are a sign of a buck's bedding area. This core area will be located on elevated ground, close to cover, and have a commanding view of the surrounding area. A hunter's chances for tagging a buck improve greatly, if he or she knows the primary bedding area of a buck. **See Back Tracking/Backtrail/ Bench/Core Area/Deer Sign/Habitat/Home Range/Stand Placement/Tracks.**

BEECHNUT The second favorite nut or mast crop (after acorns) of the whitetail. Beechnuts have a buttery taste and are a high-calorie, high-energy food source. The availability of beechnuts is limited because of unpredictable yearly production. Beech trees blossom every year and produce the triangular shaped, burry hulls, but only fill out the meaty nuts inside every two to five years. Various factors, such as lack of proper moisture, poor soil fertility, or early frosts, can limit nut production. In years when the nuts do fall, turkeys, opossums, squirrels, raccoons, blue jays and other large birds will rival the deer for their consumption.

Beech trees are easy to identify in the woods. The tree itself has gray bark that is relatively smooth. After the first frost, beech leaves turn yellow but do not fall off. They then turn golden and ultimately brown in color; but still do not drop. After all the other leaves have fallen, a beech tree will still have its adornments. In fact, the beech leaves will not drop until spring's new buds come forth.

Beechnuts falling to the ground will literally carpet the forest floor. Interestingly, the nut drop often occurs during a two-to-three week period in late October and early November that corresponds roughly to the peak breeding period of the rut. Particularly in the middle and upper Southern states, hunters near a beech tree that is dropping nuts will find hungry does, *and* their amorous suitors, whitetail bucks. The sound of beechnuts falling to the ground should alert the hunter because whitetails, too, hear this and will not yield to the other animals who also seek out this highly nutritious nut. **See Acorns/Deciduous/Food/Hardwoods/Mast/Nuts/Oaks.**

BEGINNER'S LUCK Behavior by a neophyte hunter that causes a wise old buck to make a mistake. Being in the right place at the right time and being lucky enough not to make any noise, leave any scent, or move so as to be detected, could result in the beginning hunter tagging his or her first buck. **See Planning/Preparation.**

BENCH A natural-occurring terrace or shelf-like, flat area along a hillside where deer can travel without being silhouetted against the sky. Benches are often a preferred bedding site for whitetails. **See Beds/Corridor/Deer Sign/Habitat/Silhouette/ Skylined/Stand Placement/Terrain/Travel Corridor.**

BENCHREST A stationary surface at a firing range where shooters can sit down, stabilize their firearms, and accurately adjust their sights so that the firearm hits close to where they are aiming. **See Accuracy/Bipod/Deer Camp/Preparation/Shot Placement/Sighting In/Zeroing In.**

BERGMANN'S RULE A biological principle that states that the farther north one goes from the equator, the larger members of any warm-blooded animal species will be. The reason for this observed phenomenon is that more body volume is needed for the animal to survive the increasingly colder winters as one goes north. Also called the borealis effect. **See Body Weight/Borealis Effect/Latitude.**

BEZOAR STONE Also called a "madstone," this calcified mass is found in the reticulum (the second of its four stomachs) of ruminants. It is formed when an indigestible object is coated with layers of calcium. **See Calcification/Reticulum/Stomach.**

BIFURCATE The splitting of antler tines into one or more points. Whitetail antlers typically do not branch out as do mule deer's antlers but rather each tine grows out of the main beam. **See Antlers/Browtine/G-1/G-2/Main Beam/Points/Rack/Spread/Tines/Trophy.**

BINOCULARS Optical equipment used to enhance a hunter's vision. Binoculars are useful to scan the field from a distance so as not to spook game or alert them to your presence, or to glass (watch) mast-producing trees to help you decide where to hang a tree stand. They also can be an important tool to confirm what you have seen or failed to see with your naked eyes. It is recommended that the hunter use at least an 8X model for hunting in thick cover but a 10X model if he hunts in fields or more open terrain. **See Accessories/Equipment/Glassing/Laser/Night Vision/Optics/Range Finder/Scope/Shot Placement.**

BINOCULAR VISION Seeing with both eyes, which allows for depth perception and judging of distance. Because predators have their eyes located facing forward and thus can focus intently on their prey, they possess better depth perception than do animals of prey, which typically have their eyes placed on the sides of their heads. **See Eyes/Night Vision/Predator/Prey/Vision.**

BIODIVERSITY A wide variety of flora (plants) and fauna (animals). To be biologically successful, a habitat must have a biodiversity in order to allow for symbiosis, evolution, and/or indirect support for each species to fully develop and flourish. The greater the diversity of a biomass, the greater the chances of habitat success for any one species. **See Biomass/Crossbreeding/Dispersal/Diversity/Habitat/Inbreeding.**

BIFURCATION of Antlers

Mule Deer - Yes

White-tailed Deer - No

BIOLOGIST (DEER/WILDLIFE) An academically, behaviorally, or observationally trained observer and professional scientist who interacts with wildlife, with a particular emphasis on the ungulates of the cervidea family: that is, the white-tailed deer. Usually employed by a state's department of conservation or natural resources, their services are often called upon to manage the deer numbers for the state, set hunting quotas, issue management tags, review habitat and so on. Your regional biologist should be able to tell you exactly when the rut will occur in your area. **See Aerial Survey/Age of Deer/Balance of Nature/Balanced Herd/Carrying Capacity/ Conservation Department/Deer Check Station/Doe Permit/Ethics/Fair Chase/Game Warden/ Habitat/Herd Size.**

BIOMASS In the case of white-tailed deer, the entire vegetative choice of food; including grasses, forbs, mushrooms, nuts (acorn, beechnut, and so on), lichens, buds, browse, leaves, apples, and persimmons. **See Alfalfa/Biodiversity/Browse/ Buds/ Food/Food Plot/Forbs/Mushrooms/Nuts.**

BIPOD Handy, two legged supports usually attached to the front stock of a rifle. They are useful in open areas where natural gun rests are scarce. **See Accuracy/Benchrest/Rest/Shooting Sticks/Shot Placement.**

BIRTH/BIRTHING TERRITORY The act of producing offspring. The first year that she is of breeding age, a doe usually gives birth to one fawn. Thereafter, two fawns are usually born, and triplets are not unheard of. When she is nearly ready to give birth, a doe will drive off her previous fawns in order to prevent any chance of her new fawns imprinting on another deer. She will seek out her "birthing territory," excluding all others from it both for the privacy during the birth, when she is very vulnerable, and later to protect the hidden fawns until they are ready to travel with her. **See Afterbirth/Doe/Fawn/Gestation/Imprinting/Nursing/Placenta/Twins/Yearling Buck.**

BLACK BEAR See Bear.

BLACK FLIES Also called "No-See-Ums," a tiny black biting insect of the northern forest that gets under your collar or up your sleeve, and produces an irritating itch where it has bitten you and taken a little of your blood. They seemingly exist by the millions as they swarm around you, looking for a bare piece of skin to ravage. Be careful of scratching their irritating bites, as the then-open sores can easily become infected. **See Hunting Maladies/No-See-Um/Parasites.**

BLACK POWDER An explosive mixture made up of sulfur, saltpeter, and charcoal used as the propellant in firearms such as flintlocks, muzzleloaders, and so on. Black powder must be ignited from a spark (for example a flint spark or firing cap) or electrically in the new in-line muzzleloaders. **See Firearm/Foot-pounds of Energy/ Gun/Gunpowder/Knock Down Power/Muzzleloader/Pyrodex.**

BLAT Sound made by a young deer who wants contact with its mother because it is stressed, desires to nurse, is injured, and so on. A hunter imitating a fawn in distress can often attract a maternalistic doe. **See Blat/ Calls/Communication/Fawn/Nursing/ Sounds in the Deer Woods/ Vocalization.**

BLAZE ORANGE A bright orange color on clothing, hats, safety vests, and so on that readi- ly identifies its wearer as a human because it is an unnatural color in the woods. It is a good idea to wear this color, whether it is required by law or not. States that mandate hunter orange or blaze orange usually require 144 square inches (twelve inches by twelve inches) of the color for safety's sake. Since deer have more rods in their eyes and not as many cones, they are less apt to differentiate colors such as hunter orange. **See Camouflage/Color Blind/Early Blur/ Eyes/FluorescentOrange/Safety/Vision/Visual Closure.**

Blaze orange hat and shirt

BLEAT Sound usually associated with a doe indicating her readiness to breed. **See Body language/Breeding/Calls/ Communication/Sounds in the Deer Woods/ Vocalization.**

BLEEDING Loss of blood when muscles or internal organs are punctured by an arrowhead or bullet. **See Blood/Blood Trailing Dogs/Exit Wound/Hemorrhaging/ Hydrostatic Shock/Knock Down Power/Shot Placement/Tracks.**

BLIND/GROUND BLIND A shelter made from branches, brush, or camouflaged mesh, and placed by hunters near a trail, water source, or scrape in hopes of ambush- ing a deer. **See Camouflage/Ghillie Suit/Stands.**

BLOOD/BLOOD SIGN/BLOOD TRAIL Blood marks left by a wounded deer. Sometimes even fatally hit animals do not leave spots of blood before they travel thir- ty feet. When you do discover some blood, it is best to mark that discovery with some readily identifiable marker, such as toilet paper (best because it is biodegradable and does not have to be retrieved) or surveyor's tape (you must retrace your steps and retrieve all pieces). Blood on the ground or sprayed against a tree trunk or bush can relate a lot of information to a hunter; such as the direction the deer traveled, how fast it was moving, where the deer was hit, and how hard it was hit. For archers, finding the arrow first can speak volumes about the shot. The color and consistency of the blood provides this information. For example:
    A. Heart or arterial blood is maroon-colored and often lumpy looking when

exposed to air. This blood has already circulated through the body and is oxygen-depleted, so it is dark and thick. This generally means a fatal hit. The deer is not going far.

B. Lung blood is newly recharged with oxygen, so it is usually bright pink, and most often frothy or bubbly. This is a fatal shot if both lungs were hit. With only one lung pierced, though, the deer will often be able to travel far and long before it succumbs, thus making for a rather difficult trailing job.

C. Muscle blood is the typical red, sticky consistency that we often associate with blood. Sometimes it even demonstrates evidence of clear fluids. You should wait for a while before following the deer's trail. You do not want to let this deer know that

Bloodtrail

it is being pursued. If you immediately push this deer, it could run into the next county, its blood trail could peter out, and you might still lose it. It would be better to sit down, review events in your mind, and think carefully how you wish to proceed. If it is rapidly getting dark outside, you may wish to wait until morning. Picking up a trail at night means that you will probably spook the deer and ultimately lose it.

D. Gut shot blood is often punctuated with green or brownish fluids and bits of stomach matter. The deer will hunch over after this shot, act sick if walking, and instinctively head for water as a source of relief.

See Bleeding/Blood Trailing Dogs/Deer Search, Inc./Downed Deer/ Hemorrhaging/Paunch Shot/Tracking/Wounded Game.

BLOOD-TRAILING DOGS Hounds specially trained to track wounded deer. In some states, using these dogs is illegal. In other states, these highly trained animals provide a useful service, after hunters have lost the trail of their mortally hit quarry. Recent research tells us that hunters alone generally find mortally wounded deer that ran only fifty to sixty yards from where they were hit. Wounded deer that traveled one hundred yards or more were often difficult for hunters alone to track and recover. Success in finding a mortally wounded whitetail who traveled over 150 yards after being struck decreased tremendously without the aid of blood-trailing dogs.

Often these dogs have bells tied around their necks so that their handlers can follow their movement, if they are not kept on a leash during the search. With some breeds, their baying signifies having found the previously lost animal. **See Automobile-Deer Accidents/Bleeding/Blood/Deer Search, Inc./Dogs/Downed Deer/Ethics/Feral Dogs/Wounded Game.**

BLOW See Deer Blow.

BLOW DOWN Trees toppled over by wind, tops left by logging operations, and so on that provide cover and security for deer. **See Beds/Cover/Security/ Terrain/Wind.**

BLUE TONGUE See Epizootic Hemorrhaging Disease.

BLUFF CHARGE A show of dominance by a whitetail buck, usually preceded by stomping and snorting. (Not unlike human teenage boys showing off in front of teenage girls). **See Aggression/Dominance/Fighting/Sparring.**

BLM See Bureau of Land Management.

BOB See Head Bob.

BODY HARNESS Safety equipment for hunters using a tree stand. Hunters who fall out of a tree stand often die or break their necks or backs. Select a full body harness, rather than just a single belt or rope around your waist. The full harness will hold you upright and distribute your body weight, if you fall, across your chest and pelvic girdle. Belts or ropes can leave you hanging upside down, cut off your air supply and suffocate you. Two belts are always better than one. **See Fall Prevention Device /Harness/Ladder Stand/Safety(Hunter)/Stands/Tree Stand.**

BODY LANGUAGE Body actions and gestures used to communicate. For example, within a buck's world, the "pecking order" or social hierarchy is established mostly by body language during the spring and summer months, when the bucks are still in velvet. By the time his velvet is shed, a buck knows his rank and status within the bachelor group.

The following are other observable whitetail forms of communication and their possible meanings:

• If a doe's tail is raised horizontally and straight back, she is ready to bolt.

• If her tail is held out level, but off to one side, a doe is visually signaling that she is receptive to be bred by the attending or trailing buck.

• If a buck's ears are laid back, and the hair on his neck and shoulders is bristled and erect, then he is expressing his dominance and aggressive intentions. Dominant bucks usually realize that most of the time all they have to do to scare off lesser or submissive bucks is to exhibit some aggressive body language.

• If a deer wags its tail, it is alarmed or uneasy about something in its immediate world.

• If a doe waves its tail occasionally while feeding, it wants to keep other deer from getting too close or signal her position to her fawn.

• If a tail wag is accompanied by a foot stomp and staring, either a buck or doe is trying to get some object that it cannot clearly identify to move and reveal itself.

• If a doe, while feeding some distance from her fawn, casually flips her tail, she is keeping in touch with the fawn. A more nervous flagging tells the fawn either to come closer or get ready to run. **See Alarm Snort/Alert Snort/Communication/Deer Blows/Ears/Flag/Foot Stomp/Head Bob/Hierarchy/Tail.**

BODY SIZE/WEIGHT White-tailed deer can weigh anywhere from under one hundred pounds to over four hundred pounds. The farther north one goes, the heavier bodied are the deer (see Bergmann's Rule). Northern whitetails are heavier, have a larger chest girth, and have longer hind feet than Southern deer. It is not uncommon for a Maine, New York (Adirondack), or Saskatchewan buck to weigh in field dressed between 200 to 250 pounds. Field-dressed weight is approximately three-quarters of a whitetail's live weight.

Vermont deer hunter Wayne Laroche has performed field studies that relate the width of a deer's hoof to its live weight. His gauge for this measurement—called a Trackometer—is now on the market.

The American record was set by Carl Lenander Jr. of Minnesota in 1926, with a deer field dressed at 402 pounds; its estimated live weight was 511 pounds.

The North American record was set by bowhunter John Anwett of Ontario, Canada, in 1977 with a deer field dressed at 431 pounds on government certified scales.

See Bergmann's Rule/Borealis Effect/Dressed Weight/Fat/Field Dressing/ Hog Dressed/Live Weight.

BOLT A term used in deer behavior and archery.

A. Deer behavior. The sudden running away of a white-tailed deer, having been spooked by a strange sound, smelling danger, or visually identifying some threat.

B. Archery equipment. The short, stiff arrow used in crossbows for practice and hunting.

BOLT ACTION In a rifle or shotgun, a mechanism for injecting live ammunition and extracting spent cartridges. It involves a top mounted "bolt" that is usually raised and pulled back,. A fresh cartridge is inserted, it is then pushed forward and turned down to lock it in place. **See Autoloader/Firearms/Lever Action.**

Bolt Action

BOLUS See Cud.

BONDING Ways animals interact with each other to re-enforce a bonding or social order, such as a mother doe licking or grooming the coat of her fawn, two bucks attending to each other's head and neck—areas that they cannot groom themselves. **See Dominance/Grooming/Hierarchy/Imprinting/Licking/Social Bonding.**

BONE MARROW The jelly-like material found inside of a deer's long bones that produces blood cells. Large whitetail predators will often break open the larger bones in order to lick out this richly nutritious material. **See Blood/ Predators.**

BONING Taking the meat off of the bones of a deer to make transporting the meat home from your hunting area easier. The boning saw and boning knife are tools of adequate size and sharpness to handle the hardness and size of the largest bones. **See Accessories/Equipment/Field Dressing/Knife/Recipes/Venison.**

BOONE AND CROCKETT CLUB (B&C) North America's oldest hunting and conservation club, started in 1887 by Teddy Roosevelt. It was named after two early frontiersmen: Daniel Boone and Davey Crockett. The club is one of several record keeping organizations that offer a method to measure and systematically score deer antlers for ranking and comparison purposes. It emphasizes antler size and symmetry, and its cumulative score—after deductions for irregularities—is based upon the combination of antler tines and beam length in inches. The minimum score needed to enter the B & C record book is 170. The B & C Club recognizes two whitetail categories, typical and nontypical, and only two subspecies of whitetail: *Odocoileus virginianus couesi* (Coues Deer) and all 28 other subspecies of *Odocoileus virginianus* lumped together as one.

BOONE & CROCKETT CLUB SCORING

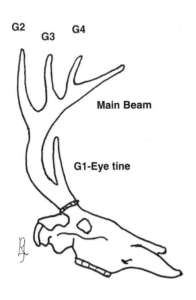

G2 G3 G4

Main Beam

G1-Eye tine

In the Typical category, judging is based on the sum of the lengths of the two main beams of antlers, the lengths of all normal points (must be one inch or more), the greatest inside spread between the right and left antlers, and the circumference of the main beam. Deductions are made for the difference in symmetry between the left and right antlers.

In the Nontypical category, for nonuniform, nonsymmetrical rack, the same guidelines are used as with typical racks, except that all points are added to the total score. The minimum entry score is 195.

The official address for the Boone and Crockett Club is 250 Station Drive, Missoula, MT 59801, (406) 542-1888 **See Buckmaster Whitetail Trophy Records/Burkett System/Drying Period/Grand Slam of Deer/Green Score/ Net Score/Nontypical/Pope & Young Club/Safari Club International/ Scoring/Typical.**

BORDER SCRAPE See **Boundary Scrape**.

BORE/BORE SIZE The inside diameter of a pistol, rifle, or shotgun barrel. It can be referred to as caliber in pistols and rifles, but shotguns use the term "gauge." **See Caliber/Gauge/Pistol/Rifle/Shotgun.**

BOREAL FOREST/BOREAL WOODS The northernmost forests in North America, Asia, or Europe. Although not numerous, the deer living in these woods can be monstrous in size, as per Bergmann's Rule. Going further north, the trees start to become shrublike and ultimately vegetation of any height ceases as perpetual snow covers the arctic tundra. **See Bergmann's Rule/Climax Forest/Latitude/Snow.**

BOREALIS EFFECT See **Bergmann's Rule.**

BOSS BUCK See **Alpha Buck.**

BOTTLENECK A portion of the landscape that is easier to travel on because the terrain or the obstacles on both sides (for example, a ravine, flowing river, lake, or cliff) forces the deer to travel through it. **See Draw/Funnel/Ravine/Saddle.**

BOUNDARY/BORDER SCRAPE An early-season scrape found along the edge of a buck's territory, usually along a field's edge, fencerow, or logging road. These are usually the first scrapes made, occurring about five to six weeks before the rut's peak. Speculations about the purpose of these scrapes conflict: they are made to "test out" the doe population in the area; they are made only by the dominant buck early in the season and not revisited by him; they are only made by bucks of lesser dominance, and therefore not worthy of hunting over and so on. The experts all have an opinion on these scrapes, but the scientific jury is still out on their purpose. **See Buck/Communication/Does/Dominance/Overhanging Branch/Primary Scrape/Rut/Scent Check/Scrape/Secondary Scrape.**

BOW AND ARROW Whether a traditional longbow or a modern compound, a device used to propel an arrow that has been nocked on the bowstring, drawn back, and then let go. The arrow, tipped with a sharp hunting point (broadhead) is used to bring down a deer. **See Archery/Arrowhead/Arrow Speed/Arrow Weight/Draw Weight/ Feathers/Finger Release/Hemorrhaging/Mechanical Release/ Release.**

BOWHUNTING   Using a bow and arrow to hunt game animals. Bowhunting is a short-range, non-firearm hunting sport. **See Archery/Bow and Arrow/Fred Bear/Howard Hill/Saxton Pope/Art Young.**

BOW SLING   A strap, rubber tube, or leather thong attached to the bow riser that an archer puts his or her hand through while holding the bow. It prevents the bow from being dropped after the shot is taken. **See Accessories/Archery/Bow and Arrow/Equipment.**

BRAINWORM   A parasite that infects a whitetail's brain but apparently causes it no harm. The parasite's eggs hatch in the whitetail's lungs and are expelled through its droppings, where they are picked up by ground snails and slugs, which in turn are ingested by other whitetails and the parasite's reproductive cycle starts all over again. **See Parasites.**

BREATH/BREATH ODOR   Human mouth odor, which deer can detect. A human exhales approximately 250 liters of breath per hour. This can spread a lot of human scent downwind. To reduce the bad odor of your breath, brush your teeth with odor-free toothpaste or baking soda (also found as an odor neutralizer in toothpaste). Taking chlorophyll tablets or sucking on a piece of apple are other means of controlling mouth odor. Some hunters have even started utilizing a camouflaged charcoal-activated mouth mask with scent-free properties. **See Apple/Chlorophyll/Scent.**

BREEDING/BREEDING PHASE/BREEDING SEASON   The time of year when white-tailed deer mate. From a whitetail buck's perspective, breeding season lasts from the time it peels its antlers of velvet until it casts those antlers during late winter. The rise in testosterone throughout its body has caused the buck to strengthen his neck muscles by false fights with bushes and saplings (September) and eventually sparring with other bucks (October). He has advertised his availability, virility, and dominance by leaving his scent on scrapes, rubs, and licking branches (late September to October). He has even left his bachelor group and expanded his range so as to monitor the does' receptivity to being bred (late October to early November).

However, does establish the actual time for breeding. A few does will be ready to breed in October, but this only serves to fuel the bucks' frenzy and desire. This period is often called the "false rut." With too few does actually ready to breed at this time, a buck increases his travel range in search of any receptive doe that smells right to him. In the northern range of where the white-tailed deer lives, between seventy to seventy-five percent of the does come into estrus in November. This is perfect timing on Mother Nature's part. It assures that the fawns will be born in late May and June when there is ample green food available to help the does produce the thick, rich milk (colostrum) needed for the fawn to grow quickly and then convert to eating the lush green plants themselves. Fawning at this time also reduces the likelihood of a late killing freeze and gives the fawn a chance to mature enough to survive its first winter. **See Artificial Insemination/Chase Phase/Copulation/Crossbreeding/Gestation/Glands/Impotence/Inbreeding/Overhanging Branch/Post-Rut/Rut.**

BREEDING HUB Areas high in "buck sign," such as licking branches, scrape lines, and rub lines. This is alleged to be an area of the buck's home range where he will concentrate his efforts at breeding all available and ready does, an area where he will fight to keep his right to breed there. **See Breeding/Dominance/Fight/Rut.**

BRENNEKE SLUG A popular style of shotgun slug originally designed in 1935, incorporating a massive cylindrical piece of lead attached to a fiber wad. Distinctive and pronounced fins surround the slug, which impart spin to the projectile head. This slug style is incompatible with rifled barrels found in most modern shotguns. **See Ammunition/Foster Slug/Sabot/Shotgun/Slug.**

"BRIGHT EYES" THUMBTACKS Reflective heads that are used as trail markers or as a nighttime aid for navigation to a stand. They are visible but not conspicuous during daylight hours, but after dark glow brightly when struck by a flashlight beam. **See Accessories/Equipment/Trail Markers.**

BROADHEADS Sharp hunting arrow tips with two or more cutting edges that slice through the hide, muscle, and vital organs. The arrow shaft is just a means of delivering the "business end" of the arrow (broadhead) to the deer. Broadheads with large cutting diameters do not penetrate as well as smaller ones but can provide larger initial cuts for more hemorrhaging (bleeding). The more an arrowhead cuts, the more a wound will bleed, the easier the blood trail will be to follow, and the sooner the deer will be recovered. Broadheads may be of two types: (a) fixed broadhead and (b) mechanical broadhead. **See Arrowheads/Arrow Speed/Arrow Weight/Feathers/Helical Fletching/Hemorrhaging/Mechanical Broadhead.**

BROADSIDE SHOT A shot taken when a deer is standing directly in front of you with its full body length perpendicular to a direct line from you to the deer. This is usually the preferred shot to take on a white-tailed deer as it affords a hunter a chance to penetrate the vital organs for a mortal hit. **See Backstop/Shot Placement/Wounded Game.**

BROWSE/BROWSE LINE In many northern areas, freezing temperature and heavy snow force the whitetail to change its diet from eating succulent, highly nutritious herbaceous forage (green plants) to subsisting upon less-nourishing buds and the woody end branches or tips of trees and bushes. Practically all of this food is comparatively low in protein, digestible energy, and other essential dietary constituents. In a brushy or woody area where the deer have heavily eaten the buds and branch tips of every tree to a certain height, one can actually notice this "browse line." It is also sometimes referred to as a "highline." **See Conifer/Deciduous/Evergreen/Forage/Forbs/Hardwood/Herbaceous/Land Management/Nutrition/Overbrowse/Starvation/Yarding.**

BROW TINES Also called G-1s or eye tines. On a buck mature whitetail buck, these are two single antler points that project straight up from the head between and separate from the main beams of the antlers. As defensive equipment, the browtines appear to fill in the gap between the main beams of the antlers, thus protecting the head while sparring for dominance or during actual fighting. **See Antlers/Bifurcate/Eye Tine/Forkhorn/G-1/G-2/Hierarchy/Main Beam/Rub/Shed/Spike.**

BUCK The male of the *Cervidae* species, which usually sports antlers grown on a seasonal basis for expressing dominance and establishing breeding rights then cast off (shed), only to be grown again for the next breeding season. **See Antlers/Bachelor Buck Groups/Button Buck/Dominance/Hierarchy/Rack/Rut/Testosterone/Trophy.**

BUCK FEVER Also known as "the shakes," a malady that has different symptoms in different hunters but usually is exemplified by sweaty palms, nervousness, and "stupid actions" such as punching holes all around the deer, ejecting the shells without actually firing the firearm, and so on. In short, it is the freezing up of thought and action, failure to shoot straight, or to shoot at all! While these actions have physical consequences, their source is in the mind of the hunter. These symptoms occur when a hunter sees a buck deer and have been blamed for more missed shots than any other cause.

One way of lessening the effects of this malady is to train yourself as to what you expect to see when a deer approaches. Just as professional athletes visualize in their minds how they will make the winning touchdown, basket, or pole vault, deer hunters can mentally go through the steps they will take to effectively harvest a whitetail. Obviously, this visualization should occur before one actually sees a deer coming. New hunters have to learn to shoot under pressure, ignore the antlers once they have decided that this is the buck they want to shoot, pick their spot in the deer's vital zone and shoot. The time to get nervous is after your deer is down! Caution: This affliction can strike at any time, and is known to affect the experienced hunter as well as the novice. **See Antlers/Archery/"Jumping the String"/Hunting Maladies/ Movement/Patience/ Pressure.**

BUCK POLE Also called a "meat pole." That special area, whether it be a horizontal tree limb or a wood or metal bar lashed between two trees, located outside the deer camp, where the successful hunter hangs his or her deer for aging, skinning, butchering, or just showing off. **See Aging Meat/Buck Pole/Butchering/Deer Camp/Skinning.**

BUCK RUB Brush, saplings, trees, fence posts, and even telephone poles, where whitetail bucks thrash and "rub" their antlers. They do this at first to help remove the itchy, drying, and annoying velvet from their newly hardened antlers; later they do this to strengthen their neck muscles for sparring and dominance purposes, and ultimately they continue making buck rubs in order to display their dominance for the breeding arena (rut) and as a visual and chemical signpost for all to see that this is their territory. **See Rub/Scentpost/Signpost/Velvet.**

BUCK TRAIL Does and fawns often travel about twenty-five to forty yards back from the edge of a bench, which enables them to see the area below them. However, another fifteen to twenty yards farther back from this highly visible trail will be another fainter trail, better hidden and used by bucks. This trail has had less hooves on it less often and thus does not show up as readily. It is usually upwind from the usual doe trail. However, by paralleling the more visible does' trails, a buck can monitor who has used that trail recently. Dark, recessed areas, such as under thick evergreen cover,

BUCK TRACK VS. DOE PRINT

Center Line · Center Line · Front Hoof · Dragging Hoof Marks · Hind Hoof · Hind Hoof · Dragging Hoof Marks · **DOE TRACK** · Front Hoof · **BUCK TRACK** · **WOUNDED BUCK TRACK**

Doe's Hind Hoof Overlaps Front Hoof   Buck's Smaller Hind Hoof Does Not Overlap Front Hoof

that are hard to see into, will often hold buck trails. Mature bucks did not get that way by making mistakes and exposing themselves in the open. **See Corridor/Cover/Deer Run/Edge/Path/Spoor/Tracks/Tracking/Trail/Travel Corridor/Travel.**

BUCKHORN SIGHT A rear sight aiming device that has a "V" cut in the center; it has sides or wings that are roughly deer antler shaped, in which the front sight or "bead" is rested. **See Firearm/Peep Sight/Rifle/Shot Placement.**

BUCKSHOT Large, oversized, round BBs of 00 (double aught) or 000 (triple aught) size, packed in a large shotgun shell. With only a few "pumpkin balls" being thrown at bucks, the idea is to wound, cripple, or shock a buck, leaving a bloodtrail for followup. The advantage of buckshot is that you can use a smoothbore shotgun and swing easily on deer through the brush, usually at shots of thirty yards or less. **See Ammunition/Bore/Bore Size/Bullet/Calibre/Gauge/Knock Down Power/Shotgun/ Slug.**

BUCKSKIN See Deerskin.

BUCK-TO-DOE RATIO The number of male deer in a herd compared to the number of females. The ideal buck-to-doe ratio is one to one. A realistic ratio is three adult does for every adult buck. This ratio, however, does not allow for intense competition among bucks because a doe will always be available for a buck to tend. When there is a balanced or equal buck-to-doe ratio, buck competition will be intense as several bucks will compete for the receptivity of any doe coming into estrus. Since a buck could breed ten or more does during the overall rut season, the area could have high doe to buck numbers and still show population growth. Hunters harvesting does help with quality deer management programs and create better hunting opportunities for bucks by keeping the ratio closer to the ideal (one buck to three does). Harvesting does helps make the rut more intense as bucks will actively compete for each doe that comes into heat.

The buck-doe ratio definitely affects the success of hunting over scrapes. If the doe population greatly exceeds the buck population, the bucks will still make scrapes out of instinct, but they will rarely return to them. With so many does around, a buck has no need to wait at a scrape to meet a receptive doe. If hunters use calls immediately before or immediately after the peak of the rut, when estrous does are few, mature bucks will regularly approach the calls. During the rut, scrape hunting is less successful, because the bucks are too busy tending the receptive and soon-to-be receptive-to-breed does. **See Balanced Herd/Calls/Does/Doe Harvest/Dominance/Quality Deer Management/Rut/Tending.**

BUDS The small end or lateral protuberance (growth) on the stem of a plant that is an undeveloped shoot. It will develop into a flower or possibly a new branch. Deer instinctively know that this is the high-energy part of the plant, its most nutritious part, and that it will provide them with nutrients and energy after the green plants have died off or stopped growing because of cold weather. Buds are the natural food supply for white-tailed deer through the winter and before the spring "green up." **See Biomass/Browse/Cud/Food/Forbs/Graze/Nutrition/Overbrowse.**

BULLET/BULLET SHAPE/BULLET WEIGHT A projectile used in a firearm. With such a wide range of cartridges available hunters must test and make their own choices on what to use. Often states mandate the minimum caliber that can be used on whitetails.

In rifle cartridges, the seven most popular calibers are .243 Winchester, .270 Winchester, .30-30 Winchester, .30-06 Springfield, .300 Winchester Magnum, .308 Winchester, and 7mm Remington Magnum.

Handguns obviously have a shorter range and less knockdown power than rifle cartridges. The smallest caliber recommended to use with deer-sized game animals is .35 caliber, which is the legal limit in several states (e.g., New York). Three of the most popular calibers for handgun hunting are .357 Magnum, .40 Magnum, and .44 Magnum.

Use the heaviest (e.g., 150- to 165-grain) suitable bullet in a given caliber that you can shoot with accuracy and consistency. A well-made, heavy bullet has more authority on quartering shots commonly found in deer hunting. Quartering shots are when the deer is angling to or angling away from the hunter. There is a lesser chance of taking out both lungs with this type of shot. Even with a poorly placed shot, a heavy bullet usually does more damage and has a better potential to turn a bad shot into a recoverable deer. **See Ammunition/Ballistics/Caliber/ Factory Loads/ Firearms/Foot Pounds of Energy/Gauge/Handloading/Kinetic Energy/Knock Down Power/Rifle/Shotgun.**

Winchester Bullet

BUREAU OF LAND MANAGEMENT (BLM) A federal agency that is responsible for addressing the use of public lands. Of interest to the deer hunter are maps it regularly publishes usually by state. The bureau's state maps show all of the BLM-managed land in that state and often designate which areas are open to public hunting. Types of useful maps offered by the bureau include resource area maps and the surface management maps. Most of these maps use a scale measurement smaller than that used on the U.S. Geological Survey topographical maps. **See Aerial Photographs/Contour Lines/Global Positioning Satellite/Maps/Orienteering/Orthophotoquad/ Survival/Topographical Maps/United States Geological Survey.**

BURN Sometimes called a "clearing," an open space usually resulting from a fire whether ignited naturally (by lightning) or by humans—on purpose or accidentally. These areas usually allow increased forage for whitetails as the shady canopy of leaves from the trees is removed and the undergrowth starts replenishing itself. For several decades after a burn, the area will support active whitetail use and thus, decent hunting. **See Clear-cut/Climax Forest/Edge/Habitat/Regeneration/Terrain.**

BURR An outgrowth located at the base of an antler at the pedicle level, where the antler joins the skull. It is also referred to as the coronet, because it looks like a crown around each antler's base. This area can be very prickly, with many protrusions, hence the name "burr," and is often responsible for the shredding of bark and/or interior fibers when a buck rubs a tree. **See Antlers/Browtine/Burr/Forkhorn/Genetics/Keratin/ Main Beam/Photoperiodism/Rub/Signpost/Testosterone/Velvet.**

BUTCHERING The act of cutting up a whitetail (after first field dressing it) into the many fine cuts of meat (e.g., roasts, loins, chops, steaks, and so on) to be enjoyed as tablefare, and grinding the less desirable meat into venison burger and sausage. **See Aging Meat/Field Dressing/Gambrel/Jerky/Recipes/Venison.**

CUTS FOR BUTCHERING YOUR DEER

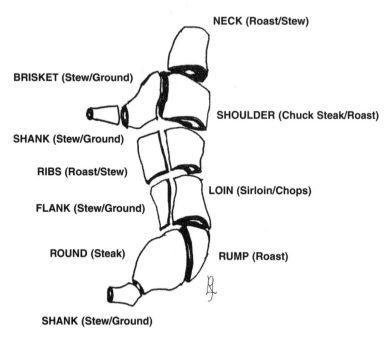

NECK (Roast/Stew)

BRISKET (Stew/Ground)

SHOULDER (Chuck Steak/Roast)

SHANK (Stew/Ground)

RIBS (Roast/Stew)

LOIN (Sirloin/Chops)

FLANK (Stew/Ground)

ROUND (Steak)

RUMP (Roast)

SHANK (Stew/Ground)

BUTTERFAT The fatty nutrients in all mammal mothers' milk that provide the baby with energy to grow rapidly and gain weight. The colostrum or doe's first milk for her young is especially rich in this creamy, fat-laden nutrient. **See Colostrum/Fawn/Milk/Nursing/ Singleton/Twins.**

BUTTON BUCK A male fawn from the summer birthing time. It is difficult to see the "buttons" or small knobs on the fawn's pedicles, as they are covered by hair. Hunters are usually disappointed that they have shot a buck fawn as that action takes a future antlered deer out of the herd. Thoughtless hunters sometimes leave a button buck in the field, rather than claim it as a legitimate kill. Remember, fawns are square-shaped, while adult deer look rectangular, that is, longer in body length than they are tall. **See Age of Deer/Fawn/Pedicle/Spike/Testosterone/Yearling Buck.**

CABIN FEVER The claustrophobic feeling of being closed up inside a house or workplace with no chance of getting outside to the hunting grounds. There are primarily two types of cabin fever:

      A. The summer version usually occurs before the fall hunting season when a strong mental pull calls you to look over the hunting cabin, walk the hunting grounds and so on.

      B. The winter version occurs after the fall hunting season, during late winter or early spring, when you feel the need to check the cabin for winter damage or look for sheds or any other excuse to leave home or work and go back to the hunting cabin. **See Buck Fever/Camp/Hunting Maladies.**

CACTUS BUCK A buck whose antlers look like cactus plants, the result of hypogonadism caused by undescended or undeveloped testicles or because the buck has been castrated. The testosterone released from his adrenal glands starts the antler growth but is not enough to finish the process of velvet shedding and antler hardening. **See Antlers/Castration/Hypogonadism/Impotence/Testes/Testosterone.**

CALCIFICATION Figuratively, "turning to bone"; with whitetails, the hardening of the antlers under the velvet. Male whitetails begin to grow antlers from their pedicles soon after the vernal or spring equinox. These knobby outgrowths are covered in that warm-to-feel, blood vessel-enriched velvet. For the next four months, as spring wears on and into the summer months, the antlers continue to grow. The buck has guarded them well, as they are living tissue and thus vulnerable to injury. Around the beginning of August, photoperiodism again sends new chemical messengers into the buck's bloodstream. The burrs at the base of his antlers begin to protrude and cut off the rich blood supply that was nourishing this rapid tissue growth. The antlers start to harden, the velvet begins to peel off, and the buck starts feeling that his new headgear makes him "King for a Day." Once he has sensed that his antlers have hardened fully or "calcified," he will begin thrashing brush, saplings, and so on, in an attempt to strengthen his neck muscles in preparation for sparring for dominance in the prerutting season.

    A calcified, stony mass (bezoar stone) found in the reticulum (fourth stomach) of ruminants is formed when an indigestible object is coated with layers of calcium. **See Antlers/Bezoar Stone/Pedicles/Photoperiodism/Reticulum/Rut/Sparring/ Velvet.**

CALIBER The barrel bore size, gauge, diameter, or cross-section of a bullet usually measured in hundreths of an inch. This measurement gives the bullet and the firearm's corresponding barrel diameter its name; such as .41 , .270, or .22. The larger the caliber, usually the greater the knockdown effect on the target. States usually mandate a minimal size of bullet for hunting white-tailed deer. **See Ammunition/Black**

Powder/Bullet/Firearm/Foot Pounds of Energy/Handgun/Handloading/Kinetic Energy/Knock Down Power/Muzzleloader/Rifle.

CALLS/CALLING Tactics used by hunters to bring deer into an area or draw them closer for a shot. Prerut is the best time to rattle for bucks. The peak of the rut is a good time for doe breeding bellows or the deep grunts that lure in hormone-drunk bucks or those defending their territory. Deer vocalization calling equipment, such as grunt tubes, estrous calls, fawn bleats, distress calls, and rattling antlers, are all designed to convince deer that you are one of them or to pique deer's curiosity so that they come closer to investigate the source of the sound. Does and predators are especially attracted to fawn distress calls. The doe will answer any fawn distress call out of maternal instinct.

Almost all adult bucks are call shy. They are naturally cautious by nature, and if they have heard hunters calling before, they will be doubly so. Bucks circle downwind and sniff for danger while trying to pinpoint the odors of other deer. They become extremely wary if they do not see other deer in the vicinity. Making your calls and rattling techniques sound submissive will draw the attention and aggression of bucks of all sizes, especially the dominant buck, who knows that all he has to do to scare off a submissive buck is to exhibit aggressive body language and give off a little "snort wheeze" or two. Try using a "confidence call," such as a doe bleat or a fawn bleat. These usually signify to a weary buck that "The coast is clear! Come on in!" **See Alarm Snort/Alert Snort/Blat/Bleat/Communication/Deer Blows/Grunt/ Snort Wheeze/Sounds in the Deer Woods/Vocalization.**

CAM Out-of-round, rotating string pulleys or guides on the end of bows. A bow may also have just a single cam. They are noisier than wheels, but they usually make the bow shoot faster. **See Arrow Speed/Bow and Arrow/Equipment/Wheels.**

CAMOUFLAGE Covering that lets deer or hunters blend in with their background.

A. Deer. The white-tailed deer has evolved an excellent system for blending in with its environment. The natural dark color on its back and sides make its body look inconspicuous, hard to see against the forest floor and gray-barked trees. The

Camouflage

buck's antlers, legs, and general body form are not easily distinguished from among the saplings, trees and shrubs of its surroundings. Looking uphill at a whitetail silhouetted against the brightness of the sky, the deer's white stomach appears to blend in with the lighter background. Even a fawn's spots at birth (cryptic coloration) are made to blend it in with the dappled sunlight that often permeates its hiding spot. A fawn's lack of scent in its first few days of life (before it can run away from predators) is another way of keeping it safe, by hiding its presence. **See Fawn.**

       B. Hunter. Outer clothing designed to allow hunters to blend into the background, thus reducing their visibility to deer. The rule is to choose a camouflage pattern that matches the background that you are hunting in. Examples of camo-clothing patterns are Trebark, World War II, tiger stripe, Vietnam, snow. **See Back Cover/Blaze Orange/Blind/Clothing/Equipment/Face Mask/Face Paint/Foul Weather/Head Net/Layering.**

CAMP See Deer Camp.

CANINES See Dogs.

CANOPY Also known as the "overstory," the top layer in a forest where the branches of the trees have grown so thick with leaves that they tend to block out most sunlight from reaching the forest floor or understory, thus limiting growth of vegetative plants. **See Cover/Edge/Habitat/Understory.**

CAPING The careful skinning of a deer so that its head, neck and possibly front shoulders can be mounted properly by a taxidermist. It is always better to leave more skin than you think that the taxidermist will need for a mount. **See Field Dressing/ Follow-Up/Mount/Taxidermist.**

CAR-DEER ACCIDENTS See Automobile-Deer Accidents.

CARBOHYDRATES Starchy or sugary nutrients extracted by consuming organisms, such as the white-tailed deer, from plants that provide it as ready energy for heat and fuel for muscle exertion. Excess intake of carbohydrates can then be turned into body fat for winter survival during the lean months, when food is not readily available. **See Cellulose/Energy/Fat/Protein.**

CARNIVORE A meat eater; an animal that has its eyes facing forward (not on the sides). A predator hunts, stalks, and kills its food source, which is usually an herbivore. **See Carrion/Eyes/Herbivore/Predator/Roadkill/Winterkill/ Zoophagous.**

CARRION The remains or bodies of dead animals left to putrefy (rot) and often fed upon by scavengers. By not following up on each shot, whitetail hunters contribute to the number of dead, and thus wasted, animals. Left to rot, the remains become a source of disease transmission to other species. Fortunately, nature has created a system of cleaning up this waste through opportunist meat eaters, scavengers, and so on. **See Carnivore/Die-Off/Predators/Roadkill/Winterkill/Zoophagous.**

CARRYING CAPACITY A biological limitation of the ability of the land to support a herd of deer throughout the year but most importantly through the winter. Only a certain number of deer can live adequately on any particular piece of land. If an area becomes greatly overbrowsed, winter die-off of the young (smallest) and the weakest deer will occur, cutting the herd back to a size the land can support, thus ensuring the survival of future generations. Habitat and the general health of the deer population will be preserved if whitetail numbers are kept below the number the land can support. **See Aerial Survey/ Balanced Herd/ Browse/Browseline/ Census/Deer Yard/ Die-Off/Habitat/ Herd/Herd Size/ Home Range/Over-browse/Quality Deer Management/ Winterkill/ Yarding.**

Castings

CASTS/CASTINGS Also called "shed," the last act of a buck's antler cycle. When the buck's testosterone level falls below a certain minimum level to maintain the antlers, the pedicle demineralizes and the antlers fall off. It is believed that this casting of antlers occurs roughly the same time each year for each individual buck. After the antler has fallen off, the pedicle looks like an open wound—often bleeding. However, it soon heals, only to begin the cycle of antler growth all over again within a few months. **See Adrenal Gland/Antlers/ Castration/Horn/Pedicle/Shed/Testosterone/Velvet.**

CASTRATION The removal of a buck's testicles, usually through some freak accident of nature, such as jumping over a fence, sparring or fighting injury, etc. The resultant loss of testosterone production capabilities has an adverse effect upon antler development, breeding rights, dominance, etc. **See Adrenal Gland/Antlers/Cast/Cactus Buck/Dominance/Fighting/Hypogonadism/Impotence/Injury/Testicles/ Testosterone/Velvet.**

CELLULOSE The carbohydrates making up the cell walls of plants, that provide nutrition from browse to the white-tailed deer. **See Browse/Food/Nutrition.**

CEMENTUM The annual growth layers of a deer's tooth that biologists use to accurately age the deer. This is done by extracting the tooth, cross-sectioning it, and then counting the cementum layers. **See Age of Deer/Teeth.**

CENSUS The act of counting individuals within a certain sector. Conservation departments and wildlife biologists need to know a reasonably accurate number of whitetails within a specific area, if not the whole state, so that carrying capacity is not exceeded, hunting quotas can be established, and deer management permits issued. **See Aerial Survey/Balance of Nature/Balanced Herd/Carrying Capacity/ Die-Off/Herd Size/Winterkill.**

CERVID/CERVIDAE A scientific family classification for all deer. The United States and Canada contain approximately seventeen subspecies of the white-tailed deer. **See Deer/Ruminant/ Subspecies/White-tailed Deer.**

CHARCOAL SUIT A recent development in human odor control using microscopic pieces of charcoal embedded into hunting clothing, to filter, contain, or control the dispersion of human scent, are now being embedded into hunting clothing. **See Camouflage/Hygiene/Scents.**

CHASE PHASE A period during the rut. In those areas with a well-defined rut, the chase phase occurs at the very end of the scraping period and just prior to does entering into estrus—usually during the week prior to peak breeding. Hungry does will regularly visit food sources and bring the sex-crazed bucks with them. From the doe's perspective, this phase ensures that she has a buck ready when she is ready to breed. The doe begins to give off scent signals a day or two before actually entering estrus. These signals are picked up by any buck around her and the chase phase is on. This is a time when a buck will not eat or sleep and will doggedly defend his place near the doe so as to be the one to actually breed her. Since the doe is not quite yet ready to be bred, she will be constantly moving. You can be sure that the bucks

Chase Phase

will be nearby and a couple of days of nonstop chasing is the norm. Morning and evenings see intense action, but bucks look for does all day long during this period. **See Breeding/Breeding Phase/False Rut/Flehmen/Late Rut/Prerut/Rut/Seeking Phase/ Tending Phase/Testosterone.**

CHEATER POINTS Side pointing tines on a buck's antlers that extend beyond the main beams and can thus increase the greatest outside measurement score. **See Antlers/Boone and Crockett Club/Burr/Drop Tine/Green Score/Net Score/ Nontypical/Pope & Young/Scoring/Spread/Typical.**

CHEMICAL SIGNPOST White-tailed deer communicate to each other most effectively through smell. They are able to identify specific individuals and determine dominance, ability to breed, direction of travel, danger, and so on. Deer put their glandular secretions in scrapes, on rubs, on overhanging branches, and anywhere else that other deer might come across them. These are the chemical postal service of the whitetail's world. **See Communication/Flehman/Forehead Gland/Overhanging Branch/ Pre-Orbital Gland/Rub/Rub Line/Scents/Scrape/Signpost.**

CHLOROPHYLL The substance in leaves that makes them look green. It is a catalyst in photosynthesis for producing oxygen and simple sugars as plant food. Once killed by frost chlorophyll is no longer active and allows the leaf to display its true color—the yellows, oranges, and reds of fall.

Chlorophyll also has an inherent odor eliminating characteristic. It is sometimes ingested by hunters in pill form. In doing so, hunters attempt to reduce their body odor to help avoid being detected by a deer's nose. **See Autumn/ Breath/ Camouflage/Deciduous/Hardwoods/Herbivore/Human Odor/Leaf Drop/ Leaves/Photosynthesis/Scent.**

CHRONIC WASTING DISEASE (CWD) A deadly brain disease of cervidae currently seen in the western states of Colorado, Wyoming, Nebraska and the Canadian province of Saskatchewan. CWD literally consumes the animal and causes it to waste away. CWD has been found in some elk, mule deer, and white-tailed deer over the previous three decades. It has no known cure and is always fatal. When found in game farm animals, they are immediately put under quarantine and destroyed so as to not transmit the disease to other game farm animals or animals in the wild. **See Cervid/ Diseases/Epizootic Hemorrhaging Disease/Game Farm.**

CIRCADIAN/CIRCADIAN RHYTHM The "internal clock" that regulates the body's daily rhythm and activities including sleep and alertness and body temperature. It is believed to be controlled by the amount of light received through the eye. It is photoperiodism on a daily basis. **See False Rut/Lunar Influence/Moon/Photo-periodism/Prerut/Quarter Moon Phases.**

CLEAR-CUT/CLEARING Whole hillsides or strips of a wooded area cleared of all trees, and most brush, often due to a logging operation. This area is then allowed to rejuvenate through natural succession of plant growth over three to five years from the initial cutting. As the plants and trees return, this area becomes a prime habitat for deer as it offers them cover, food, and security. **See Burn/Cover/Edge/Terrain.**

CLIMAX FOREST The last and final phase of the regeneration of land, when it has gone through reseeding of grasses and forbs, to bushes and shrubs, to softwoods, and finally to hardwoods comprising tall, mature trees. A climax forest holds valuable timber resources that logging operations desire. Their clear-cutting operations open the way for new, successive plant growth. The understory is usually cluttered with old growth and decaying branches and trees, such that if a fire were to start, it would progress from tree to tree, resulting in a major burn or clearing of the climax forest, returning nutrients to the soil and preparing to start the succession of plant growth all over again. **See Boreal Forest/Canopy/Regeneration.**

CLIMBER/CLIMBING TREE STAND Many hunters prefer a climbing tree stand because of its portability (mobility) and ease of use. As the conditions (e.g., wind direction, changing food sources) and stages of the whitetail's breeding season change (e.g., pre rut, rut), so too can hunters alter their strategy and stand placement to fit those conditions. A climber is usually carried in and out the very same day of the hunt. The downside of a climber is that it can often be noisy while being put up thus alerting deer to something invading their home territory. In addition, since it has many more parts than a hanging stand or ladderstand, more creaks and groans are possible while a hunter is sitting in it. Be sure to use a climber only on rough-barked trees, never on a smooth-barked tree, where it could easily begin to slide down the tree trunk while you are still in it! **See Accessories/Equipment/Ladder Stand/ Noise/Permanent Stand/Portable Stands/Safety Harness/Sounds/Stands/ Tree Steps.**

CLOTHING Garments used for hunting. Hunters should make a practice of carrying an extra sweatshirt, pair of gloves, and pair of socks in their backpacks every time they go afield. Wool, even when wet, retains the best insulating (warmth) capabilities of any clothing material. Fleece comes in a close second. Warm, dry, and quiet are the watchwords to go by in shooting clothing for hunting.

Laying out the proper clothing for the next day's hunt starts the night before when you check the next day's weather forecast. The wise hunter dresses in layers for total flexibility and adaptability to changing weather conditions, amount of exertion, and so on. It is always better to wear too much clothing rather than too little. The standard rule is "You can always take it off, but you cannot put it on if you do not have it with you." It is best to keep hunting clothes out of the house so that they do not absorb household or human odors. Likewise, hunters should not wear their hunting clothing while filling up their gas tank nor while eating bacon and eggs at the Greasy Spoon Diner on the way to the hunting grounds. Spilling coffee down the front of a hunting jacket while driving is also a mistake. **See Accessories/Camouflage/Footwear/Foul Weather/Layers/Pacs/Preparation/Rubber Boots/Scent.**

CLOVEN HOOVES The split, heart-shaped toes of deer, goats, sheep, and so on that is made of chitinous material called keratin (much like human fingernails). **See Artiodactyla/Dewclaws/Feet/Hooves/Keratin/Splayed Track/Tracks.**

COCK FEATHER The odd or different colored fletching on an arrow. The cock feather is usually pointed down between the prongs of an arrow rest. Traditional archers and some compound bow shooters use solid rests and the cock feather is then pointed straight out to the side. **See Archery/Arrow Speed/Bow and Arrow/Feathers/Helical Fletching/Nocking.**

COLOR-BLIND It was once generally believed that deer see only in shades of white, gray, and black, rather than in distinct colors. Deer researchers have recently confirmed that whitetails have many more rods (low-light receptors and motion detectors) in their eyes than they do cones, which are responsible for seeing color. They have now discovered that deer are responsive to colors in the yellow and blue ranges. Deer see more deeply into the blue range but are not sensitive to red hues as are humans. The white-tailed deer's eye also does not possess the ultraviolet light filter that is present in the human eye. These phenomena allow the hunter to wear red or blaze orange in the woods, colors which are readily observable to other hunters, but not so readily to deer. **See Blaze Orange/Eyes/Fluorescent Orange/Retina/Rod Cells/Safety/Ultraviolet/Vision.**

COLOSTRUM The initial milk produced by a doe or other mammal for immediate consumption by her baby. This extremely rich milk provides the best start for newborn fawns. Biologists believe that the maternal doe's consuming the placenta or afterbirth tissue stimulates the colostrum's production. **See Afterbirth/Baby Teeth/Birth/Butterfat/Does/Fawn/Nursing/Placenta.**

COMMUNICATION The exchange of messages and information.

     A. Deer. Deer communicate through sounds, scents (smell), and their body actions. Fecal droppings, urinary deposits, pheromonal emissions, and other scent markings are common along a deer trail. By walking singlefile over their trails, deer communicate several messages to the deer with them. By casual tail flicking, a deer lets the others behind it know that all is well and that no predators have been spotted. When startled, deer emit a scent from the glands (interdigital) between their toes. Other deer walking that same trail will smell the fear-induced scent and they too will become alerted to possible danger. **See Alarm Snort/Alert Snort/Blat/Body Language/Deer Blows/Foot Stomp/Grunt/Head Bob/Kairomone/Pheromone/Vocalization.**

     B. Hunter. Two-way radios with a range of two to five miles are the latest and greatest means for hunters to communicate with each other. Nonverbal hand signals, previously agreed upon can prove invaluable to drivers in a deer drive or to two buddies stalking a bedded deer, or still-hunting together. **See Allomone/Calls/ Kairomone/Radios/Scent/ Sounds in the Deer Woods/ Whistles.**

COMPASS   A directional device that always points north but that can allow a hunter to consistently travel in other directions. A compass provides direction, a sense of safety, and convenient and valuable infor- mation, if used properly. If already lost, hunters cannot use a compass to point them back to the car or truck, as will a GPS unit. It can, however,

Compass

keep hunters from walking in circles as so easily happens when lost. The compass never lies—trust it, believe it. **See Aerial Photographs/Bureau of Land Manage- ment/Contour/GPS/Maps/Navigation/Orienteering/Orthophotoquad/ Scouting/Survival/Topographical Maps.**

COMPOUND BOW   The most modern type of archery equipment that utilizes cables, cams, pulleys, or wheels to provide a mechanical advantage for holding, sighting, and shooting much farther than traditional archery equipment. The mechanical advantage is mainly due to the reduction in holding the string back in place while aiming. The arrow coming out of a compound bow is actually accelerating at first and thus travels farther in its flight before gravity ultimately pulls it down. With traditional archery bows, the arrow decelerates from the start of its release. **See Archery/Bow and Arrow/Crossbow/Longbow/Mechanical Release/Recurve Bow/Release.**

CONDUCTION   The transfer of body heat while lying on the ground. Whitetails do not lose much heat from their bodies in the winter. They have excellent thick winter coats that keep them from losing body heat because of the long guard hairs and the short, fuzzy or woolly undercoat. Whitetails can lie in their beds on snow-covered ground for hours. When they get up, the snow will have been compressed, not melted under them. Likewise, snow can fall heavily on them, stay in its crystalline form, and not melt from body heat loss. On the other hand, during the hot summer months, whitetails do want to lose body heat. They have lost most of the fuzzy undercoat and the long, winter guard hairs have been replaced with shorter, less insulating versions. The whitetail will stretch out on the cooler ground and allow conduction, or the transfer of body heat to the ground to occur. **See Guard Hairs/Hair/Radiation/Summer Coat/Winter Coat.**

CONIFER/CONIFEROUS FOREST Common evergreen trees. They do not lose their needlelike leaves all at once in the fall, as a deciduous tree does. Whitetail deer often forage on several conifer species (e.g., cedar, white fir, juniper, several pine trees). Often the sign of a hard winter is a browse line in a coniferous stand. **See Autumn/Browse Line/Cover/Deciduous/Edge/Evergreen/Food/Frost/Hardwoods/Nutrition/Security.**

CONSERVATION DEPARTMENT The branches of the federal and state governments that are responsible for the management of all of the natural resources under their jurisdiction, including the white-tailed deer. **See Balance of Nature/Balanced Herd/Biologist/Bureau of Land Management/Game Warden/Poaching.**

CONTACT CALL Also called "social call," sounds used by whitetails to locate other deer, inform other deer of their presence, and share information. It is expressly used by does separated from other deer or their fawns. **See Body Language/Calls/Communication/Sounds in the Deer Woods/Vocalization.**

CONTOUR/CONTOUR LINES Lines on a topographical map that connect like or similar levels of elevation. The further apart these lines are, the flatter the terrain. Likewise, the closer the lines are to each other, the steeper the terrain. Hunters that take the time and opportunity to study the topographical map(s) of their hunting areas can readily determine the existence of any terrain breaks (e.g., saddles, ravines, benches, bottlenecks) that will tend to influence deer movement. **See Aerial Photographs/Bureau of Land Management/Compass/Equipment/Maps/Navigation/Orienteering/Orthophotoquad/Scouting/Survival/ Topographical Maps/United States Geological Service.**

CONTRACEPTION Tranquilizing does with darts and then injecting them with birth control drugs as a means of controlling nuisance deer and herd size. This controversial technique has proven to be ineffective, impractical, and has even led to stress-induced death for the participating whitetails. The effect of humans eating long-lasting hormones or steroids artificially implanted in deer are also a concern. **See Artificial Insemination/Herd Size/Immunocontraception/Overbrowse/Trap and Transfer.**

CONTROLLED HUNT A methodical reduction of deer numbers within a fenced area, such as a military base, a game preserve, or a wildlife research area. Often the exact number of deer, by gender, are known within that area. Hunters are allowed in with specific instructions as to the gender and number of the deer needed to be extracted. **See Baiting/Fair Chase/Ethics/Feeder/Game Farm Buck/Guided Hunt/High**

Fence Hunting/Land Management/Managed Hunt/Outfitters/Quality Deer Management.

CONVECTION CURRENTS The cyclical circulation of warm air (thermals) and falling of cool air that contributes to local wind. Usually unique to a particular land formation, convection currents are often contrary to the prevailing winds. A large rock, ledge, or cliff could deflect the local air currents and send this wind in a different direction. Wise hunters know the prevailing wind direction but still constantly check for changing wind and adjust their stand placement accordingly. **See Cross Wind/ Downwind/Prevailing Winds/Terrain/Thermals/Upwind/Wind.**

COPULATION The act of breeding; a buck mating with a doe. **See Artificial Insemination/Breeding/Buck/Chase Phase/Does/Dominance/Ejaculation/ Estrus/Gestation/Prerut/Rut.**

CORE AREA The prime area where a buck lives and spends a good deal of time, both prior to and after the peak of the rut. It could refer to his bedroom, his feeding area, and any travel routes in between. Examples might be conifer swamps, overgrown former clear-cuts, steep wooded ridges, a cattail or willow marsh, a tangled creek bottom, or even areas of blowdowns. It might even be a thick, nasty piece of real estate in which the buck feels most safe. Your primary goal should be to hunt the buck's core area. Unless you have been observing regularly, and have not spooked him at all, you will not just be able to walk into his bedding area, set up a stand, and take him as he arises. Better to start on the outer fringes of his core area, observing deer movement and signs, and, most notably, the travel corridors. Using several stand set-ups, work your way into his core area. **See Aerial Photographs/Bachelor Buck Groups/Beds/Carrying Capacity/Dispersal/Doubling Back/Funnel/Home Range/Hunting Pressure/ Security/Stand Placement/Terrain/Travel Corridor.**

CORN/CORNFIELD A favorite food of deer. It provides them with almost everything they need—food, cover, and security. They will spend all day and all night in corn-fields, and might only leave it to get water. The key to locating these deer is to locate their source of water. The best way to hunt an area with cornfields is to learn the lay of the land by walking the fields prior to the season, locating any wet areas, gullies, and grassy or rocky knolls where the crop has not grown well. Since the deer could try to stay in the corn all day, these will all be likely bedding areas.

The most effective way of hunting deer holding up in the corn is to still hunt them. This method is especially effective after a rain or snow shower has dampened the ground and made it easier to quietly move through the stalks. Hunters must always approach likely bedding areas from the downwind position. By walking across the rows in a perpendicular or diagonal manner, they can cover a lot of ground, carefully peeking into each row and looking as far as possible in both directions. Then step into the row and look even further down the row in both directions. Then take another step, peeking into the next row to check for bedded deer. Hunters should be aware that most corn rows are not perfectly straight and are often weed clogged and thus visibility may only be a few feet at best. Even if you spook deer out of a cornfield, they will probably return another day, as the cornfield offers them everything they need.

Farmers usually try to harvest the corn as feed for their dairy cows. After the corn is harvested in the fall, the deer are forced back into the woods, where they can be hunted from tree stands. A general rule for hunting near corn is to hang your stands in the woods before the corn is cut, as deer will be less aware of any changes you make (e.g., by cutting limbs, or clearing shooting lanes), or unnatural sounds (e.g., when nailing boards, attaching tree steps, or hanging metal stands). **See Crop Damage/ Food/Food Plots/Nutrition/Quality Deer Management.**

Corn

CORNEA The outer, clear covering of the eyeball; it is shiny, transparent-looking, and moist. **See Eyes/Eyeshine/Jacklighting/Retina/Tapeteum lucidum/Vision.**

CORNER/INSIDE CORNER/OUTSIDE CORNER A back area where a crop or planted field meets a forest or overgrown thicket. An inside corner is the corner of a field that is bordered by woods. An outside corner is the corner of a wooded area that is bordered by fields. Whitetails seem more likely to enter a field near these inside or outside corners than at any other place along a field's boundary. The reasons are twofold: increased visibility and the availability of nearby bedding cover. Hunting an inside corner in the morning is difficult because you cannot approach your stand from the field for fear of possibly spooking the deer in the field before you get to the stand. Thus, you must enter the stand from the woods side. Be careful too about the wind's direction. Using a stand when the wind blows from you to the field, where you expect the deer to come from, is foolhardy. **See Beds/Cover/Security.**

CORONET See Burr.

CORRIDOR A deer's often-traveled route between its bedding area and its food plot or the trail between two or more obstacles. **See Bench/Buck Trail/Deer Run/Deer Sign/Edge/Path/Rub/Security/Tracks/Trail/Travel Route.**

COUES DEER A subspecies of white-tailed deer that inhabits the southwestern United States and western Mexico. One of the twenty-nine subspecies of *Odocoileus virginianus,* (white-tailed deer) it is generally of small stature. It is a separate category for Boone and Crockett ranking (an antler net score of 125 is required for a B&C book entry) all the other twenty-eight whitetail subspecies are grouped together by B&C. **See Boone and Crockett Club/***Odocoileus virginianus***/Pope & Young/Spread/Subspecies.**

COUGAR/MOUNTAIN LION The largest and most powerful of the North American wild cats. The cougar feeds extensively upon deer fawns and adults within its territory. **See Bear/Coyote/Predator/ Prey/Wolf.**

COURTSHIP/COURTING The act of bucks courting or chasing does which can usually be observed between four to six weeks after the bucks have started sparring or mock fighting. This is a time where the bachelor buck groups have already broken up and each buck is out on his own, feeling compelled to find receptive does for breeding. At first bucks will try to closely trail a doe; however, if it is not her time to

Cougar

breed, she will often run away or just attempt to avoid him. Later in the season, as she gets closer to being in full estrus—that twenty-four to thirty-six hours when she is willing to stand for the buck and actually mate with him—the doe will let the buck get closer to her. She will urinate more frequently, allowing the buck to perform flehmen or lip curl, which is believed to assist him in determining just how close to full estrus she is. Any other buck attempting to get close to her will be driven away by the more dominant buck. The breeding buck will raise the hair on his back and neck, walk stiff-legged toward his adversary, and lower his antlers toward this subordinate intruder. Because the hierarchy of dominance has usually been established long before this time, the subordinant buck retreats, slinks off to the perimeter, or is actively chased away, all but relinquishing any expectation to breed the estrous doe. Only occasionally do actual fights occur. These might happen between two unfamiliar adversaries, when the two bucks are evenly matched in social order, or if the tending buck has become weakened by his chasing both the doe and her other suitors or by prior fights. **See Breeding/Calls/Chase Phase/Dominance/Estrus/Flehmen/Hierarchy/ Prerut/Scrape/Spar/Tending Grunt.**

COVER Any area of thick vegetation, ranging from grasses to forest canopy that a deer uses to bed down in, hide in, or avoid predators. Areas of cover provide security, food, escape routes, and so on. Experienced hunters advise, "Locate the thickest cover, erect your stand there, and that's where the Ol' Mossyback will be." The very reason that you as a human might not want to go into that thick brush, is precisely why the buck lives there! **See Back Trail/Buck Trail/Core Area/Deer Run/Edge/ Flight/Habitat/Path/Security/Terrain/Trail/Travel Corridor.**

Cover Scents

COVER SCENTS Scents used to mask or cover up a hunter's own scent. Fox urine, raccoon urine, skunk spray, pine, hemlock, spruce, earth, and dirt are examples. They are typically applied to the bottom of boots when walking into a stand, dabbed onto clothing, worn on a scent vent, or applied to a tree branch while in the stand. **See Aromatics/ Camouflage/Hygiene/Scents.**

COYOTE A canine predator that rivals the wolf in its intelligence and exceeded it in its adaptability. The Eastern Coyote is larger and heavier (fifty pounds) than its western cousin (thirty-five pounds). The coyote is believed to be the killer of more deer than any other predator, just because of its sheer numbers and extensive range overlapping that of the whitetail's range. A coyote usually kills a fawn by biting its neck, head, or spinal area. It is estimated that fawn mortality can reach seventy percent where predator numbers are high. **See Bears/Canine/Carrion/Die-off/Predator/Prey/Winterkill/ Wolf.**

Coyote

C

CRAB APPLE A deciduous, thorny branched tree that produces a golf-ball size fleshy fruit, usually over two-to-four-year intervals. Early in the growing season, this soft mast is sour. After ripening, it falls to the ground and attracts animals who use it as a food source. An orchard of crab apples is often found around abandoned homesteads. **See Apple/Deciduous/Food/Frost/Grapes/Hardwoods/Mast/Oaks/Pawing/ Pears/Persimmon.**

CREEK/CREEK BOTTOM The natural lowland area, including and bordering a small, flowing body of water that provides security, water, food, and cover to whitetails. Hunters can use a creek to quietly access their stand or hunting area and keep their entry and exit scent trail to a minimum. **See Aerial Photographs/Aquatic Vegetation/Terrain/Topographical Maps/Water.**

CREPUSCULAR Creatures such as deer whose periods of greatest activity occur during the changing levels of daylight—dusk and dawn. Their activity level is also greatly affected by the weather and the moon phase. **See Barometer/Dawn/Diurnal Activities/Dusk/Lunar Influence/Moon/Nocturnal/Rut/Rut Suppressants/ Weather.**

CROP DAMAGE The amount of damage that deer inflict in many agricultural areas. The average whitetail consumes between eight and fifteen pounds of food per day. Whether dear eat the plant itself or the seeds of soybeans, corn, wheat, rye, and oats, or the silage-producing crops of alfalfa or clover, that is a lot of loss per animal— every day—for a farmer to bear. In an area of high deer numbers, landowners may give permission to hunt more readily because of this damage to their livelihood. **See Alfalfa/Apples/Carrying Capacity/Food/Fruits//Herd Size/Land Management/ Landowners/Permission to Hunt/Predator.**

CROSSBOW The French response to the powerful body armor or mail-piercing arrows of the English longbow. It was a short weapon, built of an extremely strong and difficult-to-pull-back bow mounted horizontally onto a "gunstock," with a trigger mechanism for releasing the short, stiff arrow known as a bolt. Using crossbows to hunt whitetails is legal in some states. Handicapped hunters, otherwise unable to hunt deer, can apply for their use under special circumstances. Crossbows can be very accurate and effective at ranges beyond that at normal archery equipment. **See Archery/Bow and Arrow/Compound Bow/Firearms/Longbow/Recurve Bow/Release.**

CROSSBREEDING Copulation outside of an individual's immediate or related family members. Whitetail males one to two years old are forced out of their mother's home range, which prevents inbreeding and subsequent reduction in genetic diversity. This dispersal of young males is a two-way street as other males from different matriarchal (doe) lineages will move into the nonrelated doe's territory and interbreed with her or her daughters. **See Biodiversity/Breeding/Copulation/Dispersal/ Genetics/Inbreeding.**

CROSS WIND Any breeze, moving air current, or wind that is not straight in your face or 180 degrees directly behind you. It can be crossing your path from any angle from the side. **See Air Currents/Barometer/Convection Current/Down Wind/ Prevailing Wind/Storms/Thermal/Upwind/Weather/Wind Chill.**

CROWDING A situation when the size of a herd exceeds the carrying capacity of a habitat. Stress is put on both the herd size, individual deer, and the land, itself. Too many deer and too little food leads to overbrowsing of the treeline, disease, and eventually some die-off of the weak and the young. The stress of too many deer compacted together has been observed to lead to an increase of antisocial activities. **See Carrying Capacity/Herd Size/Overbrowsing/Stress/Yarding.**

CRUST/SNOW CRUST The hard, icy cover of snow; that has melted and then refrozen. Whitetails have a difficult time walking and more particularly running in deep snow as their sharp hooves puncture through the crust and their bodies sink into the snow. Moving through deep snow expends a great amount of energy for the deer. Other animals, with better adapted feet for traveling on the snow, appear to easily walk across a heavily crusted snowfall. **See Safety/Snow/Winter.**

CUD Balls or mounds of quickly chewed grass, browse, and so on that a deer has rapidly gorged itself on, stored in the first of its four stomachs, and then regurgitated up later while in its daytime bed to be more thoroughly chewed up and prepared for further digestion. The now thoroughly chewed cud or bolus will then be passed into the deer's other stomach chambers for completing the digestion process. A new cud will then be regurgitated and worked on. **See Beds Area/Bolus/Food/Digestion/ Regurgitate/Rumen.**

CULL/CULLING The purposeful removal of certain members of a population, such as females (does), for the express purpose of reducing the herd size and possibly protecting the environment from overbrowsing, the spreading of disease, and so on. **See Carrying Capacity/Herd Size/Doe Harvest/Quality Deer Management/ Spikes.**

CWD See Chronic Wasting Disease.

DAWN The time just before sunrise, the beginning of daylight. It is usually a time of active deer movement, as they are returning from the feeding areas to their daytime bedding areas. **See Crepuscular/Diurnal Activities/Dusk/Sunrise.**

DECIDUOUS FOREST Broad-leafed trees that usually drop their leaves at some point after the first frost in autumn. Before they fall (that is how the season got its name), their leaves revert back to their real colors; that is, the bright yellows, oranges, and reds, are no longer masked by the green of the chlorophyll. This shutting down of the chlorophyll means that the trees are no longer producing "food" to store in their roots. **See Acorn/Autumn/Browseline/Chlorophyll/Conifer/Evergreen/ Hardwoods/Leaf Drop/Oaks/Photosynthesis.**

DECIDUOUS TEETH The "milk teeth" of the fawn. They soon are replaced with incisors and molars so that the young deer can eat vegetative materials. **See Colostrum/Cud/Food/Molars/Nursing/Teeth/Udder.**

DECOY Models or silhouettes resembling a deer that enhance a hunter's calling by giving the deer something to visually cue on when they arrive at the scene. Deer decoys work well in open fields as well as dense cover.

These visual aids can be used to maneuver and stop rutting bucks. A small buck decoy can serve as a visual attractant and confidence builder to a live buck. If you place a doe or small buck decoy on a field edge within bow range of your tree stand, a rutting buck can see this simulated deer from several hundred yards away. He will try to slip into the woods to approach it. Soft grunt calls or rattling sometimes enhances the setup.

Find a spot where the wind blows from heavy cover into a field. Erect your tree stand on the inside edge of the cover line with your back to the field. Place a decoy fifteen to twenty yards inside the cover and directly upwind of your stand. If the cover is heavy along the field edge, this setup works well to give an incoming buck confidence to approach your calling. The open ground behind you forces the buck to move toward your calls in a cross-wind direction

Decoy

because he will not want to expose himself out in the open and thus will avoid crossing the open ground to try to sniff out the situation.

When a buck comes creeping toward your calls, he is looking for another deer. If he sees the doe decoy, he either relaxes and stops or is sexually attracted enough to investigate "her." If you are using a buck decoy, he gets mad at the territory infringement of this new male interloper and starts to swagger toward the fake buck. A buck decoy must always face toward the stand. The reason for this is that as a buck approaches another male (real or decoy), he always circles around it, checking for deer scent, and comes in head to head. If the decoy faces the stand (and you), the buck will present you with a broadside shot. With his attention riveted upon the decoy, this is your best opportunity to take him. Make sure that your decoy is scent-free, that you have securely anchored it to the ground (you don't want the wind to knock it over forcing you to get out of your stand and possibly spooking your buck), and that it can be easily seen by approaching bucks.

Place a doe decoy about twenty to twenty-five yards upwind from your stand; face "her" away from you and your stand as a buck approaches a doe from behind in order to check out her estrous status. A deadly effective trick is to add movement to your decoy by attaching a clean white handkerchief to the decoy's tail and running an attached mono-filament fishline from the handkerchief to your stand.

Caution: Never carry a decoy into the woods without using some sort of blaze orange covering or concealing it in a bag. It is certainly not worth having another hunter spot your decoy, thinking it is a live deer, and take a shot at you. **See Ethics/Equipment/Safety/Sportsmanship.**

DEER BLOWS The low, sharp, nasal, whooshing sound one hears when a whitetail has been alerted by an intruder and seeks to get a response back, identify the intruder, or warn other deer in the area of potential danger. This sound is often heard when an alerted deer bounds away. The terms blow and snort are often used interchangeably. **See Alert Snort/Blow/Calls/Communication/Noise/Sounds in the Deer Woods.**

DEER CAMP Often referred to as the annual get-together of deer hunting buddies. Occasionally, this gathering is for the express purpose of shedding the shackles of society and returning to their early Pleistocene roots as pursuers of wild game. Whether it is a tent pitched somewhere, a mobile home pulled off the road, or a permanent building specifically built for sheltering the hunters from the elements, "deer camp" takes on an aura of humankind's return to the instinctual drive to hunt deer. **See Benchrest/Camp/Rituals/Sighting In/Zeroing In.**

DEER CHECK STATION Also called "registration stations," these mobile checkpoints are used by conservation officers and state wildlife biologists to spot-check on the health of the deer herd, and get a rough idea about hunter success in an area. **See Age of Deer/Biologist/Conservation Department/Game Warden/Herd Size/ Land Management.**

DEER DIARY
See Hunting Log.

DEER DRIVE
See Drive.

DEER FENCE A fence that is too high for a deer to jump over, usually at least eight feet high. Whitetails have been reported to easily clear six-foot obstacles in a single leap. A deer fence that tempts whitetails to jump it is dangerous to the deer, just as are high-strung strands of barbed wire. Many a good buck has caught its leg in a fence, got hung up, and died because it could not free itself. landowners often use high fences to keep deer out of their vegetables, orchards, or valuable nursery stock.

Deer Fence

Game managers have used high deer fences to keep control of their deer herd, and govern its genetics, buck-to-doe ratio, and so on. **See Controlled Hunt/ Fence/Funnel/Game Farm/Game Warden/High Fence Hunting/Managed Hunt.**

DEER MANAGEMENT PERMITS "Licenses" to take an extra deer, also referred to as "antlerless deer permit." They are issued by state conservation authorities as a management tool to keep deer herd numbers in check (i.e., below the carrying capacity of the land) by focusing on taking does. Often they are issued for use during a specified time during the hunting season. Some areas of the country issue these permits to farmers who have had extensive crop depredation (damage) as a means of reducing future crop damage. **See Biologist/Conservation Department/Doe Permit/Game Warden/Herd Size/Land Management/Management Permit.**

DEER RUN Highly visual paths used repeatedly by deer that look like bare-earth trails through the woods, across hillsides, and so on. They usually lead to bedding or feeding areas. **See Buck Trail/Cover/Deer Sign/Edge/Path/Security/Tracks/ Trail/Travel Corridor.**

DEER SEARCH, INC. An organization originally established in New York State in the 1980s to help hunters locate wounded or lost deer. Using blood trailing dogs, licensed handlers assist ethical sportsmen recover lost, mortally wounded deer. Deer Search, Inc. does not allow its services to be used as a deer driving technique on live deer, but only for the recovery of dead deer. **See Blood Trail/Blood-trailing Dogs/Dogs/ Downed Deer/Ethics/Sportsmanship/Wounded Game.**

DEER SIGNS Anything that indicates a deer has used an area or passed through it. Deer signs include oval-shaped beds, droppings, rubs, scrapes, shed antlers, sightings, sounds, and tracks. Before crops are harvested, deer signs tend to be widespread and diluted. Once farm crops are harvested, deer signs tend to become concentrated in heavy cover, travel corridors, and bedding areas. Wet weather often washes tracks and droppings away. After a rain or snowfall, a hunter can usually assume that deer signs are fresh and that a deer recently has been in the area. **See Beds/Browseline/Buck Trail/Deer Run/Dewclaws/Drag Marks/Fecal Dropping/Overbrowse/Rubs/ Scrapes/Tracks.**

DEERSKIN The tanned hide of a buck or doe (usually without the hair). It is generally soft, supple, and used for making quality leather gloves and other accessories. Because it stretches so easily, and so much, it must be "toggled" by experts in leatherworking before larger items of apparel (e.g., coats, jackets, pants) can be made from it. Deerskin colors range from pure white to almost totally brown; with a golden tan being the most popular and usual color. **See Tanning.**

DEER YARD A particular area where deer traditionally feel safe and generally find food. An annual migration usually occurs in northern and mountainous climates, where the snow reaches depths that make travel difficult and exhaustive, when the temperature plummets and predators threaten. By "yarding" together and with a multitude of deer traveling the same paths, deer are able to keep the snow packed underfoot, thus expending less energy to get at what food is available. The tragedy of a deer yard is that the deer usually do not leave its security even when the available food is depleted and fresh food may be only a short distance away. Weakness caused by starvation and disease can lead to a die-off or severe reduction in numbers. The fawns, the sick, and the starving will weaken and die first. **See Carrying Capacity/Die-Off/Habitat/Predator/Security/Winterkill/Yarding.**

DEFECATE/DEFECATION The act of anal elimination, dropping pellets or scat, releasing solid bodily waste materials. **See Deer Sign/Droppings/Scat.**

DEFENSES Techniques animals use to protect themselves from danger. White-tailed

deer rely upon the three S's: smell, sight, and sound (arguably in that order of importance) as their first line of defense. Once alarmed, or having identified danger, they
then use their legs in a "fight or flight" reaction. Whitetails also use their characteristic
tail to alert others of possible danger and to lead fawns out of harm's way. **See
Ears/Eyes/Fight or Flight/Hearing/Nose/Security/Vision.**

DEMOGRAPHICS The study of the particular characteristics and makeup of a population of flora or fauna. The demographics of a whitetail population might include
herd size, number of each gender, number of adults and fawns, frequency of drop tine
observance, existence of albinism, and so on. **See Diversity/Herd Size.**

DEWCLAW Two, functionless, chitinous (hard, fingernail-like), knobby projections
located on the backside of a whitetail's front and back legs. The dewclaws on the front
legs are larger and lower (closer to the main hooves) than those on the hind legs,
which are located several inches above the main hooves. Their name reportedly came
from their not touching the ground, only the dew on the grass. Dewclaw marks can
easily be seen in deer tracks in deep mud or snow. They are the symbolic equivalent
of a human's index and pinkie fingers. **See Artiodactyla/Cloven Hooves/Deer
Run/Deer Sign/Feet/Hooves/Keratin/Tracks/Trails.**

DIAPHRAGM The internal body membrane made up of muscle and connective
tissue, specifically the partition separating the chest and abdominal cavities in a white-
tailed deer and other mammals. **See Field Dressing/Guts/Internal Organs.**

DIE-OFF A mass reduction of deer numbers, usually late in a severe winter, when the
carrying capacity of the land has been exceeded. Without hunters to manage the deer
herds, deer will reproduce to the extent that starvation will occur, resulting in a massive die-off. Warning signs of impending die-offs first become noticeable in small,
emaciated deer, often infected with parasites and noticeable fawn mortality. Hunters
often contribute to this situation by refusing to shoot does. (Remember: you cannot
eat horns!) Hunters should not hesitate to take a doe in order to reduce the herd size,
as one doe removed actually accounts for a dozen or more deer (the doe herself and
her progeny) that will not become part of the overpopulation problem. **See Balance
of Nature/Carrying Capacity/Green-Up/Habitat/Herd Size/Overbrowsing/
Predators/Winterkill/Yarding.**

DISEASE Illnesses that affect an animal. Whitetails, being mammals, are affected by
a myriad of diseases, as listed below. One of Mother Nature's ways for reducing an
overcrowded herd is through infectious disease. This natural method for culling out
the old and the infirm often ultimately strengthens the genetic diversity and thus survivability of the deer population. **See Anthrax/Chronic Wasting Disease/
Epizootic Hemorrhaging Disease/Ixodes Tick/Liver Flukes/Lyme Disease/
Parasites/Survival of the Fittest/Ticks.**

DISNEYFICATION The attitude held by some people that wild animals possess human traits as portrayed in Walt Disney cartoons. These anthropomorphic attitudes fuel anti-hunter sentiments, and their holders don't fully understand the truth or the consequences of these improper ideas about wild animals and proper management. **See Anthropomorphic/Anti-Hunter/Bambi Syndrome.**

DISPERSAL The period in early September when the groups of bachelor bucks that have been together all summer begin to thin out or disappear. What is happening is that they have traveled to new areas several miles from their birth area and established a new core area or home range. Ready-to-give-birth does drive off their previous year's fawns (yearlings) and any other females from their claimed birthing areas. This is to prevent any chance of newborns imprinting on other deer and to keep foreign scent out of the area, thus increasing the fawn's chances of survival. **See Bachelor Buck Groups/Biodiversity/Birth/Crossbreeding/Habitat/Home Range/Imprinting/Inbreeding/Lead Doe.**

DISSIPATE Allowing one's scent to leave an area before you use or hunt it. **See Cross Wind/Downwind/Scent/Wind.**

DIURNAL ACTIVITIES Daytime activities as opposed to nighttime. It has been repeatedly observed that cooler weather provides a stimulus for an increase in deer's daytime activities. This cooler weather does not initiate the onset of the rut as some believe, but people see more deer then because the rut and the accompanying cooler weather prompt deer to move around during the daytime. Likewise, if the weather becomes unseasonably warm, deer have been known to become very inactive and bed down during the day. Bucks then breed at night when the air has cooled down and they can be more comfortable in their sexual exertions. Whether breeding occurs at night or during the day, the rut will always occur. **See Barometer/Crepuscular/Lunar Influence/Moon/Nocturnal/Rut/Rut Suppressants/Storms/Weather.**

DIVERSITY Differences between members of a species that allow for genetic growth and species improvement. When referenced to the total environment, the greater the variation of plant and animal life within an area, the greater the opportunities for all to survive. **See DNA/Genes/Heredity.**

DNA (DEOXYRIBONUCLAIC ACID) Located within the nucleus of each cell of the body, the gene code governing everything about an organism. Passed on from the genes of the male and female parents, this genetic code is responsible for continuing the traits and characteristics of a species and for the evolution of those characteristics that leads to better survivability. **See Biodiversity/Demographics/Diversity/Genes/Herd Size/Heredity/Inbreeding.**

DOES The female deer of the whitetail species, sometimes called "flat-tops," "propeller-heads," "nannies,"and "skillet-heads." Does actually control the world of the

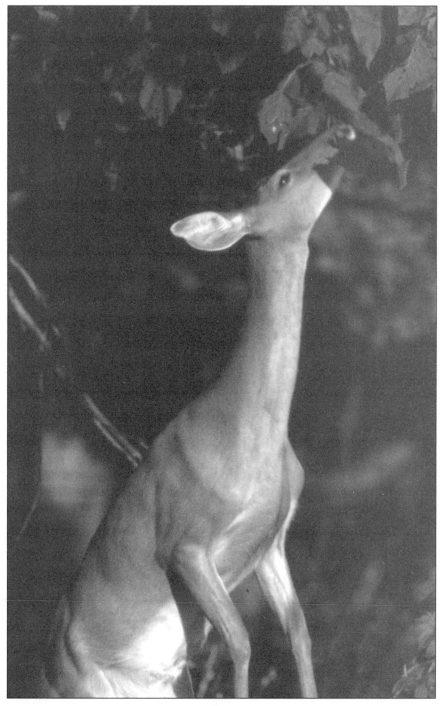

Doe

white-tailed deer. Does are usually able to breed and conceive during their second year (one and one-half years old). An older doe and her female fawns usually stay together as a family grouping. The doe is the primary instructor for her fawns, who are totally dependent upon her for their nourishment and security. The key to finding bucks during the breeding season (estrus/rut) is to locate the does. The doe population is the main determinant for wildlife biologists setting up harvest or bag limits for the hunting season. **See Alpha Buck/Birth/Doe Harvest/Dominance/Gestation/Head Bob/Herd Balance/Lead Doe/Quality Deer Management.**

DOE HARVEST Deer researchers now tells us that it is necessary to abandon the "buck only" concept of whitetail hunting. In fact, in order to keep the deer herd from overpopulating the land and thus adversely affecting their own numbers and health, approximately twenty-five percent of does should be harvested by hunters during the season. Too many does puts pressure and stress on the whole whitetail population in an area. In fact, a lot of does and too few bucks extends the rut because the bucks cannot breed all the available does. This results in a later-than-normal breeding for some does and later-than-normal fawn birthing times, not to mention the toll that this extensive breeding takes on the fat reserves and recovery time for the bucks. Winterkill will claim many of the reserves-depleted breeding bucks.

By killing off twenty-five percent of a habitat's does, a good land steward can keep a deer herd's numbers in check. Thus, it is better to harvest a significant number of does than not enough whitetails in order to keep the herd numbers below the carrying capacity of the land. It takes longer for an overbrowsed habitat to repair itself than it does for whitetails to replenish their numbers. Those hunters practicing quality deer management concepts of regularly harvesting does will begin to see a better buck-to-doe ratio, intensified rut activities, and an overall healthier herd. **See Balanced Herd/Browseline/Buck-Doe Ratio/Carrying Capacity/Doe/Herd Size/Overbrowse/Quality Deer Management.**

DOE PERMITS These licenses to take an extra deer are also referred to as "Antlerless Deer Permits." They are issued by state conservation authorities as a management tool to keep deer herd numbers in check (i.e., below the carrying capacity of the land) by focusing upon taking does. Often they are issued for use during a specified time during the hunting season. Some areas of the country issue these permits to farmers who have had extensive crop depredation (damage) as a means of reducing future crop damage. **See Biologist/Deer Management Permit/Doe Permit/Conservation Department/Herd Size.**

DOGS Members of the canine family. Whether household pets or feral (wild), dogs are a major irritation and source of danger to deer. Sometimes running alone or often in pairs or packs, dogs chasing deer cause undue stress, exhaustion, and sometimes death. Dogs observed running or chasing deer are often tempting targets to hunters, trappers, even game wardens.

Dogs can also be of benefit to deer hunters, as in their use for trailing wounded deer. Deer-trailing dogs usually have bells attached to them, so that their handlers can follow their trailing efforts and ultimately find them and the recovered dead deer. **See Blood-trailing Dogs/Deer Search, Inc./Feral Dogs/Hamstring/Hounds/ Predation/Wounded Game.**

DOMINANCE A hierarchical social order. The white-tailed deer's world revolves around the quest for food, cover, or sex. The seemingly constant search for food, especially during winter or starvation times, or during the breeding season (rut), forces all members of a deer herd into their individual social ranking. Does establish their dominance by flailing or striking out at another deer's head with their forelegs. Dominant does get the choicest food, the best and most secure fawning areas, and are often bred first by the dominant buck, thus assuring the best genes of one gender match up with the best genes of the other.

Bucks settle any disputes over dominance before the rutting season actually begins. The size, weight, age and condition of his antlers all help a buck establish his dominance during the sparring contests or actual fighting that occurs during the breeding season. Yearling bucks and those past their prime (over seven years) must wait by the sidelines to get a chance to breed a doe in heat. The top buck deer, who establishes his dominant position by winning every sparring contest and any actual fight, has first rights to any estrous doe.

The dominant bucks entering the time of the rut will have fat packed along their spines from abundant foraging of fall vegetative browse and will not have much time to spend eating. They will be too busy fending off rival bucks for the privilege of breeding a doe in estrus at the right time. The sexual drive, good health, and the fighting spirit of a mature buck assures the continuation of his genes and thus the best of the species. **See Aggression/Agonistic Behavior/Alpha Buck/Bachelor Buck Group/Eye Contact/Fighting/Flailing/Hierarchy/Sparring/ Testosterone.**

DOUBLE-BARRELED RIFLE/SHOTGUN A firearm with two barrels, either side by side or one over the other, giving the hunter two shots before having to reload. Loaded with 00 (double aught) or 000 (triple aught) buckshot, the shotgun can be very effective at bringing down a whitetail at close range. They were the preferred firearm before autoloaders, pumps, and lever action firearms arrived on the deer-hunting scene. **See Autoloader/Firearms/Lever Action/Over-Under/Pump Action/ Rifle/Shotgun/Side-by-Side.**

DOUBLE LUNG A deer hit in both lungs. Whitetail hit in one lung can travel for quite a distance, but if a deer is hit in both lungs, your trailing chore will be short as the deer will soon asphyxiate or collapse and die through lack of oxygen to the brain. **See One Shot Kill/Wounded Game.**

DOUBLING BACK A deer's behavior when alarmed, spooked, shot at, or pressured in any of a myriad of ways. White-tailed deer will usually not run out of the familiarity of their home range. Very often, they will circle around their own trail, often even heading back in the direction that they came from, and check to see if predators are trailing them. A trailing hunter should parallel a spooked deer's trail by about twenty yards to the side. The hunter just might catch the deer watching its back trail. **See Backtracking/Back Trail/Core Area/Escape Route/Home Range/Security/ Tracks/Trails/Travel Corridor.**

DOWNWIND A negative hunting condition, in which the wind is blowing from the hunter toward the deer. Any hunter scent that is on the air currents will travel directly to the deer's nose. Since deer try to always travel with the wind in their noses, they will smell the hunters, know their location, and will not travel toward them. **See Cross Wind/Prevailing Winds/Scent/Thermals/Upwind/Wind.**

DOWNED DEER A deer that has been shot at and runs away. The hunter is left with the major question of follow-up: how and when to pursue and find the deer. It is absolutely the hunter's responsibility and moral obligation to recover the deer. The first question facing the hunter/shooter is "Do I immediately pursue this wounded animal or do I wait a reasonable amount of time and let it stiffen up?" Most hunters were taught to let a wounded deer run off and wait at least half an hour so that the deer can lie down, bleed out, stiffen up, and die. To answer this question, hunters must realistically re-examine the shot in their minds, considering where the deer was hit, its reaction to the shot, the direction that it ran, whether other hunters are nearby, and the existing or impending weather conditions. Each of these factors will have an impact upon decisions about when and how to follow-up on a wounded deer. **See After the Shot/Blood/Blood-Trailing Dogs/Dogs/Follow-Up/Lantern/Rigor Mortis/ Shot Placement/Stiffen Up/Tracking Wounded Game.**

DRAG MARKS Long, narrow marks between deer tracks made in the snow, usually a solid indication of a buck. Does tend to walk more daintily than bucks. They will pick up their front legs clear of the snow and just leave the footprint itself. Button bucks, spikes, and mature bucks, tend to "drag" their hind legs as they walk, lifting them just enough to clear the ground. **See Buck/Deer Sign/Dewclaws/Tracks.**

DRAG ROPE A useful piece of equipment that every deer hunter should have along when afield. Generally about six-to-eight feet long, the rope is used by itself, coupled with handles or a stick found nearby, to tie the head and forefeet, of a whitetail together for ease of dragging it out of the woods. **See Accessories/ Equipment/Fanny Pack/Follow-Up/Wounded Game.**

DRAW A term used in archery and land formation.

    A. Archery. To pull a bow back, as in "draw the arrow." **See Anchor Point/Bow and Arrow.**

    B. Archery. The distance from the nocking point on a bowstring to the front of the bow riser, or arrow rest.

    C. Land formation. A depression, gully, or ravine. **See Funnel/Gully/ Ravine/Saddle/Terrain.**

Draw

DRAW WEIGHT The amount of effort needed to pull a bow back. The usual draw weight of a hunting bow is between fifty to seventy pounds. The same amount of effort is needed to hold a recurve or longbow at full draw. A compound bow, due to the design of its cams or wheels, allows the user to hold the bow at full draw with less effort. This is known as the let-off. The advantage of the compound bow is that many have a let-off of one-third to one-half the resistance at full draw. For example, a compound bow with a draw weight of seventy pounds and a let-off of fifty percent, requires on enough energy to pull thirty-five pounds. **See Arrow Speed/Arrow Weight/Bow and Arrow.**

DRESSED WEIGHT The weight of a deer carcass after the lungs, heart, liver, stomach, intestines, and all supporting viscera have been removed. Dressed weight can be safely estimated at two-thirds of the weight of the deer when it was alive. Comparisons:

Dressed Weight (lbs.)	Relative Live Weight (lbs.)
80	120
90	135
150	200

See Bergmann's Rule/Body Weight/Fat/Field Dressing/Hog Dressed/Live Weight.

DRIVE/DEER DRIVE/DRIVERS A tactic most useful when deer will not budge from their thick sanctuary or escape cover. Using this technique, a group of hunters splits into two groups: drivers and posters. The drivers walk through the holding cover, trying to push the deer toward the posters, who sit tight and ambush the deer as they emerge. Obviously, safety is of paramount concern here, as all parties must known exactly where each of their partners are so that no one is accidentally shot.

A well set-up drive will work almost anytime. It is absolutely crucial to choose the right area for staging a deer drive. Daytime bedding areas are the usual choice. The driving area must offer some predictability as to where the deer will go when pushed. Certainly, if a natural funnel is present, this area should be closely watched by the posters because deer are apt to follow the contour of the land, which should lead them past the posters. Drivers should stay close enough together so as to prevent deer from slipping through the gaps. Posters should be positioned so that they sit directly into or quartering into the wind in a place that offers a clear shot. Safety first! Deer drives should be carefully planned: Everyone should wear hunter-orange clothing and always be absolutely aware of each other's position.

The following six guidelines for a deer drive should be taken into consideration:

A. Before hunters start a drive, they should all carefully go over a topographical map or aerial photos of the land, explaining the drive thoroughly to all parties and pointing out the location of each hunter, particularly the watchers.

B. Standers/watchers should approach their spots silently and from downwind, well before the drive starts.

C. Drivers should move downwind, letting their scent blow into the drive.

D. Drivers should move deliberately, quietly and slowly, pausing frequently and nearly still hunting the cover.

E. As drivers move through an area, they should check every deer-size clump of cover, walking through it, kicking it, and so on.

F. Both watchers and drivers must meet at a previously agreed upon point and time. Everyone is to be accounted for before the drive wraps up. See Escape Routes/Hunting Pressure/Push/Stand/Standers/Watchers.

DROOL/DROOLING The act of dribbling spital or saliva all over by bucks during the rut, particularly in pursuit of an estrous doe. See Rut/Salivary Glands.

DROPPINGS Deer feces, or pellets. They can show up anywhere and range from black, to brown, to green in color, depending upon what the deer is currently eating.

Droppings

Deer droppings can be disklike in shape or elongated pellets with a small spike of fecal material at one end. They can be individual and loosely scattered around in a rough circle or an amorphous mass. Deer droppings should not be confused with rabbit pellets, which are usually perfectly round (no indentations or spikes) and are most often light brown in color.

Most often observed are pellets ranging in size from one-third to one inch long. The general rule of thumb is the larger the pellet, the larger the deer. Observing a lot of droppings scattered over a confined area usually indicates a deer's core living area. This would be an excellent place to hunt. Be sure, though, that you do not hunt so close to this core area that your entry or exit will spook the deer. See **Anus/Core Area/Deer Sign/Droppings/Home Range/Scat/Spoor.**

DROP TINE/DROP POINT Downward growing point on a mature buck's antlers. Drop tines are unusual, usually associated with a "nontypical" rack, and therefore attractive to the trophy hunter. See **Boone and Crockett Club/G-1/G-2/Genetics/Main Beam/Net Score/Nontypical/ Pope & Young/Rack/Scoring/Spread/Trophy Rack.**

Drop Tine

DRYING PERIOD The required sixty-day holding time before any rack can be officially scored for possible entry into the record books. The rack is likely to lose several inches from its green score. **See Boone and Crockett Club/Green Score/ Mount/Net Score/Pope & Young/Rack/Scoring/Taxidermist/Trophy.**

DUSK That mystical time when the sun is beginning to set. Deer will again leave their beds and head to the feeding areas, where they will feed off and on throughout the night. Hunters locating themselves overlooking a trail that leads to a feeding area will have an excellent chance at a deer. Keep in mind that nasty weather conditions will often cause deer to begin feeding during late afternoon, well before dusk. **See Crepuscular/Dawn/Evening/Sunset/Sunrise.**

EARS The third most important sensory organ, after the nose and eyes, that a deer uses for defense and security. Deer are highly sensitive to sounds, particularly a strange sound in their world. The average mature deer's ear reportedly has about 24 square inches of surface area with which to capture sounds. The ears rotate to focus and concentrate on a new sound for any signs of danger. **See Alarm Posture/Alarm Snort/Alert Snort/Blow/Body Language/Communication/Flag/Hearing/ Sounds in the Deer Woods/Vocalization.**

EARLY BLUR See Visual Closure.

EARPLUGS/EARMUFFS Protective gear used to muffle or shield the ears from harsh sounds such as a gunshot, as repeated exposure to gunshot blasts have been proven to harm a shooter's hearing. Hearing augmentation devices (e.g., Game Ears/Walker's Ear) are available that actually protect a hunter's ears from sound of the shot but amplify any surrounding sounds so that the hunter can hear better as game approaches. **See Ears/Equipment/Hearing/Safety/Sounds in the Deer Woods.**

EASTERN COUNT A method used by hunters east of the Mississippi River to count the points (one inch or more in length) on both side of a buck's antlers. This is different from the western count, where points are counted on only one side. For example, a "six pointer" in the east has possibly three points on each side or maybe two on one side and four on the other for a total maximum number of six points between the two antlers. A "six pointer" by western count could refer to either a total of eleven or twelve points available to score. **See Boone and Crockett Club/Points/Pope & Young/Rack/Spread/Western Count.**

EDGE Ecological terrain where one type of vegetation meets or blends into another type; that is, the place where two or more habitat types come together. Another name for an edge is an ecotone. Examples in clude a hedgerow between cultivated fields; a cornfield alongside an overgrown drainage ditch; a marshy, cattailed creek bottom next to a wooded hillside; and a pine forest spur jutting into a deciduous forest. Edges are important to whitetails for security and cover, as well as food. Edges are potential sources of soft mast such as berries, wild grapes, and other fruits. **See Buck Trail/ Ecotone/Escape Route/Habitat/Hunting Pressure/Topographical Maps/ Trail/Transition Zone/Travel Corridor.**

Edge

EHD See Epizootic Hemorrhaging Disease.

EJACULATION The action of a male's sexual organ releasing sperm and semen after stimulation, whether through the breeding act or some form of autoerotic masturbation. See Artificial Insemination/Breeding/Buck/Copulation/Dominance/Rut/Scrape.

ENDEMIC Native to or naturally occurring in a specific place. Exotic game species from Africa or Europe are not endemic to the United States. See White-tailed Deer.

ENDOCRINE SYSTEM A collective category of glands (e.g., adrenal, pineal, pituitary, and testes) that release their specific hormones and other secretions internally, where they affect specific behaviors (in the whitetail they trigger breeding, grow antlers, start lactation, and so on). These are opposed to the glands of the exocrine system, which exude their secretions outside the body (e.g., pre-orbital gland). See Adrenal Gland/Glands/Pineal Gland/Pituitary Gland/Testes/Testosterone.

ENERGY/ENERGY CONSUMPTION In the case of animals, the amount of energy for normal body functioning, maintenance, and survival that comes from food. Equilibrium exists if animals get all their energy from their daily food supply. However, problems arise, particularly during the lean times of winter, when animals like the whitetail must avoid predators, free-ranging dogs, hunters, and so on and live off their reserves of body fat. Too much energy expended in fight-or-flight situations or maybe in pursuing belly-filling but nonnutritious food sources can lead to starvation or weakening before spring "green-up" occurs. See Die-Off/Green-Up/Starvation/Winterkill/Yarding.

EQUINOX See Autumnal Equinox/Vernal Equinox.

EPIZOOTIC HEMORRHAGING DISEASE (EHD) A disease of the white-tailed deer that usually results from overcrowding. It gets its name because the deer appear to lose bodily fluids directly from their tissue and they bleed internally from their organs. Their tongues turn blue, and they are constantly thirsty and drinking during the early stages of it in an attempt to replenish lost body fluids. See Chronic Wasting Disease/Diseases/Parasites.

EQUIPMENT The large variety of gear available to a deer hunter. It would not be possible to list every piece of equipment in this field manual! The following statements are not to be construed as passing judgment on anyone's equipment nor do they purposely endorse anyone's product. They are simply based upon what I have used or have amply discussed with my hunting compatriots. .

    A. Backpack. Handy for carrying most of the above equipment to and from your stand, a pack can be as small as a fanny pack or as large as a frame pack if you should need to pack out meat.

B. Broadhead. The larger the cutting diameter of a broadhead, the more blood will flow, the better the blood trail will be, and the sooner your deer will die and you can recover it. Cutting corners for weight reduction at the expense of the killing power of your broadhead is foolish. State hunting regulations usually specify the size of a legal broadhead. The minimum I use is 100 grains, and the maximum is 125 grains. **See Arrowheads/Hemorrhaging.**

C. Calls. These sound-making devices are used by the hunter to simulate communications between deer, often with the intention of bringing the deer in closer for a shot.

D. Camouflage. The key to excellent camouflage is to eliminate the solid outline of a person's figure while at the same time blending well with the surroundings. Most of the more popular brands of camouflage clothing on the market today have patterns that dissolve a hunter's solid outline into a maze of open spaces and twisted sticks and leaves. The desired effect is actually an optical illusion. A deer looking at a combination of blurred background and detailed foreground images has a hard time focusing on both at the same time. The animal is unable to pick out a single outline. With these detailed and contrasting foregrounds combined with large background patterns, a hunter in the shadows or in dappled sunlight can disappear into the woods.

E. Carbon versus aluminum arrows. The type of arrows you use is strictly your choice. Carbon arrows are lighter, thus usually faster. They are also more forgiving if your shot tickles a tree, whereas aluminum will usually bend or kink. You must match your arrows to your bow for the most efficient and effective combination.

F. Footwear. For long treks, traditional leather lace-up or hiking boots (particularly in the early season) are most comfortable. Late-season standhunters need cold-weather PAC boots with felt liners. All rubber, knee-high boots help keep your scent off the trail, on the way to and from your stand, thus decreasing a deer's chances of becoming alert to your presence. Felt overboots are used to muffle the sound of your walking for silent entry into your hunting area. Thin-soled boots and hunting sneaker let stillhunters and stalkers feel the ground, branches, and loose rocks beneath their feet in order to avoid them.

Footwear

G. Outerwear. Dress in layers so that you can peel off or add layers to suit the conditions. Soft, quiet clothing is ideal for still-hunters, bowhunters, and stalkers. Warm clothing is the key for stand-hunters. Hunter orange is mandatory when walking, carrying out game, and so on. **See Calls/Communication/Sounds in the Deer Woods/Vocalization.**

H. Scents. Cover scents are designed to mask human odor with a naturally occurring smell; such as pines, apples, cedar, fox, raccoon, or skunk scent. Remember deer learn that skunks use their spray when they feel threatened. Attractant scents, such as

Scents

buck urine, does-in-heat scent, and apple or other food scents take advantage of a buck's tendency to investigate the odors of other deer, particularly during the rut.

I. Two-Way Radios. Ideal for hunting remote areas with a buddy, calling for assistance, and so on, these communication devices often have a range of two to five miles (depending upon the terrain).

J. Survival or First Aid Kit. Extremely handy to have in case you get lost or are injured, these kits should be carried by hunters any time that they are in the field. The recommended minimum components of any survival kit are a "space blanket" (an extremely thin, highly flexible metallic sheet that reflects warmth, body heat, and harsh elements); a butane lighter or waterproof matches and a candle; a length of string or rope; some high-energy food; and water.

K. Other Useful Equipment. You may also want to take along a compact camera for real-time pictures, rubber gloves for field dressing deer, rain gear, a range finder, a seat cushion, a thermos, trail markers, a hunting knife, a folding saw used for cutting bones and clearing shooting lanes, a drag rope, a safety harness, a global positioning system for locating a stand or downed game. **See Accessories/Archery/Binoculars/Knife/Rifle/ Safety/Shotgun/Stands.**

ESCAPE ROUTE The path that a deer takes to get out of danger and to its safe haven. White-tailed deer are creatures of habit that act and react to stimuli and events in their immediate environment. When feeling threatened, a deer will choose to escape the immediate area, and then head for one of its known sanctuaries. Unless a deer is severely frightened, it will take the pathway that leads it to safety without having to exert a lot of energy. Terrain often dictates where an escape route will go. Saddles or dips that cut between two steep inclines, ridges with flat benches, or the head of a steep ravine all offer good intercept spots on a deer's escape route. **See Back Trail/Doubling Back/Fight or Flight/Flag/Hunting Pressure/Opening Day/ Security/Terrain/Travel Corridor.**

ESOPHAGUS The ribbed tube inside a whitetail's throat that leads from the pharynx to the stomach. It delivers food directly into the stomach to start digestion. This internal part is one of the first parts to spoil and possibly taint the venison. It is recommended to remove this tube as far up into the throat as possible. **See Field Dressing/ Internal Organs/Throat/Windpipe.**

ESTRUS/ESTROUS CYCLE The time in heat of does and other mammals. They produce sexual substances called pheromones, which can easily be detected by a buck as he smells the air and permit him to detect the sexual status of a doe. The doe will usually stay in heat for about twenty-four hours so the buck must detect her upcoming receptivity early and then stay with her, fending off all rival bucks who will also want to breed her. Does not bred during their first estrous cycle come into heat about twenty-eight days later and can then be bred by a buck. Breeding must be well timed so that fawn dropping will occur at the optimal time of abundant food, usually 189 to 222 days later. Late-season spotted fawns may be the result of breeding from the previous post peak rut season, or they may be a signal that the herd is hard pressed for food. Healthy does, having been bred during the peak of the previous year's rut, and with all other conditions being equal, will usually fawn earlier than does foraging on poor browse. **See Attractant Scent/Breeding/Does/False Rut/Metatarsal Gland/ Pheromones/Rut/Tending/Testosterone.**

ETHICS A set of values or moral principles. An ethical deer hunter knows that poaching, violating game laws, and disregarding the rules of fair chase have no place in the true sport of deer hunting. Any game taken without following the rules of fair chase cannot be displayed with pride before any other knowledgeable hunter. The ethical hunter, for example, should pass up a poor, low-percentage shot rather than risk wounding or losing a deer. Only hunters who have strictly followed all the game laws and regulations for their hunting area and have shown the highest respect for their quarry can be called ethical hunters. **See Bait Hunting/Blood Trailing Dogs/ Controlled Hunt/Downed Deer/Fair Chase/High Fence Hunting/Managed Hunt/Night Vision/One Shot Kill/Wounded Game.**

EVERGREEN The group of conifer or cone-bearing trees that never seem to lose their leaves but remain green all year. **See Browseline/Canopy/Conifer/Cover/ Deciduous/Food/Nutrition.**

EXIT WOUND The hole on the opposite side of an arrow or bullet entry point where the projectile left the deer's body. A low exit wound in the chest cavity, produced by a shot from an elevated stand, usually provides an earlier blood trail and thus an easier trailing job. The internally collecting blood will leak out sooner, rather than building up, filling the chest cavity, and then dribbling out. **See After the Shot/ Approaching Downed Deer/Bleeding/Field Dressing/Hair/Tracks/ Wounded Game.**

EXPOSURE See Hypothermia.

EYE(S) Organ(s) of sight. A deer's eyes are located on the sides of its head because it is a prey animal and must constantly be on guard for predators. Deer do not have red eyes. The red glare one sees at night in a deer's eyes is a reflection of the headlights or spotlight off the tapeteum cells at the rear inside of the deer's eyes. Glazed-over eyes on a downed deer usually means that it is dead. However, never assume anything! **See Binocular Vision/Eye Contact/Eye Shine/Movement/Outline/ Retina/Rod Cells/Security/Silhouette/Tapeteum lucidum/Vision.**

EYE CONTACT/EYE AVERSION The act of looking directly into another creature's eyes, something whitetail avoid. Both bucks and does have a defined rank within their social hierarchy. As an animal matures, it usually moves up in the pecking order for dominance. Subordinate deer avoid the presence of more dominant deer (e.g., the alpha buck) to the point of avoiding direct eye contact. Even when a group of deer are bedding, their eyes will always be pointed in different directions not only for security purposes, but also to avoid direct eye contact. **See Alpha Buck/ Dominance/Eyes/ Hierarchy/Predator/Pressure/Survival/Tapeteum lucidum/Vision.**

EYE SHINE The glow or bright reflection one sees when shining an artificial light at night into the eyes of white-tailed deer. It is the reflection off the back layer of the deer's eye. **See Eyes/Jacklighting/Poaching/Retina/Tapeteum lucidum/ Vision.**

EYE TINE Officially designated the G-1 tine on a buck's antler. It is also referred to as the brow tine. **See Brow Tine/G-1/G-2/Spike.**

FACE MASK Usually a camouflaged netting or other material that is used to break up the outline, shininess, and light color of hunters faces thus reducing the chance of their being discovered and identified by a deer as a predator. **See Camouflage/ Equipment/Face Paint/Head Net.**

FACE PAINT Usually a cream-based, easily removed camouflage paint available in green, brown, black, and sometimes gray, that hunters put on their faces, ears, neck, and hands in order to break up their features and look less humanlike. Face paint generally works better for most hunters than does a head net as it does not get in the way of their vision. Some hunters complement face paint by wearing sunglasses in order to prevent the whites of their eyes, and possible blinking movements from betraying their presence. **See Camouflage/Face Mask/Head Net.**

FACIAL RUBBING This act of a buck apparently wiping his face on a branch overhanging a scrape, after he has urinated in it. What he is actually doing is depositing his scent from the various glands on his forehead, around his antlers, and next to his eyes. All of these identify him and his level of dominance in the herd. Any other buck or doe that comes across this scrape will know who was there. **See Dominance/Forehead Gland/ Glands/Nasal Gland/Overhanging Branch/Pre-Orbital Gland/Primary Scrape/Scrape/Scent.**

Face Rubbing

FACTORY LOAD Bullets professionally manufactured. They are usually more accurate, consistent, and more practical than handloading for the average hunter. Factory loads also usually foul less frequently than handloads which are reloaded from spent or used casings. **See Ammunition/ Bullet/Caliber/Handloading/Rifle/Shotgun.**

FAIR CHASE A set of rules that ethical hunters use in the pursuit of quarry. Some trophy rack scoring systems (e.g., Boone and Crockett Club, Pope & Young) will not accept the candidacy of antlers not acquired under the concept of fair chase. Examples of nonfair chase might be deer struck by motor vehicles, shot in high-fenced enclosures, shot over bait, jacklighted at night, or taken out of season. **See**

Baiting/Blood Trailing Dogs/Boone and Crockett Club/Controlled Hunt/ Ethics/Guided Hunt/High Fence Hunting/Managed Hunt/One Shot Kill/ Pope & Young/Sportsmanship.

FALL See Autumn.

FALL-PREVENTION DEVICES Safety belts, full safety harnesses, climbing belts, and so on, which should always be used when climbing up a tree, while in the tree stand, and when coming down in order to prevent an accident. Approximately ten percent of tree hunters report that they have fallen, had their stand or a branch break, or had some other potentially injurious accident happen. **See Climber/Equipment/Harness/ Ladder Stand/Permanent Stand/Portable Stand/Safety/Stands/Survival/Tree Stand/Tree Steps.**

FALSE RUT/FIRST RUT Also called "preliminary rut" or "prerut." A phenomenon exhibited in late-occurring rut years that ushers in a brief flurry of noticeable buck activity but without a reciprocating interest on the doe's part. Does establish the actual time for breeding. Nature uses this prerut or false rut to get the bucks' attention and to alert them to the soon-to-come breeding season. This is likened to "priming the pump." A few does will be ready to breed in October, but this only serves to fuel the bucks' frenzy and desire. With too few does actually ready to breed at this time, the bucks increase their travel range in search of any receptive doe that smells right to them. From this point on, the bucks will think more about sex than they will about eating. They also become less secretive and engage in fewer survival-honed activities. **See Breeding/Chase Phase/Dominance/Estrus/Late Rut/Prerut/Post-Rut/ Primary Rut/Rut/Testosterone.**

FANNY PACK A smaller version of a backpack, usually worn around the waist that might contain these items for easy access:

• Compass	• Flashlight	• Neck Warmer	• Foot/Hand Warmers
• First Aid Kit	• Whistle	• Water Bottle	• Back-Up Release
• Candles/Matches	• Knife	• Granola Bars	• Extra Dragline/Haul line
• Scent Lure	• Branch Saw	• String 18-24 inches long	
• Lighter			

FAT/BODY FAT Food reserves stored, in the whitetail, mainly along the backbone,and sometimes around the kidneys and liver. Unlike beef cattle, deer do not store any fat within their muscles, thus keeping them free and strong for running from their enemies. They have developed seasonal eating habits that allow them to eat extremely well during the summer and fall, and add body fat as a cold-weather reserve. This fat allows them to survive the leaner winter months when food is less readily available. Likewise, a dominant buck going into the rut with fat packed along its spine does not spend much time eating as he is totally preoccupied by servicing does, and defending his breeding rights from other bucks. **See Body Size/Dressed Weight/Field Dressing/Follow-Up/Gamey Taste/Live Weight/Recipes/Venison.**

Fawn

FAWN A young deer. From birth, deer begin their lives very well camouflaged. The whites spots on a fawn give it a dappled effect that allows it to merge with the light and dark shadows of the forest floor. Fawns are relatively scent-free and the doe keeps it that way by staying out of view except when the fawn is nursing. Fawns instinctively move very little and stay exactly where the does place them. This behavior has definite survival advantages that allow the fawn to go undetected by predators. The fawn will begin to lose its spots by late summer as its coat adjusts to the coming breeding season. Generally, a female fawn will not breed her first season as she is too young. Late-season spotted fawns are a sign that the herd is stressed for food, as healthy does drop fawns earlier than does eating poor browse. **See Afterbirth/Age of Deer/Baby Teeth/Blat/Birth/Blat/Lead Doe/Nursing/Placenta/Singleton/Twins.**

FEATHERS The natural wing or tail feathers from a large bird, used as vanes or fletching at the rear of a hunting arrow, which stabilize the arrow in flight. Most arrows have either three or four vanes and a "cock feather," all of which are entirely the archer's choice. Helical or offset fletching can be right or left oriented, depending on the direction that the hunter wishes the arrow to rotate. **See Archery/Arrow Speed/Arrow Weight/Bow and Arrows/Feathers/Helical Fletching/Nocking.**

FECES/FECAL DROPPINGS See Droppings.

FEEDER A mechanical device timed to dispense corn, alfalfa pellets, and so on and used to attract and feed deer on a regular basis. In about half of American states where deer hunting occurs, baiting, hunting over bait, or salt blocks, or using mechanical feeders is legal. In other states, this is not allowed. Be sure that you know the hunting laws for the area that you are hunting in! **See Baiting/Ethics/Fair Chase/Jacklighting/Poaching/Pope & Young/Scoring/ Trophy.**

FEEDING Eating habits. White-tailed deer usually feed twice a day.

A. Midday. Deer usually have a minor feeding period at midday, when they will leave their bedding area, perhaps defecate, and nibble on acorns or browse near-by. This feeding is very brief and always not too far from their beds. Because of this movement and because hunters are often leaving the woods for lunch or to get warm and may disturb the deer, midday is a good time to be watching for deer movement. If the moon is out during the daytime, that is usually a signal that the deer will be active and feeding. This is a good time to be on stand at midday.

B. Night. Deer do the bulk of their feeding at night. They leave their daytime beds approximately one to two hours before dark and make their way down toward their feeding areas. **See Crepuscular Activity/Lunar Influence/Moon/Orchards/Weather.**

FEEDING AREAS One of the best places to hunt deer (others are travel routes and bedding areas). The best way to find a feeding area is to go where deer food is, such as a stand of oak trees, agricultural fields, an abandoned apple orchard, or even an area with abundant browse. Follow a well-worn deer trail and see where it takes you. (Remember the general rule that trails leading uphill usually lead to bedding areas and trails going downhill typically lead to food.) Very often there are nighttime beds and scattered droppings all over. Look for evidence that the deer have been actually eating the food. Since deer do not have upper

Feeding

teeth, they tear off buds and twigs (browse), thus leaving a telltale jagged edge. This ragged cut is easily distinguished from a rabbit's nibblings as rabbits neatly and cleanly snip off their food with both upper and lower teeth.

It is difficult to enter a feeding area in the morning because you will more than likely spook every deer on your way in. The only deer that you will see will be does and fawns as the bucks will have already left the feeding area before light. In addition, keep in mind the general rule that deer will feed heavily during an approaching storm front. **See Alfalfa/Browseline/Deer Sign/Fields/Food/Food Plot/Orchard.**

FEET On white-tailed deer, cloven hooves. The front hooves are generally larger than the hind hooves. **See Cloven Hooves/Dewclaws/Hooves/Splayed/Tracks.**

FENCE/FENCEROWS A barrier that defines the set boundaries of a field. It can be made of wooden or metal posts, trees, rails, barbed wire, or brush. Fencerows are excellent spots to ambush deer as the fence tends to funnel or direct their travel. Look for deer hair on barbed-wire fences as this indicates preferred locations where deer cross the fence. **See Bottleneck/Deer Fence/Ethics/Funnel/High Fence Hunting/Managed Hunt.**

FERAL DOGS Wild canines that probably were household pets at one time and ran away or were purposefully abandoned from by human owners. These canines have reverted to their native instinct for survival and will chase anything that is food. Hunters have reported seeing beagles, German shepherds, basset hounds—essentially any breed of dog—chasing and baying while running deer. Often the dogs run in packs and cooperate in wearing down a deer until it is too tired to defend itself. They try to hamstring it, eviscerate or disembowel it, and then wait for the deer to die before consuming part of it or even abandoning it. Some hunters feel a moral obligation to shoot any dog chasing a whitetail, regardless of whether it has a collar on it or not. **See Blood Trailing Dogs/Canine/Dogs/Ethics/Free-Ranging/Hamstring/Hounds/Predator/Sportsmanship.**

FETUS The unborn young of a mammal such as a doe, still in her uterus. (Does usually have one fawn the first year and twins thereafter.) **See Afterbirth/Breeding/Fawn/Gestation/Placenta/Twins.**

FIELD A wide stretch of open, cleared land, set off or enclosed for raising crops or pasturing livestock. **See Alfalfa/Deer Fence/Feeding Areas/Fence/Food/Food Plot/Orchard/Soybeans/Terrain.**

FIELD DRESSING The initial process of preparing a downed deer for ultimate consumption. It entails opening up the white underside of the deer's visceral area, removing the windpipe, lungs, heart, liver, stomach, intestines, kidneys, bladder, anal tract, sex organs, and any internal blood from the wounded area. (Wash out with clean water if possible.) The purpose of removing these organs is to prevent their spoiling

Field Dressing

or contaminating the meat of the deer. Hunters do not need a machete or bowie knife (twelve or more inches long) to field dress a deer. In fact, such large knives are overly cumbersome. The best knife is three to four inches long and could be a folding, pocket knife, or a straight-shaft model. Hunters should also carry a one- to one-and-a-half foot piece of strong string or twine to be used to tie off the bladder and prevent urine being spilled onto the meat and also to tie off the small intestine and anal tract to prevent fecal contamination of the venison. **See Aging Meat/Back Straps/Dressed**

Weight/Fat/Field Dressing/Gamey Taste/Hog Dressed/Esophagus/Live Weight/ Rigor Mortis/Sternum/Venison.

FIELD POINT/PRACTICE POINT/TARGET POINT Arrow points made for practice shooting only and maintaining the hunter's shooting proficiency during the off-season. These arrow tips are not broadheads and definitely should not be used for deer hunting. They will not accomplish what the hunter wants an arrow point to do, that is, to cut widely and deeply, causing as much bleeding as possible, and/or damage to a vital organ. **See Arrowheads/Broadheads.**

FIGHT OR FLIGHT The moment-of-decision time when a startled prey animal must decide whether it can easily get away from a source of danger (flight) or that it must face and confront its attacker (fight). **See Adrenal Glands/Aggression/Escape Route/Flail/Flight/Instinct/Spooked.**

FIGHTING Both does and bucks can engage in aggressive action. Does will defend their fawns, their immediate food supply, or their birthing areas. Bucks will fight as a last resort, if necessary, in order to establish or reassert their dominant breeding status. This dominance hierarchy was usually established over other bucks much earlier in the fall. A fight usually occurs between two equal-sized bucks that have not met before. **See Aggression/Aggressive Snort/Agonistic Behavior/Alpha Buck/ Dominance/Fight or Flight/Flail/Hierarchy/Locking of Antlers/Rut/ Sparring.**

FINGER RELEASE Using the fingers to release an arrow. Hunters can use two or more fingers to grip, draw, and hold a bowstring, until ultimately straightening them out and releasing the arrow. **See Anchor Point/Bow and Arrow/Mechanical Release/ Nocking Loop/Nocking Point/Release.**

FIREARM A mechanical device, typically referred to as a gun, that uses an explosive charge to propel a bullet out a barrel toward a target. **See Black Powder/Bullet/ Caliber/Foot Pounds of Energy/Gun/Gunpowder/Handgun/Hydrostatic Shock/Knock Down Power/Muzzleloader/Rifle.**

FIRST AID Basic knowledge of how to handle the various medical situations that may confront hunters or their buddies. Wise hunters always carry with them, and know how to use, a first aid kit. **See Backpack/Burns/Equipment/Foul Weather/Freeze/Hypo- thermia/Inclement Weather/Safety/Survival/Temperature/Weather.**

FLAG/FLAGGING An erect tail, the most readily observed whitetail signal for danger used as a visual communication to other whitetail in the immediate area. When a deer's tail goes erect, a deer usually bounds away toward cover. It is this white signal waving back and forth as the whitetail doe bounds away that allows her fawns to keep track of and follow her into the woods. It also puts all other deer on alert. A buck will hold its tail erect and stiff, with hair muscles flaring to make the white flag as large as possible. **See Body Language/Communication/Flail/Flight/Gait/Gallop/Lead Doe/Tail Flick/Trot/Walk.**

Flag

FLAIL/FLAILING Aggression displayed by does toward other deer—including bucks—by rearing up on their hind legs and striking out with their front legs, usually at the head or neck of the other deer. This behavior is observed when they are defending their fawns, a birthing area, or critical food source. Bucks will also flail with their front legs in the springtime as well as during the summer while their antlers are in velvet and highly vulnerable to injury. **See Aggression/Agonistic Behavior/Alpha Buck/Antlers/Dominance/Fighting/Hierarchy/Lead Doe/Sparring.**

FLASHLIGHT A useful but controversial tool for hunters. In some states, it is illegal to carry a lit flashlight into deer woods as the presumption is that the hunter is jacklighting deer. (Check your local state laws.) However, a lit flashlight can prevent hunting accidents as hunters walk into or out of the woods. The sounds of their footsteps will not be confused with those of a deer when accompanied by such a light. When a hunter is lost or injured and has to spend the night in the woods, having a flashlight can be comforting. Needless to say, having a light at night is also useful for signaling for help or providing a beacon for late incoming hunters. **See Backpack/Equipment/Ethics/Fanny Pack/Safety /Survival.**

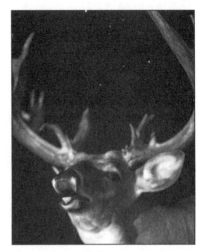
Flehmen

FLEHMEN A behavior that bucks use to determine when and if a doe is ready to be bred. The combination of scent making and scent detection is one of the whitetail's most effective means of communication. During the breeding season (rut), a buck's hormonal and sexual systems are running in high gear as he pursues does to breed. Sexual pheromones from an estrous doe's urinary tract stimulate the limbic or pleasure-seeking portion of the buck's brain. These pheromones are carried on the air currents and indicate her status for breeding. The buck curls his upper lip back, inhales deeply and pulls the pheromone-laden, urine-based air currents over the moist, sensitive tissue within his nostrils. This act seems to intensify his sexual arousal even more. **See Chase Phase/Flehmen/Glands/ Lures/Nasal Gland/Nose/Pheromone/Rut/Scents/Scent Checking/Scrape/ Urine.**

FLETCHING See Feathers.

FLIGHT The moment when a startled or alerted prey animal decides that it should immediately get away from a source of danger, rather than face and confront its attacker. Usually, the white tail of a deer rises to alert, thus signaling others of its intended flight and the whitetail then bounds off to cover and safety. **See Adrenal Glands/Alarm Snort/Alert Snort/Communication/Cover/Escape Route/ Flag/Safety/Spooked/Survival.**

FLINCH/FLINCHING The sudden jerking of a firearm or bow in anticipation of a sharp recoil or fore-arm snap. This is a common cause of poor shot placement or even missing altogether. **See Buck Fever/Hunting Maladies/Shot Placement.**

FLOAT HUNT Using a canoe or small steerable rowboat to catch a deer in its natural state near water. This is possible only in remote areas, where whitetails do not experience a lot of human hunting pressure. Too much human pressure causes the whitetail to avoid open areas and stay back in denser, less visible areas. Once float hunters have acquired their trophy, the watercraft is a convenient means for transporting the deer out of the hunting area. Some hunters work in tandem, leaving vehicles at both the entry and the exit points of the river or creek. **See Guided Hunt/Water.**

FLUKES See Liver Fluke.

FLUORESCENT ORANGE The generally accepted standard clothing color for deer hunting safety afield. It is the same as blaze orange but with fluorescent dyes imbedded in it which increases its brilliance by a factor of three. **See Blaze Orange/Safety(Hunter).**

FOG Visible water vapor, one hundred percent humidity, that looks like low-flying, ground-hugging clouds. When traveling to one's stand in the morning, fog can reduce the chances of being observed by deer. Conversely, the hunter is also less likely to see deer. The accompanying high moisture content also reduces hunter noises, such as footsteps or leaves crunching. Caution: Heavy fog can contribute to a hunter becoming disoriented or lost. If this occurs, it is best to sit down and wait for the fog to clear. Usually the sun "burns off" any morning fog. **See Inclement Weather/Safety/Survival/Weather.**

FOLLOW-THROUGH The crucial time after a shot release when a shooter must maintain stance and aiming technique. Maintaining concentration on the target helps to reduce the chances of flinching, minimizes movement of the firearm or bow, and increases the shooter's ability to see where the shot went and its effect on the target.

From the moment your arrow strikes the deer to the time your deer disappears, you must listen and watch carefully. What you do during these precious seconds will improve your ability to recover your deer. An animal's reaction to your shot and all of the related clues are important to piecing together what really happened. The following five follow-through activities should be stringently paid attention to:

A. You should be able to describe what sound the arrow made upon impact: Paunch shots or minor muscle hits will produce almost no sound at all. Lung, heart, liver and other vital organ hits sound like practice shots on pumpkins-a dull "thunk" Hits to bones produce a loud "crack," not unlike a homerun. Ham shots, that is, to bones with thick muscles around them, sound more like a "crunch" than a crack The standard rule is to wait for thirty minutes before trying to pick up the blood trail to recover your deer. It will have succumbed to the effects of bleeding by that time and died or, if it has "stiffened up," it will be unable to get up to flee and you can finish it off if necessary.

B. You should be able to tell whether the arrow stayed in the deer or not. Experienced bowhunters prefer bright, easy-to-see fletchings. White, although easiest to see under low-light conditions, is not really the best vane color. It is too easily noticed by deer because it is their alarm warning color. Bright yellow, reds, and oranges are also highly visible to the hunter and should be able to be readily picked up whether it is bounding along with the deer in its flight or has passed through it and is stuck in the ground.

C. You should be able to tell where the arrow hit. Given the speed of today's bows, an archer might not be able to readily see the arrow passing through the deer. When light is low and the deer whirls around to "jump the string" and escape, you might not see the impact spot.

D. You should be able to describe the body language of the deer as it exited the immediate area. Its reaction to a hit in the lungs or heart area can be described as an all-out scramble for safety with its body held close to the ground. A high hit just below the spine could be in that non-vital zone where no organs exist, yet the deer exhibits the same reaction. Deer hit there sometimes stumble and some actually fall. However, this area is not lethal and usually the deer survives. Paunch or rear loin hits cause the deer to run away in an initial burst, then slow down, and finally walk away with their bodies hunched up, but their heads held low. A hunter is advised to wait three hours after a ham shot before picking up the deer's trail and six hours after a paunch or gut shot.

E. You should be able to tell the place where you last saw the deer and the last sounds that you heard associated with that deer: No matter how and where the deer leaves the area, you should carefully note where you last saw and what you last heard about that deer. Blood usually begins to fall to the ground between fifty to one hundred yards from the spot where it was hit. Laying a trail with a piece of toilet tissue paper on each blood spot allows you to see the deer's direction of travel. If you lose the blood spoor, you can easily return to the last-known findings.

Longstanding advice to archers was always to "watch your arrow fly to the target." That is actually poor advice, in that you are taking your eyes off the target in order to follow the arrow vanes, degrading your concentration, and ultimately making for a poor shot. Wise hunters stay fixed upon the aiming point so that they will see the arrow actually hit the deer. By holding steady on your sight plane, and following through on your aim, you will maintain your accuracy. You should not "pluck" your bowstring and fling your string hand away from your face, lower the bow too quickly before the arrow leaves the rest, nor anticipate the string release and blink or shut your eyes before the actual release. The best archers continue to see the target through the bowsight until the arrow actually hits the deer. Seeing your arrow hit is vital to knowing whether you will be tagging your animal or simply making it all the wiser. **See Body Language/Ethics/Follow-Up/Jumping the String/Shot Placement/ Sportsmanship/Wounded Game.**

FOLLOW-UP After the shot, keep your eye on the deer and observe it until it either falls down, lie down, or walks out of sight. Keep listening for a while and you might hear it collapse. Do not assume that you missed. You owe it to your quarry to follow up after every shot, even if you are certain that you missed. The best advice is to thoroughly check for any evidence of a hit (e.g., blood, hair, stomach contents, tallow on the arrow shaft and/or vanes).

A. Bowhunters know that arrows kill by hemorrhaging, not by hydrostatic shock as with a bullet. Because an arrow can slice cleanly through the soft tissues and not hit bone, an animal may not even realize that it has been hit. It may feel discomfort, but because it had no prior reason for alarm, the now wounded animal may just keep doing what it was doing prior to the shot. Bowhunters should always attempt to find their arrows before leaving an area. Not only are arrows expensive and reusable, but they can also be hazardous (possibly to you or the next hunter in the area) if just left lying around. More importantly, the recovered arrow can provide a wealth of information about the shot that you took. If it is totally clean—no blood, no fat globs or streaks, no hair attached, no green paunch or stomach contents attached—then maybe you missed. If any of the above evidence exists on your arrow, you should be able to combine it with insights from your observation of just how the deer reacted to your shot to surmise the extent of your quarry's injury.

B. Firearm shots dispatch game by their shock value. These shots should also always be followed up on. Bits of hair, gobs of fat, green stomach contents, a sudden voiding of feces, and blood or tissue on the ground or sprayed against a tree or brush are all indicators of a wounded animal. As above, hunters should watch the deer until they see it go down, bed down, or hear it fall and then wait for a reasonable amount of time so that the animal can expire. How the deer reacts to your shot can say volumes about where and how fatal the hit was. **See After the Shot/Approaching Downed Deer/Downed Deer/Doubling Back/Hydrostatic Shock/Paunch Shot/Shot Placement/Sportsmanship/Tracking/Wounded Game.**

FOOD (Deer) An important part of deer's life. The hunter that understands how deer are attracted to food, has a distinct advantage in hunting these majestic animals. Deer are creatures of habit Not normally grazers, they are browsers of twigs, buds and mostly cellulose materials. An adult white-tailed deer consumes between eight and fifteen pounds of food per day. You can count on their being attracted to the most nutritious and best food sources available. White oak acorns are the favorite food of the whitetail. Wherever a good food source becomes available (e.g., when acorns start dropping), that is where you will readily find the deer. During summer and early fall, agricultural crops, specifically high-protein legumes such as alfalfa, clover or soybeans, are generally the biggest magnet foods for deer. Grains such as wheat, rye, oats, and buckwheat will bring deer into the open fields in the evenings during the early part of the hunting season. In the middle of the hunting season, deer will be concentrating almost exclusively on sources of high carbohydrates such as corn, sorghum, and winter wheat. This is a good place to locate a buck because he needs to put on weight before engaging in the rut.

An examination of the ten favorite foods of deer show that five farm crops are within the grouping. In fact, farmers often consider deer to be detrimental to their crops. Winter wheat will not attract deer for feeding until later in the wintertime, as it needs time under the cover of snow to sprout and grow. Southern deer biologists report that kudzu, a vine, is a mainstay source of food for the whitetail, at least until the leaves fall off after a good frost. **See Acorns/Alfalfa/Apples/Aquatic Vegetation/ Beechnuts/Browse/Feeding Area/Food Plot/Forage/Forbs/Mast/Nuts/Oaks/ Orchard/Pears/Soybeans.**

FOOD (Hunter) An important factor to a hunter's stamina. Take the time to eat a good, hearty breakfast before going out to hunt in the morning. A hungry stomach is a noisy stomach. Hunger, combined with bone-chilling cold, will soon convince you to give up and leave the woods. If you are not out in the deer woods, you are not going to shoot a deer. Quick energy foods, high in carbohydrates and simple sugars, allow hunters to stay out in the field all day, thus increasing their chances of seeing deer, particularly during the rut when deer activity will be continuous. A thermos bottle of hot tea, soup, or broth, coupled with the above-mentioned "fuel for the furnace," can convince a hunter to stick it out just a little longer, and that could make all the difference of eating venison back straps that evening. In addition, remember that apples are Mother Nature's toothbrush. Pack an apple or two with you to control your breath odor as well as to provide a good snack while waiting for your deer to show up. **See Hygiene/Nutrition/Scents.**

FOOD CHAIN An ascending order of organisms, from the simple one-cell plants and animals to green plants, plant-eating animals, carnivores, and ultimately to humans. The whitetail fits right in the middle of the hierarchy. They eat plants and, in turn, are eaten by predators, including humans. **See Alfalfa/Apples/Aquatic Vegetation/ Bear/Cougar/Coyote/Predator/Prey/Wolf.**

FOOD PLOTS The practice of augmenting deer food supply by purposefully planting attractive food sources. These food plots provide more succulent and nutritional foods than nature does alone. During the stress of winter or during a year of poor mast production, these food plots can help a deer herd get through lean times. Some hunters utilize food plots to attract and hold deer near their property for hunting. See

Food Plot

Alfalfa/Biomass/Browse Line/Buckwheat/Corn/Forage/Habitat/Land Management/Nutrition/Orchards/Quality Deer Management/Soybeans.

FOOT-POUNDS OF ENERGY Bullets kill by producing shock to the body. A measurement of the knock-down power of bullets. Bullets lose foot-pounds of energy as they travel the distance to their target. No matter what the distance, be it forty yards or four hundred yards, a bullet must have between 1,000 and 1,200 foot-pounds of energy at the point of impact in order for it to do its intended job of dispatching or putting down a deer for good. See Ammunition/Ballistics/Black Powder/ Bullet/Caliber/Firearm/Gauge/Hydrostatic Shock/Kinetic Energy/Knock-Down Power.

FOOT STOMP Behavior of a deer that senses that something is amiss or that danger might be present. A deer will raise its front leg, then forcefully stomp it on the ground. As with the head bob, the deer is hoping to startle the suspected danger into moving and thus being identified. Other deer in the near vicinity will feel this stomp and become alerted also. In performing this stomp, the deer also deposits an alarm scent from the interdigital glands between its hooves onto the ground, which will forewarn any other later passing deer that there was danger identified at this spot. See Alarm Snort/Alert Snort/Blow/Calls/Communication/Head Bob/Sounds in the Deer Woods.

FOOTWEAR Gear that hunters wear to keep their feet dry and warm. Wearing socks that wick moisture away from the feet helps keep them dry and prevents blisters from forming. Changing your socks at midday will feel like a luxury out in the field after a tough morning of activity. Do not skimp here and buy cheap boots, as you will regret not paying just that little more for quality footwear. Boots that keep moisture out, let your feet breathe somewhat, are rubber bottomed, keep you from depositing your scent on the ground, and are lug soled for nonslip tree climbing, etc., are worth looking for and purchasing. Your feet will thank you many times over! See Clothing/Equipment/Foul Weather/Inclement Weather/Pacs/ Rubber Boots.

FORAGE Food taken by grazing or browsing. White-tailed deer are opportunistic eaters. In the springtime, whitetails are grazers, gorging themselves on any herbaceous (green) plant that they can find. As spring turns into summer, they turn to browsing on newly sprouted fibrous shoots. **See Browse/Food Plot/Forbs/Green Up/Habitat/ Herbaceous/Nutrition/Orchards/Overbrowse/Starvation.**

FORB Any herbaceous plant that is not a grass or grass-like but is rather a broadleaf plant. Forbs preferred and consumed by whitetails include wild onions, common weeds, and so on. **See Biomass/Browse/Food/Food Plot/Forage/Habitat/Herbaceous/ Nutrition/Starvation/Yarding.**

FOREHEAD GLANDS Certain glands located between a buck's antlers on his forehead that deposit his specific and individualized scent onto a rub. When a buck starts to rub trees in late summer/early fall, it is more than just to remove the now-drying velvet from his antlers. He is also creating a "signpost" that tells all the other deer in the area that HE is present. **See Chemical Signpost/Deer Sign/Glands/Nasal Gland/Overhanging Branch/Rub.**

FOREST A tract of wooded land, densely covered with trees and underbrush. Where the trees or overstory has been removed through fire, prolonged flooding, or logging a clearing or opening may exist. This opening, exposed to copious sunlight, will soon regenerate with ground cover, plants, brush, shrubs, then on to trees. **See Burn/Clearcut/Clearing/Glade/Logging/Woods.**

FORKHORN A whitetail antler rack that totals four points (eastern count), that is, two points—an inch or longer—on each antler. **See Antler/Bachelor Buck Groups/Buck/Fawn/Hierarchy/Rank/Rub/Shed/Spike/Velvet.**

FOSTER SLUG Designed for a smooth-bore shotgun, a deer slug made from a soft piece of lead, die-punched into a U-shaped cup. The rounded head of the hollow projectile is thicker than the sides, theoretically thus providing stability in flight. **See Ammunition/Bore/Brenneke Slug/Full Bore Slug/Sabot/Shotgun/Slug.**

FOUL WEATHER Bad or inclement weather. Do not let a little rain or snow keep you from rendezvousing with your next deer. Only during extremely inclement weather (e.g., horizontal rain or snow, intense lightning) should you give up hunting, as the deer, too, will be in some sort of heavy cover or thick shelter and not active. Remember, deer live outdoors all the time and are used to a little inconvenience. A slight rain or snow can help cover a hunter's scent by driving it immediately to the ground and not allowing its dispersal to the surrounding countryside. Only extreme weather conditions change deer movement patterns, e.g., eighteen inches or more of snow, gale force winds (47 to 54 miles per hour on the Beaufort scale).

Be prepared to protect your body and equipment from bad weather. Anticipate its coming and dress correctly for it. Dressing in layers, keeping a spare set of socks, watchcap, gloves, and even a dry change of clothing in your backpack, wearing rain gear (no plastic slickers, nylon shells, or other noisy material), and using air-activated toe and/or hand warmers can give you the confidence to stay in your stand longer.

Realize also that taking a shot in heavy rain or snow will require you to start tracking a wounded animal immediately, as hoof prints and most, if not all, of the blood trail will soon be washed away. Laying down a line of toilet tissue at regular intervals of blood sign will allow you to preserve the direction of the blood trail. You stand an increased chance of spooking, jumping, or pushing your deer, thus causing it to run further than it normally would, but you increase your chances of finding a mortally hit animal, rather than lose it for lack of spoor or a blood trail. **See Freezing/Fronts/Frost/ Gortex/Hypothermia/Inclement Weather/Layers/Prevailing Winds/Rubber Boots/ Survival/Thinsulate/Yarding.**

FOX A member of the canine or dog family, related to but smaller than a wolf, possessing a more pointed muzzle, shorter legs, and a bushy tail. Fox are not capable of taking down a standing whitetail but often account for cleaning up the internal remains from field dressing, and/or carrion from roadkill or natural die-off. **See Canine/Carrion/ Cougar/Coyote/Die-Off/Predator/Roadkill/Winterkill/Wolf.**

FREE RANGING Any wild animal in its natural setting outdoors, not under a human's control, as are pets. **See Dogs/Ethics/Fair Chase/Feral Dogs/Sportsmanship.**

FREEZE/FREEZING A freeze or frost following a rain that often hardens the forest floor, making it very noisy for hunters to walk on. Once at their stands, hunters should try to remain as quiet as possible, not only to prevent deer from hearing their movements, but also so that they can hear the crunching of deer traveling in the woods. **See Ambient Temperature/Foul Weather/Frost/Hypothermia/Ice/Inclement Weather/Rain/Sleet/Snow/Weather.**

FRESHENING A buck's reactivating a scrape, that is, pawing the leaves and debris away, urinating onto his tarsal glands (inside hind legs), placing his hoof print and interdigital scent into the scrape, and reworking his scent into the licking branch located above the scrape. **See Hind Legs/Hocks/Metatarsal Gland/Mock Scrape/ Overhanging Branch/Scent Checking/Scrape/Scrape Line/Tarsal Glands/ Urine/Working a Scrape.**

FRONT A zone where two air masses come together.
    A. Low Pressure Front. Usually associated with unsettled or changing weather. Whitetails sense the change (falling) in the barometric pressure with the coming of a storm and often will be observed feeding earlier than usual in the evening hours. **See Barometer/Foul Weather/Movement/Pressure/Temperature/Weather.**
    B. High Pressure Front. Usually associated with good or improving weather. The barometric pressure is on the rise. **See Barometer/Movement/Pressure/Storm.**

FROST A light coating of ice crystals that forms on everything outdoors when the nighttime temperature falls below thirty-two degrees fahrenheit. Moisture in the air condense onto a cold surface forming frost. **See Autumn/Deciduous/Foul Weather/Freeze/Hardwoods/Hypothermia/Ice/Snow/Survival.**

FRUIT A favorite food of white-tailed deer. They are particularly fond of apples, pears, persimmons, and other available fruit. Whitetails have been known to travel miles from their core area (home range) when apples start falling from the trees. **See Apples/Crop Damage/Food/Mast/Orchards/Pears/Persimmons.**

FULL-BORE SLUG NonSabot-type shotgun slugs, whose diameters, gauge, and caliber must come close to fitting the bore or gauge of the barrel, be it 12, 16, 20, or .410. These slugs generally utilize a fiber or plastic wad behind the lead to seal off the propelling gases and allow that energy to expel the slug. **See Ammunition/Bore/ Brenneke Slug/Foster Slug/Sabot/Shotgun/Slug.**

FULL MOON The biggest and brightest round reflection of the moon as occurs when the sun is directly in back of Earth and in front of the Moon (a perfect line-up results in a lunar eclipse). Every 29.5 days, Earth's only natural satellite—the Moon—completes a full lunar cycle as it rotates around Earth. This cycle of lunar faces is a series of reflections of the Sun's rays as it shines on the Moon as seen from Earth. The differing shape of the Moon during the cycle is the result of the Sun shining at the Moon's surface at an angle and reflecting directly (180 degrees) back at Earth. To whitetail hunters, the second full moon after the autumn equinox is known as the "Rutting Moon" or "Hunter's Moon." It has been theorized by several well-known whitetail authorities that this is the cue that sets the rut into action. **See Autumn Equinox/Equinox/Harvest Moon/Hunter's Moon/Lunar Influence/New Moon/Photoperiodism/Waning Moon/Waxing Moon/Vernal Equinox.**

FUNGUS/FUNGI Any of a variety of saprophytic or parasitic lower plants that often grow on the forest floor (e.g., mushrooms, toadstools) and serve as food for whitetails. These plants, lack chlorophyll and cannot make their own food as can most other plants. Fungi feed off of decaying wood and other organic matter. **See Food/ Mushroom/Soft Mast.**

FUNNEL A funnel, sometimes misnamed a "saddle," is any occurring feature that directs a deer to travel through it or that has the effect of diverting its travel route. Examples of funnels are peninsulas of woods or thickets that connect two woodcuts, a ravine on a hillside that allows a deer to travel down it out of sight, a fence line that converges upon thicker cover, or maybe even a hedgerow between two fields. A funnel must offer some degree of security and connect one or more places where a buck desires to be. A funnel offers some indication as to where a buck might go when he leaves his bed. Wise hunters have to be careful of wind currents as swirling eddies of wind caught in a funnel could carry their scent right to the buck. **See Aerial Photographs/Bottleneck/Draw/Saddle/Terrain/Topographical Maps.**

G

G-1 The brow tine or eye tine of a buck's rack, if he has them. Otherwise, it is the first point from the pedicle. **See Antlers/Beam/Brow Tine/G-2/Main Beam/ Mass/Net Score/Rack/Scoring/Spread/Sticker Point/Typical.**

G-2 The second tine or point on a whitetail's antlers. The brow tine is designated as a G-1. The G-2 is usually the longest tine off of the main beam. **See Antlers/Beam/ Boone and Crockett Club/Brow Tine/G-1/Net Score/Pope & Young/Rack/ Sticker Point/Trophy/Typical.**

GAIT Speed of locomotion. A white-tailed deer has basically three: the walk, the trot, and the gallop. The walk can range from slow steps taken while and nibbling morsels to many determined steps taken in one direction. When trotting, a deer holds both its head and tail up while waving its flag from side to side. When galloping, a deer takes long leaps without touching the ground, often reaching speeds over thirty miles per hour. **See Flag/Gallop/Trot/Walk.**

GALLOP A gait in which a whitetail takes long leaps without touching the ground and often reaches speeds over thirty miles per hour. **See Escape Route/Flag/Gait/Trot/ Walk.**

GAMBREL A triangular device shaped like an upside down coathanger that is used to hang a whitetail up on the meat pole at deer camp. By cutting a slit completely through the loose skin near the deer's rear hocks (do not sever the tendons) and inserting the upward bend of the gambrel ends through them, a deer can easily be positioned for butchering, skinning, or aging. **See Buck Pole/Butchering/Field Dressing/Hocks/ Tendon.**

GAME FARM A game farm where bucks have been imported for their large rack and breeding potential. Big-antlered whitetail are now big business. Many game farms utilize high, escape-proof fences to keep their whitetail bucks within their perimeters. Would-be trophy hunters sometimes patronize these farms. These shooters seek out a controlled hunt because they have little time to hunt, little access to public land, a lot of money to pay the high fees of the game farm, and/or physical limitations. Be aware that a "trophy" deer or "game farm buck" taken under unethical circumstances may not be accepted under the rules of fair chase as prescribed for by the Boone and Crockett Club. **See Baiting/Boone and Crockett Club/Controlled Hunt/Ethics/Fair Chase/ Guides/High Fence Hunting/Managed Hunt/Outfitters/Sportsmanship.**

GAME WARDEN An officer of the law responsible for enforcing a state's game and conservation laws. Game wardens are conservation officers with the power to arrest

ONE-MAN HANGING DEER

Gambrel slit in hind leg (do not sever tendon)

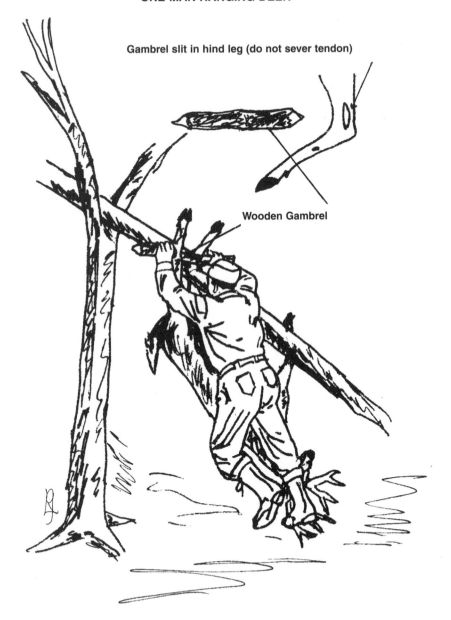

Wooden Gambrel

Gambrel

game-law breakers and unethical hunters. **See Biologist/Conservation Dept./ Deer Fence/Ethics/Fair Chase/High Fence Hunting/Outfitters.**

GAMEY TASTE A sour, poor taste in a piece of venison that results from improper handling and/or preparation of the meat during field dressing, butchering, packaging, or cooking. If handled properly, venison is food "fit for a king" with no wild taste whatsoever. To keep venison from tasting gamey, here are some recommendations: Remove all hair, even a single strand, from the meat as burnt hair gives the venison a pungent, smoky taste. Remove as much fat as possible because deer fat is sour tasting, unlike beef's sweeter aroma and taste. Cut away bloody tissue that is slimy and black-looking. Venison cuts include roasts, chops, steaks, shanks, sausage, deerburger, and stew meat. **See Aging Meat/Back Straps/Fat/Field Dressing/Jerky/ Popiteal Gland/Recipes/Tenderloins/Venison.**

GAUGE The size or bore of the barrel of a shotgun and/or the slug being used. The barrel and the slug size must match, just as with any firearm. Deer loads are usually 20, 16 or 12 gauge, although 28 gauge and .410 slugs are not unheard of. The smaller the number, the larger the actual slug size. **See Ammunition/Bore/ Buckshot/Bullet/Caliber/Foot-Pounds of Energy/Kinetic Energy/Knock-Down Power/Shotgun/Slug.**

GENES/GENETICS Genetic make-up, which comes from both of an animal's parents. The potential for a large-racked buck comes from the traits of his father and his mother. In addition, a buck must live beyond his first eighteen months (the first two hunting seasons) and have adequate nutrition to supply the needs of his body and his antlers. **See Antlers/Drop Tine/Habitat/Inbreeding/Main Beam/Net Score/ Nontypical/Pope & Young/Rack/Trophy/Typical.**

GESTATION PERIOD The time that a fetus spends in a doe's uterus after she is bred by the buck (approximately 190 to 210 days). By February, a pregnant doe sometimes has difficulty finding adequate food to support her developing fawn. The final three months of development are critical for the unborn fawn, and failure of a doe to find adequate food could affect the fawn's survival. The process is biologically correctly timed so that the fetus is nourished by the doe's body during the cold, inclement weather, and is born during spring "green-up" (usually May and June) so that the lactating doe can accumulate as much nourishing food as she needs. The gestation period for deer is about seven months long (November/December to May/June). It is interesting that the whitetail's breeding and fawning times roughly correspond to the winter and summer solstices, the shortest and longest days of the year. **See Birth/ Breeding/Copulation/Doe/Estrus/ Fawn/Fetus/Ovaries/ Rut.**

GHILLIE SUIT A camouflage suit made of a multihued and multistrand fabric that looks like a bush. It was developed in the military for sniper use, but has been slowly adapted and adopted by deer hunters as an excellent form of concealment. **See**

TARSAL GLAND (inner side of rear leg)

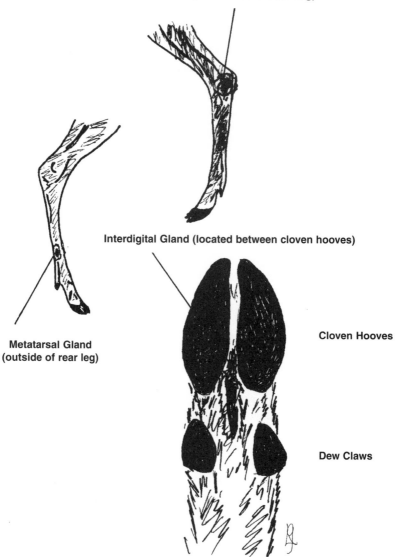

Interdigital Gland (located between cloven hooves)

Cloven Hooves

Dew Claws

Metatarsal Gland
(outside of rear leg)

Glands

Blind/Camouflage/Face Mask/Face Paint/Head Net/Layering/Outline/
Silhouette/Skylined/Vision.

GIBBOUS MOON The period when Earth's natural satellite is more than half illu-
minated, but less than full. See Full Moon/Moon/Waning Moon/Waxing Moon.

GIRDLE/TREE GIRDLE To remove a complete circle of bark from around a tree,
often causing it to die because it can no longer transport vital fluids up to its leaves or
down to its roots for storage. Some trees and fence posts have been rubbed so frequently and aggressively by whitetail bucks that they have become hourglass shaped.
See Rub/Rut/Scent/Signpost.

GLADE An open space surrounded by woods or an opening in a forest. Glads are often overgrown with ferns, leeks, forbs, and grasses. See Burn/Clearcut/Field/Forest/Glen.

GLANDS (External) The exocrene system, made up of glands that secrete odor-pro-
ducing substances that assist deer in communicating with other deer. Most of a buck's
glandular secretion deposits are made to attract does for breeding and to warn other
bucks to stay out of his territory.

   A. Forehead. Located between the antlers on the forehead, this gland is used
by a buck to create a "signpost" that tells all the other deer in the area that he is present. These glands deposit his specific and individualized scent onto the rub. The buck
also enjoys licking his own scent off.

   B. Interdigital. Deer have scent glands between their toes. When startled,
deer deposit a scent on the ground that serves to warn other deer that danger was
recently discovered at that spot. Scent left behind as a deer walks allows another deer
to follow its trail.

   C. Metatarsal. A gland located on the outer side of each hind leg of a white-
tailed deer. It is represented by a darkish tuft of hair, but its functions are not yet
known to hunters nor biologists.

   D. Nasal. Glands located near the nose and mouth area of the whitetail,
whose function has not yet been determined.

   E. Preorbital. Glands near a buck's eyes that emit a scent, often rubbed on a
licking branch near a scrape.

   F. Tarsal. Glands on the inside knee joints of a buck that he urinates on while
over a scrape, thus adding the gland's scent to his urine. It helps identify him to other
bucks and to does. See Facial Rubbing/Flehmen/Forehead Gland/Interdigital
Gland/Metatarsal Gland/Musk/Nasal Gland/Overhanging Branch/Pre-
Orbital Gland/Tarsal Gland.

GLANDS (Internal) The endocrine system, those glands that operate internally within whitetails' bodies, regulating vital aspects of their growth, survival, and reproductive needs.

   A. Adrenal glands. Located near the kidneys, this gland produces sex hormones, steroids needed for bodily metabolism, and adrenaline—also called "epinephrine."

B. Gonads. See Testes.

C. Pineal gland. Located at the base of the brain, this gland is often refered to as "the seat of the soul," because of the amount-of-daylight-affecting-the-eyes information that it receives, thus initiating and regulating production of breeding-related hormones.

D. Pituitary gland. Located within the brain, producing many endocrine secretions that govern body functions, including growth and sexual development.

E. Testes. These primary male sex glands produce the hormone testosterone and sperm and are located within the scrotum, which hangs between the rear legs and dangles beneath the body proper. **See Adrenal Glands/Endocrine System/ Gonads/Pineal Gland/Pituitary Gland/Testes/ Testosterone.**

Glassing

GLASSING Watching deer from a long distance, such as at a field's edge or from a road. Glassing can be an effective method of providing the hunter with information as to the size and makeup of a deer herd. Of particular interest is the sighting of a nice buck. A good pair of binoculars allows the hunter to pick out deer in the shadows of dawn or at dusk. They are particularly useful to the trophy hunter who is only interested in a particularly good rack. Glassing also allows a hunter to survey deer entry points, terrain features, and so on. **See Binoculars/Ethics/Jacklighting/Night Vision/Preparation/Scouting/Sportsmanship/Spotlighting.**

GLEN A secluded narrow valley; often a convenient funneling area for observing deer. **See Forest/Forest Opening/Funnel/Glade/ Hollow/Terrain.**

GLOBAL POSITIONING SYSTEM(GPS) A handheld electronic device that allows a hunter to leave and return to a vehicle, camp, tree stand, downed deer, and so on with precise accuracy. The system uses a triangulation method with data from three or more satellites overhead so hunters are able to know just where they are at all times. **See Aerial Photographs/Compass/Contour/Maps/Navigation/Orienteering/Orthophotoquad/Survival/Topographical Maps/United States Geological Service.**

GOING-AWAY SHOT A shot when an animal is going away, exposing only the hindquarters. Do not take this risky shot. It will spoil too much meat, or worst yet, could result in a wounded, unrecovered animal. **See After the Shot/Approaching Downed Deer/Hair/Shot Placement/Wounded Game.**

GONADS/GONADOTROPISM The testes or testicles. In the whitetail buck, the term "gonadotropism" refers to acting or stimulating the male sexual organs. **See Breeding/ Cactus Buck/Castration/Ejaculation/Impotence/Luteinizing Hormone/Rut/Testicles/Testosterone.**

GORE-TEX A waterproof, yet breathable material used in boots, parkas, pants, and so on to protect the hunter from foul weather. It provides protection from the effects of moisture and wind while it remains comfortable. Its microscopic pores are too small for water droplets to penetrate yet are large enough to allow perspiration vapors to escape so that you stay dry inside and out. **See Camouflage/Clothing Foul Weather/Inclement Weather/Layers/Thinsulate]**

GPS See Global Positioning System.

GRAND SLAM OF DEER Bagging one trophy-size buck of each of the four major subspecies of white-tailed deer hunted in the United States: Virginia whitetail, Columbian blacktail, Sitka blacktail, Coues deer. **See Boone and Crockett Club/Green Score/Net Score/Pope & Young/Subspecies/Trophy Hunt.**

Grazing

GRAZE The act of eating forbs and grasses, such as when whitetails converge in an alfalfa field near dusk and fill their rumens before retiring to safety and having the opportunity to chew their cud. While grazing deer naturally picks up grit and sand particles that wear down the teeth over the years. **See Alfalfa/Bolus/Browse/Clover/ Cud/Food/Forbs/Overbrowse/Rumen/ Ruminant.**

GREEN SCORE The first measuring and scoring of a buck's antlers before the required drying or curing period (60 days) has elapsed. The final and official score is called the "net score" and will usually be smaller because of slight antler shrinkage. **See Antlers/Boone and Crockett Club/Drying Period/Mass/Net Score/Nontypical/Pope & Young/Rack/Scoring/Symmetry/Trophy.**

GREEN-UP This refers to the time during the spring of the year when the herbaceous plants first start to sprout. Deer are ravenous at this time and eagerly gorge themselves. This is a good time to glass deer and check on how the herd made it through the winter. **See Crops/Die-Off/Fawn/Food/Food Plot/Forage/Herbaceous/Nutrition.**

GROOMING One method of whitetail social interaction, when two or more deer lick each other. This is also a method for deer to display subservience or acknowledge their place as lower in the pecking order of dominance. Mothers also display their maternal instincts by licking or grooming their fawns. A doe's initial grooming of her newborn cleans the fawn after the birthing process, helps eliminate any odors attractant to predators, and helps imprint the fawn to the mother andthe mother to her fawn. **See Alpha Buck/Dominance/Grooming/Hierarchy/Imprinting/Maternal Doe.**

Grooming

GROSS SCORE After the proper drying period has elapsed, this is the largest sum total of a whitetail's antler point lengths, generally expressed in inches, before deductions are taken, resulting in a final or net score. **See Boone and Crockett Club/ Drying Period/Green Score/Net Score/Pope & Young/Scoring System.**

GROUND BLIND See Blind.

GROUND STAND See Stand.

GROUND SHRINKAGE The visual phenomenon of deer antlers that look "massive"

Grunt Call

while on the hoof but seemingly smaller once the deer has been downed. **See Antlers/Green Score/Gross Score/Net Score/Scoring.**

GROUPING The degree to which bullets, slugs, or buckshot hits the same defined area on a target. Acceptable grouping is generally within a defined circle around an aiming point. **See Accuracy/Shot Placement/Sighting In/Zeroing In.**

GRUNT/GRUNT CALL/GRUNT TUBE A deep pig-like sound bucks make during the peak of the rut while looking for does to breed with. This raspy vocal message lets does in the area know of a buck's sexual intentions. If a hunter hears this piglike sound, he should get ready to shoot, as a buck is surely coming his way. A loud, deep grunt will usually make a buck pause without scaring it away. **See Calls/Chase Phase/Communication/Sounds in the Deer Woods/Tending Grunt/Vocalization.**

GUARD HAIR One of two layers of hair on white-tailed deer. The layer closest to their skin is soft and wool-like and provides a mechanism to trap air for cooling in the summer and insulation in the winter. Deer put their legs under their bodies while lying down so as not to compress the guard hairs on their bellies, thus staying better insulated and warmer. The coarse hairs observed on deer during the winter months are long, hollow guard hairs, which are stiffer and water resistant and provide such good insulating effects that often snow will not melt off a whitetail's back, nor under its bed. **See Cape/Conduction/Insulation/Mount/Radiation/Summer Coat/ Taxidermist/Winter Coat.**

GUIDE/GUIDED HUNTS An outfitter who leads hunts. If a hunter does not have access to public land, then hiring an outfitter for a guided hunt can provide a very worthwhile experience. Be sure to ask for references and investigate the guide thoroughly, talking to both successful and unsuccessful clients. **See Baiting/Controlled Hunt/Ethics/Fair Chase/High Fence Hunting/Managed Hunt/Outfitters/ Pack Train/Poaching/Sportsmanship.**

GULLY A ravine, a draw, a trench created by water erosion. **See Draw/Funnel/ Hollow/Ravine/Saddle/Terrain.**

GUN A portable firearm that propels a bullet or projectile toward a target. Examples include a pistol, rifle, or shotgun. **See Ammunition/Bullet/Caliber/Equipment/ Firearms/Handgun/Muzzleloader/Rifle/Shotgun.**

GUN SIGHT Any device used to sight-in, or aim, a gun, providing a consistent aim point at the intended target. It usually consist of a bead on the front end and an open sight, a buckhorn V sight, fiber optic, telescopic, peep, or laser sight. **See Accuracy/ Bead/Line of Sight/Peep Sight/Trajectory.**

GUNPOWDER An explosive mixture of chemicals (potassium nitrate, charcoal, and sulfur) used for gunnery or blasting. It is the source of the propelling charge in a firearm when ignited. **See Ammunition/Black Powder/Factory Load/Handload/Muzzleloader.**

GUTTING See Field Dressing.

Gut Pile

HABITAT The place or type of setting where a plant or animal naturally or normally lives and grows, the place where it is found. Deer habitat will generally be preserved if the number of deer are kept below the carrying capacity of the land. **See Bedding/ Biodiversity/Boundary/Carrying Capacity/Core Area/Dispersal/Ecotone/ Forage/Terrain/Winter Range.**

HAIR An important way to determine exactly what part of the deer's body you hit. After taking a shot at a deer, examine any hair particles that might exist on your arrow on the ground. White hairs indicate a throat patch hit, or more likely, a low, underbelly hit; hair from the lung area will be brown, coarse and without black tips; hair from the kidney area will be long, dark brown, and possibly have black tips. **See After the Shot/ Approaching Downed Deer/Exit Wound/Field Dressing/Follow-Up/Going Away Shot/Shot Placement/Tracks/Wounded Game.**

HAMSTRING In deer, the tendon that connects the main hind leg muscles to the bone. Predators such as wolves and feral dogs try to sever this tendon as a means of immobilizing their prey, leading to its death and ultimate consumption. **See Feral Dogs/ Hind Legs/Hounds/Free-Ranging/Predator/Tendon/Wolf.**

HANDGUN Any firearm that is generally held and fired with one hand, such as a pistol or revolver, as opposed to a "long arm," such as a rifle or shotgun. **See Caliber/Firearms/Guns/Handloading/Pistol/Revolver/Rifle/Shotgun.**

HANDLOADING An effective and fun technique if you shoot a lot, need to match specific requirements for accuracy, and are unable to attain comparable factory loads. The problem is, you can buy a lot of factory loads for the price of the reloading equipment and the bulk supplies needed to set up for reloading by hand. **See Ammunition/ Bullet/Caliber/Factory Loads/Foot Pounds of Energy/Knock Down Power.**

HARDWOODS Oak, hickory, walnut, and other mast-bearing trees. Most hardwoods produce a yearly crop of nuts, except during

Hardwoods

times of extreme drought, or a later-than-usual spring frost. Hanging a stand near a mast-producing hardwood will almost guarantee a hunter's seeing white-tailed deer, turkey, and so on when the nuts are falling. After a few frosts, the leaves of hardwoods turn beautiful colors—ranging from yellow, golden, and orange to red and purple, and ultimately fall off. Hunters are often pleasantly surprised to see the amazing sight of every leaf in the woods seemingly falling off at once. Hearing the single and multiple "thuds" of falling mast should alert hunters to expect incoming whitetails, as they too hear this highly desirous food crop dropping. **See Acorn/Autumn/Beechnuts/Browseline/ Conifer/Deciduous/Mast/Nuts/Softwoods.**

HARNESS Crucial safety equipment for hunters using a tree stand. Serious accidents (falls, hangings, suffocation, injuries, death,) often occur as hunters attempt to climb up or down a tree in order to get into or out of their tree stands. Post-accident interviews with survivors indicate that they tended to be most careless while climbing up into a tree stand and next careless when climbing down out of the stand. Third were careless mistakes made while actually in the tree stand itself—a misstep, leaning too far out to make the shot and so on. It is estimated that ten percent of tree stand hunters will suffer some sort of accident during their use of this hunting tactic. These statistics lend credence to the need for using a full-restraint safety harness put on immediately upon leaving the ground and worn while going up the tree, at all times while in the tree stand, and while coming down the tree. **See Climber/Fall Restraining Device/Ladder Stand/Permanent Stand/Portable Stand/Safety/Stands/ Survival/Tree Steps/Tree stand.**

HARVEST MOON The first full moon that occurs in the fall, after the autumnal equinox, which falls around September 23. It usually corresponds to the time of the fall harvesting of agricultural crops. **See Autumn/Autumnal Equinox/Equinox/Full Moon/Hunter's Moon/Lunar Influence/Moon/New Moon/Waning Moon/ Waxing Moon.**

HARVESTING SPIKES The practice of taking bucks with only a single tine growing from their pedicles. A fawn conceived late in the breeding season may have its body and antler growth stunted enough to produce single spikes on each side for its first set of antlers. Some hunters, landowners, and/or deer herd managers consider spikes inferior bucks. This is not necessarily the case, and if given the proper nutrition and time, they may just develop into a nice-racked buck. People in some areas have tried to upgrade the quality of the deer herd by extensively harvesting spike bucks as a means of eliminating the "spike gene." This tactic has not proven to be effective, mostly because a buck deer receives its genetic input from both its mother and father and the genes contributed by does were not eliminated as well. **See Buck/Dominance/Genetics/Herd Balance/Spikes.**

HAT/HUNTING HAT Headgear for hunting that should keep you warm, keep the sun out of your eyes, and divert rain from your eyes and the back of your neck. Many hunters like to wear a blaze orange hat for safety reasons. It is, however, a matter of personal choice for hunters to decide on style and color. **See Blaze Orange/Camouflage/Clothing/Footwear/Safety.**

HAUL LINE A rope or long strap hunters use to bring a backpack, bow, rifle, or shotgun up into a tree stand, ladder stand, tree, or any elevated position after they have safely climbed up it and strapped themselves in with their safety harness. Prudent safety rules dictate that hunters never haul a loaded firearm up into a stand by any means. In order to be doubly safe, never tie the haul line to the trigger guard or trigger itself. **See Accessories/Drag Rope/Equipment/Safety/Tree Stand.**

HEAD BOB A movement a deer (buck or doe) makes when it thinks that it has seen something unusual in its immediate area. It then wants to further identify that object and confirm its suspicions with another sense. Often a deer will lower its head as if it is feeding and then rapidly raise it, just to prompt the object to move or react and thus confirm that it is a danger or threat to the deer. **See Alarm Posture/Alert Snort/ Body Language/Communication/Fight or Flight/Foot Stomp/Does.**

HEAD NET A mesh-like material placed over the face and/or head that serves to cover up the shininess of the hunter's face, thus adding to a camouflage effect. **See Camouflage/Face Mask/Face Paint.**

HEALTH The physical state of a hunter. Hunting white-tailed deer requires that hunters be in the best of health. The deer woods is no place for sick or weakened hunters, as the physical requirements are always demanding. Hunters should get a physical every year prior to beginning a conditioning program to get themselves ready to pursue the white-tailed deer. **See Arthropod/Hygiene/Lyme Disease/ Parasite/Safety.**

HEARING One of the major senses white-tailed deer use for survival. A deer's ears are constantly rotating and checking for sounds of danger. High winds dramatically reduce a deer's ability to hear or sense approaching danger. The higher the wind level, the more nervous the deer act mainly because they cannot accurately pinpoint and identify all the noises coming their way. **See Alarm Posture/Alarm Snort/Alert Snort/ Communication/Deer Blow/Ears/Sounds in the Deer Woods/Stalking/ Vocalization/Wind.**

HEART RATE The rate at which a heart is beating. The normal heart rate is calculated with an animal at rest. Once an animal is excited, agitated, or fearful, its heart is capable of beating many times faster, thus providing the animal with the capability of protecting itself through flight or fight. **See Adrenaline/Adrenal Glands/Flight or Fight.**

HELICAL FLETCHING The feathers or vanes set at an angle on the arrow, rather than on a straight line. The offsetting of the feathers or vanes causes the arrow to spin or spiral with greater stability and accuracy. The more aggressive the helical angle, the higher the spin rate, and the more stable the arrow's flight, particularly with broadheads. **See Archery/Arrows/Broadheads/Feathers.**

HEMORRHAGING Copious amounts of blood flow resulting from the cutting of major arteries or veins with a sharp instrument, such as an arrowhead or knife. **See Archery/Arrowhead/Bleeding/Blood Trail/Broadheads/Knock Down Power.**

HERB/HERBACEOUS/HERBIVORE Most green plants, often used for food by the white-tailed deer. An herbivore is a plant-eating animal, such as the white-tailed deer, as opposed to a carnivore, or meat eater. **See Browse/Carnivore/Food/Food Plot/Forage/Forbs/Green-up/Predator/Prey.**

Herd Size

HERD SIZE The number of animals in a group. As forest edge animals, white-tailed deer regulate their respective family group size in order to stay within a small and intimately known area. **See Aerial Survey/Biologist/Carrying Capacity/Core Area/ Doe Harvest/ Home Range/Lead Doe/Malnutrition/ Overbrowse/Stress.**

HIERARCHY A ranking of power that both male and female deer recognize. They often seek to move themselves up the ladder of dominance because higher ranking in the social order results in eating the best foods by dominating the food plots.

The whitetail is a highly social animal. After a fawn is about six weeks old, it starts following its mother around her home range, which it quickly learns. As the doe begins to wean her fawn, the fawn also learns what foods to eat by mimicking the doe's eating habits. Deer form several small subgroups of four or five members, which are usually the matriarchal doe (lead-doe), her yearling female fawns and her new-borns. The older fawns are not highly dependent upon her at this point but follow her around the family group's home range because of the familiarity. The social habit of walking single file through the woods allows each deer to take advantage of the others' senses for danger. By walking together, the deer are more likely to see hunters if and when they move. (So don't move!)

Summer bachelor groups of bucks begin to break up in early fall because the increasing testosterone make them agitated, independent, and aggressive. Each buck tries to establish himself as the dominant breeding buck. This leads to sparring and sometimes actual fights among the bucks. By the time a buck sheds his velvet, he knows his rank within the males of the bachelor group. **See Agonistic Behavior/Alpha Buck/Bachelor Buck Group/Dominance/Grooming/Hierarchy/Lead Doe/Rank.**

HIGH-FENCE HUNTING See Game Farm.

HIGHLINE/HIGHLINING See Overbrowse.

HIND LEGS The back legs of a white-tailed deer; sporting metatarsal glands on the outside near the hind knees. The buck is often seen urinating on his hind legs over a scrape. He is using his urine to wash and carry his scent from the metatarsal glands into the scrape. **See Freshening/Hocks/Metatarsal Gland/Scent/Scrape.**

HOCKS/HOCK GLAND The tarsal joint or region of the hind limb on a quadruped (four-legged animal) that corresponds to an ankle on a person, but is considerably elevated on the leg and bends backwards. Located at this area are the tarsal glands. A buck, arching his back, rubs his tarsal hocks together while urinating on his hind legs and thus depositing his scent into the scrape he has just worked. In the world of the whitetail, this gland is considered to be the most important. **See Freshening/Glands/Hind Legs/Metatarsal Gland/Rub Urination/Scrape/Tarsal Gland.**

HOG DRESSED Also called "field dressed," "dressed weight," or "gutted weight." A downed deer from which most of the internal organs have been quickly removed from the body cavity so that it can be lifted or transported more easily. **See Body Weight/Field Dressing/Follow-Up.**

HOLLOW A depression or a sunken area where the land has a sudden lower elevation than the rest of the terrain. **See Funnel/Ravine/Saddle/Terrain.**

HOME RANGE A deer's home area, which it knows intimately and rarely leaves. A deer's home range must be large enough to supply all of its physical and reproductive needs yet small enough to provide for its security because of the deer's total familiarity with every detail of the land. A white-tailed doe chooses an area of land, often learned from its mother, of about one-and-a-half miles in radius, or about three square miles in area and lives there. A doe keeps her family size small so as to intimately know the core area. This is one of many of the white-tailed deer's survival tactics. A buck fawn learns its mother's home range, but aggressive behavior by does and older bucks when the buck reaches yearling status (one-and-a-half years old) tends to modify or displace his original home range during the rut. Bucks tend to have a larger home range than does, and often their ranges overlap with two or more doe family clusters.

In colder, northern climates, a deer's home range tends to be larger and thus less defined than that of deer in warmer, southern climate areas. A deer's winter home range is usually about one-tenth of its summer range. **See Carrying Capacity/Core Area/ Dispersal/Deer Sign/Herd/Herd Size/Security/Survival/Yard/Territory.**

HOOF/HOOVES A deer's feet, actually two central, extended inside toenails. Its two outside toenails (dewclaws) are atrophied toenails that no longer have any use. Both bucks and does use their hooves as a defensive weapon to fend off predators (including humans). The front hooves are usually longer (i.e., larger) than the rear hooves. Deer appear to walk "knock-kneed" as they tend to walk more on the inner hoof as compared to the outside central toenail. **See Artiodactyla/Cloven Hooves/Dewclaws/ Feet/Flail/Keratin/Splay/Tracks/ Trails.**

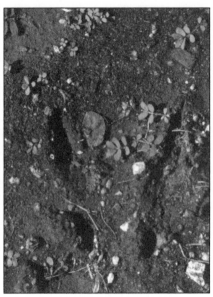

Hoof Prints

HORNS Growths made of a protein substance called keratin, a substance much like the fingernails of a human. Whitetail antlers are not horns. Horns grow on cows, sheep, and other animals and are permanent. They are not shed or cast like in the whitetail world. Whitetail antlers are true bone, grown and shed each year of a buck's life. **See Antlers/Cast/Keratin/Mass/Shed.**

HOUNDS Hunting dogs. Using dogs to hunt deer is an exciting, time-honored tradition, particularly in the deep South. In most northern states and much of the West, chasing deer with dogs is illegal. It is often cited as "unfair," "unethical," and "inhumane" by animal rights groups. However, where legal, using dogs to follow up on a lost deer is highly ethical and responsible. **See Blood-Trailing Dogs/Deer Search, Inc./Dogs/Feral Dogs/Free-Ranging.**

HSUS See the Humane Society of the United States.

HUMAN ODOR/SCENT The human smell. We stink, at least to other animals. We are meat eaters and give off the peculiar odor of a predator. In addition, humans have bad breath and odor-causing bacteria that lives off and consumes our sweat. We also smoke and touch hydrocarbons, such as oil and gasoline. The combination of all of these odors says, "Stay away from me!" to the whitetail. **See Chlorophyll/ Hygiene/Nose/Scent/Smell.**

HUMANE SOCIETY OF THE UNITED STATES (HSUS) An organization that advocates for the fair and ethical treatment of all animals. This anti-hunting group advocates for less cruelty toward animals, such as being wounded, tracked by dogs or shot at. The organization seemingly imparts human characteristics to animals and advocates for their rights as if the animals were human. This group has well-meaning intentions but is blind to the value of hunting as the best means of controlling a burgeoning deer population. **See Bambi Syndrome.**

HUNTER ORANGE **See Blaze Orange.**

HUNTER'S MOON Also known as the "rutting moon," this lunar phenomenon is the second full moon after the autumn equinox, which occurs around September 23. This full moon usually signals the beginning of the breeding period for the white-tailed deer, as does begin their estrous cycle about one week after the hunter's or rutting moon, with the peak of breeding occurring one week after that. **See Autumnal Equinox/Full Moon/Harvest Moon/Lunar Influence/ Moon/New Moon/Solstice/Waning Moon/Waxing Moon.**

HUNTING CAMP **See Deer Camp.**

HUNTING LICENSE The permission to hunt for big and small game. Hunters annually purchase licenses from their state. Depending upon state regulations, they may kill only one or sometimes more animals per license. Taking wildlife without buying a license from the state is considered poaching, an illegal act. **See Deer Management Permit/Doe Permit/Ethics/Poaching/Sportsmanship.**

HUNTING LOG A daily notebook where you can record the weather conditions, deer sightings, and other noteworthy or unusual events for use in future hunting plans. **See Planning/Preparation.**

HUNTING MALADIES Any affliction, sickness, or mind-dominating thoughts (real or unreal) that cause deer hunters to miss their shots at whitetails, travel long distances to their hunting camps out-of-season, or want to get away from the "real world." **See Buck Fever/Cabin Fever/Camp/Diseases/Foul Weather/Ground Shrinkage/ Hypothermia/"Jumping the String"/Lyme Disease.**

HUNTING PRESSURE The human hunter is a great, but unwitting, teacher of survival tactics to the white-tailed deer. It does not take more than a couple of fateful meetings with humans in the woods (including missed shots, loud noises, and human's foul smell) to teach the whitetail to avoid them at all costs. Hunters, with their loud, noise-making guns or clanking arrows hitting branches soon educate the deer to avoid any close contact with humans. Hunting pressure also causes deer to abandon coming to scrapes, at least during daylight hours. **See Core Area/Drive/Escape Route/ Home Range/Pressure/Security/Travel Corridor.**

HYDROSTATIC SHOCK The way a bullet kills. When it enters a whitetail's body, huge accompanying shock waves send vast amounts of energy through the nearby organs, sending them into arrest or shutdown. **See Bleeding/Foot-Pounds of Energy/Gun/Hemorrhaging/Kinetic Energy/Knock Down Power.**

HYGIENE Personal cleanliness that prevents any odor or bacteria buildup, which produces body odor that can betray a hunter to deer. Hunters should try to shower (or at least wash) with unscented soap before every hunt. Attention should be paid to hair, feet, and breath as these are all areas that give off odor. Never smoke, spit, or relieve yourself in any way while near your stand, as these newly dispersed scents will betray your presence. **See Apples/Breath/Chlorophyll/Health/Human Odor/Nose/ Parasites/Safety/Scent/Wind.**

HYPOGONADISM Undescended or undeveloped testicles in a buck deer. This usually leads to malformed antlers or no antlers due to the lack of testosterone production by the buck's testes. **See Adrenal Gland/Cactus Buck/Casts/Castration/ Gonads/Impotence/Testes/Testosterone.**

HYPOTHERMIA Often called "exposure," this life-threatening condition results when the core (inner) body temperature drops below a crucial point. After getting wet or chilled, the body reacts by shutting down the flow of blood to the extremities and tries to preserve functioning of the vital organs, such as the brain and heart. The solution to this dangerous situation is to get external and internal heat to the body as quickly as possible. Swallowing a warm liquid helps, as does putting the victim fully into a large sleeping bag—preferably with another person who can supply the external heat needed. It may sound ridiculous at first, but both bodies should be stripped down to their long johns or underwear for the most effective transfer of body heat within the sleeping bag. The time for modesty will come later, after the victim's body temperature has been raised and his or her life saved! **See First Aid/Foul Weather/ Hypothermia/Inclement Weather/Preparation/Safety/Survival(Hunter)/ Temperature/Weather.**

ICE A surface on which deer cannot walk or run very well because of the smooth, non-gripping nature of their hooves' chitinous material. If a deer falls on ice, it more than likely will not be able to regain its footing. The struggle to raise itself and the oft-occurring hard falls back down often cause damage to tendons or even split its pelvic girdle apart. This struggle leads to exhaustion and ultimately death through starvation or vulnerability to predators. **See Foul Weather/Frost/Hypothermia/Inclement Weather/Predator/Rain/Sleet/Snow/Weather.**

IMMUNOCONTRACEPTION Using dart-injected or oral intake (feeding) contraceptives on white-tailed does. Like trap and transfer, the idea is controversial. Although often advocated by environmentalists and others, these methods have proven to be expensive, impractical, and sometimes fatal to the subject because of the stress induced from being handled by humans. **See Artificial Insemination/Carrying Capacity/Contraception/Herd Size/Overbrowse/Trap and Transfer.**

IMPOTENCE The condition when a male of a species is unable to breed or copulate and cannot pass along his genes to a fertile female and thus procreate (have a baby). **See Breeding/Castration/Copulation/Glands/Hypogonadism/Infertility/Testes/Testosterone.**

IMPRINTING The process in which a newborn fawn identifies with the first thing that it encounters after being born, which is usually its mother. It thereafter knows her voice, her shape, her affection, and can readily identify her from all the other does. About-to-give-birth does drive off their previous year's fawns (yearlings) and any other females from their claimed birthing area. This is to prevent any chance of the newborns imprinting on other deer and to keep foreign scent out of the area, thus increasing the fawn's chances of survival. **See Biodiversity/Birth/Dispersal/Fawn/Surrogate Mother.**

INBREEDING The act of mating with a close relative, such as a young buck breeding with its mother or womb mate (sister), which results in the degradation of the gene pool. This is unhealthy and not Mother Nature's way. The solution is the natural dispersal of young bucks out of their mothers' home range, where their sisters will stay, attached to their mother in a matriarchal society. **See Dispersal/Genes/Heredity/Lead Doe.**

INCISOR TEETH The relatively sharp front teeth of a whitetail that are utilized to snip off stems of plants, blades of grass, and so on, while eating. They are not used to chew cud or grind the vegetative matter as are molars, which wear down as deer eat sand and grit along with their vegetative food. **See Age of Deer/Cementum/Molars/Teeth.**

Inclement Weather

INCLEMENT WEATHER Foul weather, which may seem nasty to a human hunter, but is generally accepted as routine for a deer. Deer tend to move normally during foul weather. They are creatures of habit who live all of their lives in ever changing weather and are used to the changes. Only very severe weather conditions cause deer to seek shelter or change their routines. **See Clothing/Foul Weather/Hypothermia/Ice/ Movement/Rain/Sleet/Snow/Weather/Wind.**

INFERTILITY The condition of being barren, sterile, unable to produce offspring. **See Breeding/Chase Phase/Copulation/Fawn/Fetus/Impotence/Rut/Triplets/Twins.**

INFRARED/INFRARED LIGHT/INFRARED SIGHT Light and heat waves that cannot be seen by humans. Body heat is given off in the form of infrared waves and the new heat-seeking technologies have allowed hunters to utilize this technology for locating wounded deer that might have become permanently lost to them. **See Accuracy/ Grouping/Shot Placement/Ultraviolet.**

INJURY Hurt or damage. White-tailed deer, being residents of our imperfect world, are subject to a variety of injuries whether from being hung up while jumping a fence, bumped by a motor vehicle, injured by a predator, or wounded by a hunter. Most seriously wounded animals do not survive the winter's harsh elements or in areas where there are significant numbers of predators. If an injured deer survives, however, it will often manifest that injury on the opposite side antler during the next growing season, resulting in a stunted or disfigured rack. For example, if a buck is bumped by a vehicle on his right backside, the effect of that contact will show up on his left side antler the next time it starts growing. **See Atrophy/Castration/Nontypical.**

INSIDE CORNER See Corner.

INSTINCT The natural aptitude, impulse, or capacity of an organism to respond to an environmental stimulus, which is largely hereditary and unalterable. It does not involve reason, but rather has its goal as the reduction of somatic tension. It is action that takes place below the conscious level. **See Adrenal Glands/Escape Route/Flail/Fight or Flight/Instinct/Sixth Sense/Spooked.**

INSTINCTIVE SHOOTER A sportsman who does not use sights, whether with a bow and arrow, handgun, or long firearm, but only points the weapon toward its target. The aiming and site picture are calculated within the shooter's mind. **See Accuracy/Gun Sight/Kisser Button/Shot Placement/Sighting In/Zeroing in.**

INTERDIGITAL GLANDS Scent glands between the toes/hooves of deer. When startled, deer deposit a scent on the ground that serves to warn other deer that danger was recently discovered at that spot. Scent left behind as a deer walks allows another deer to follow its trail. **See Alarm/Cloven Hooves/Communication/Foot Stomp/ Glands/Nasal Gland/Scent/Tracks.**

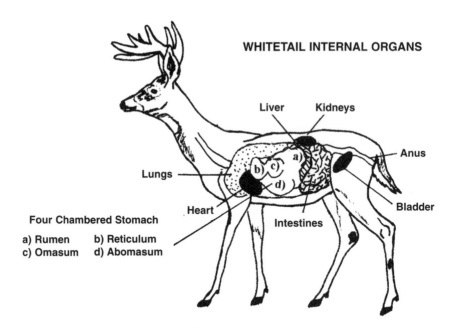

WHITETAIL INTERNAL ORGANS

Liver   Kidneys

Anus

Lungs

a)
b) c)
d)

Heart

Bladder

Intestines

Four Chambered Stomach

a) Rumen   b) Reticulum
c) Omasum   d) Abomasum

INTERNAL ORGANS All the functioning parts inside a deer's body that sustain it in life. **See Diaphragm/Esophagus/Field Dressing/Heart/Liver/Lungs/Rectum/Rumen/Sternum/Stomach.**

ISLAND A highly secure area for a white-tailed deer in a large river or lake.. Since deer are excellent swimmers, they have no problem getting to an island as a safe haven from predators—including humans. It is worthwhile taking a canoe or quiet boat to investigate an island sanctuary, as a pressured buck may head there in his attempts to avoid human contact. **See Cover/Instinct/Predator/Security(Deer)/Terrain/Water.**

IXODES TICK The deer tick that carries and causes Lyme disease. **See Arthropods/Lyme Disease/Parasites/Ticks.**

JACKLIGHT/JACKING An illegal technique of using a strong light at night to locate deer by shining the light in their eyes and then shooting them after legal hunting hours or off-season. **See Ethics/Feeders/Flashlight/Game Warden/Night Vision/ Poaching/Spotlighting/Tapeteum lucidem.**

JERKY Dried venison, sometimes flavored with spices smoked. Often carried with the hunter as a snack, whether in the woods or not. **See Back Straps/Field Dressing/Gamey Taste/Recipes/Tenderloins/Venison.**

"Jumping the String"

"JUMPING THE STRING" A deer hearing or seeing an arrow being launched from a bow and crouching, diving, or jumping out of the way to evade it. Nervous or alert animals are ready to lurch in any direction at any time and at the slightest provocation. Newly alerted deer usually crouch in order to spring forward or turn to the side, rather than dive or leap up when an arrow is launched at them. Aiming two to three inches lower on a nervous or alert animal, rather than at the normal, center heart spot as for a calm, unsuspecting deer, will usually tag it.

At a distance under twenty yards, deer are threatened by the tiniest hunter mistake and react defensively. Beyond twenty yards, deer are less likely to see you on stand, less apt to hear your bow thud during the shot, and less prone to panic and duck the arrow. However, because of the increased distance and travel time of an arrow, should the deer hear your arrow's release, it will naturally hunker down for a springing leap or turning motion. Aiming somewhat lower on the deer's body will compensate for this. **See Archery/Buck Fever/Hunting Maladies.**

K

KAIROMONES A warning pheromone or hormonelike chemical produced and released by living creatures (including white-tailed deer and humans) so that they can communicate with each other. A kairomone gives the receiver an advanced warning. Human pheromones alert deer to our presence. Kairomones result from natural biological functions such as perspiration, respiration, or glandular and hormonal secretions. **See Allomones/Attractants/Communication/Lures/Pheromone/Repellants/Scent.**

Kairomone Scent

KERATIN The fibrous, proteinlike substance that makes up the human fingernail, a cow's horns, and a deer's hooves. It is not the substance that makes up a whitetail's antlers, which are true bone. **See Antlers/Cloven Hooves/Dew Claw/Hooves/ Horn/Mass.**

KINETIC ENERGY The energy associated with motion, especially that of a bullet entering the tissue of a white-tailed deer. **See Ammunition/Bullet/Foot-Pounds of Energy/Hydrostatic Shock/Knock Down Power.**

KISSER BUTTON A disc located on the bowstring that is used as an anchor point, touched by the lips at full draw. It assists in aiming the arrow. **See Accuracy/Anchor Point/Archery/Bow and Arrow.**

KNIFE (HUNTING) A sharp, not overly big knife (a bowie knife is very cumbersome to field dress a deer with), convenient to use and easy to handle. Whether a hunter chooses a sheath or folding model is up to him or her. **See Accessories/Equipment/Field Dressing.**

KNOCK-DOWN POWER The ability of a projectile, such as a bullet or arrowhead, to "drop" an animal in its tracks. Firearms possess a greater ability to knock-down or kill a whitetail because of their shock value (hydrostatic shock). A bow and arrow kills by causing hemorrhaging or massive bleeding. **See Ammunition/Bullet/ Caliber/Foot-Pounds of Energy/Handloading/Hemorrhaging/Hydrostatic Shock/Kinetic Energy.**

LACRIMAL GLANDS See **Preorbital Glands**.

LACTATION/LACTATING DOE Milk produced by the doe, so that she can nurse her fawn, twins, or triplets, as soon as they are born. After a fawn is born, it instinctively nurses from its mother. Often, the fawns are weaned from their mother's milk before hunting season starts. However, late-born fawns might still be nursing at this time, and it is not uncommon for hunters who have shot a doe during archery season to encounter milk as they field dress the newly harvested doe. **See Fawns/ Minerals/Nursing/Teats/Udder.**

LADDER STAND A tree stand device with a built-in ladder or set of steps that extends twelve to eighteen feet into the air as it leans against a tree. While ladder stands are heavier and more unwieldy to maneuver as a completely extended unit, they are generally sturdier and more stable and thus induce more confidence in the height wary hunter. **See Climber/Equipment/Fall-Prevention Devices/Harness/Noise/ Permanent Stand/Portable Stand/Safety/Stands/Tree Steps.**

LAND MANAGEMENT Attempting to use or manage acreage to provide for the best possible deer hunting. The efforts of land owners include selective and wholesale logging, supplemental food production, mineral supplements, deer herd reduction by using quality deer management techniques, etc. **See Aerial Photographs/Buck-Doe Ratio/ Carrying Capacity/Food Plot/Habitat/Herd Size/High Fence Hunting/Land-owners/Nutrition/Overbrowse/Quality Deer Management/Soil Conservation Service.**

LANDOWNERS Those who own the land you wish to hunt on. Generally, one obtains permission to hunt on somebody's land well in advance of the season opening. When asking permission from landowners to hunt on their land, be sure to let them know that you are a responsible, safety conscious hunter who will respect their property, fences, planted fields, gates, buildings and so on. In short, assure them that you will provide them with every courtesy that they are owed as the landowner. Let them know that you will call in advance of the season just to check on any changing conditions or new concerns on their part. If you open a gate, close it! If you pack throw-a-ways in (e.g., trash, bottles), pack it back out. In fact, it doesn't hurt to pack out a little more trash than you took in. Only bring one friend at most with you, not a whole crowd. (The landowner gave you permission, not your hunting club!) Tell the landowners what vehicle you will be driving and ask them where they would like you to park and even more important where you should definitely not park. Inform landowners of any stray animals or trespassers on their land. Perhaps most important of all is the one piece of advice that might earn you the privilege of being invited back to hunt again:

offer to physically help the landowners. They probably will not accept the offer, but just your making it says that you are a worthwhile person. However, if you do offer to help, be prepared to follow through or your own credibility will be hurt and you will probably not be invited back. **See Crop Damage/Fruit/Land Management/Permission to Hunt.**

LANTERN A portable gas- or battery-operated lamp in a protective case with transparent openings. Lanterns make the best blood-trailing lights because of their wide diffusion of light. **See Approaching Downed Deer/Blood Trail/Blood Trailing Dogs/Tracks/Wounded Game.**

LASER/LASER RANGE FINDER/LASER SIGHT An acronym standing for light amplification simulated emitted radiation. This relatively new-to-the-hunting scene technology is being incorporated into all kinds of equipment for improved accuracy of firearms and bow- and-arrow systems, for visual equipment, and so on. **See Binoculars/Equipment/Night Vision/Optics/ Range Finder/Scope/Shot Placement.**

Laser Range Finder

LATE RUT Approximately twenty-eight days after the peak of the primary rut, when any unbred doe will come into estrus again. Doe fawns, born in May, can also be mature enough to exhibit signs of estrus, become sexually active, and be receptive to a buck at this time. In the northern United States, in approximately mid-December, bucks again turn their attention to estrous does and become sexually agitated for a brief period. Bucks will continue to extend their roamings through their range as they search for any unbred does that are now in heat again. Because of the fewer numbers of estrous does available to the bucks, it is not unusual to see several different bucks trailing one estrous doe. A hunter can identify a doe in estrus by the red droplets left as she urinates in the snow. Effective hunting techniques at this time of the year are rattling, tending doe calls, mock-scrape making, and using decoys. **See Late Rut/ Prerut/Primary Rut/Rut/Testosterone.**

LATITUDE The measurement in degrees north or south of the equator. The equator is 0 degrees, while the North Pole is 90 degrees north, and the South Pole is 90 degrees south. Knowing your latitude and longitude allows you to know exactly where you are on Earth. **See Compass/Global Positioning System/Longitude/Navigation.**

LAYERS/LAYERING A useful way to dress in anticipation of foul or changing weather. Rather than bulking up with heavy outerwear, it is now recommended that hunters wear multiple layers of clothing beginning with insulated or thermal underwear, following with fleece or Polarfleece, then wool, and finally ending with a waterproof outer shell/parka. The advantage of layers is that if hunters start to become overheated, they can cool down by removing several layers, or if they begin feeling cool, a layer or two can be added. **See Camouflage/Clothing/Foul Weather/Gore-tex/Inclement Weather/Thinsulate.**

LEAD DOE/LEAD DEER Usually the matriarchal or oldest female. She is usually the first deer down the pathway as she leads her fawns and other does to where the best food is or along the safest trails. She has the most experience and is the teacher of social order and all information within her home range. During the rut, if hunters see a large doe, they should be looking behind her for the trailing buck seeking to breed her. Hunters can tell a mature doe from a fawn because she is rectangular in body shape, not square like a fawn. **See Dispersal/Does/Fawn/Flag/Flail.**

LEAF DROP The reason the season—fall—got its name; when all the nuts and leaves seem to drop from the trees at once. The deciduous trees have already changed color because of the stoppage or reduction in chlorophyll production. The leaf is no longer engaged in photosynthesis or food production for the tree, so it falls off. **See Autumn/ Autumn Equinox/Chlorophyll/Deciduous/Harvest Moon/Leaves/Photosynthesis/Seasons.**

LEARNED BEHAVIOR Just as hunters try to study deer movement patterns, white-tailed deer are often able to learn where hunters will go, if they do not vary their approach to their hunting stands. The deer learns this when hunters repeat their routine. Once deer have an idea of just where the hunters are or will be, they will often avoid that area for their own safety. **See Patterning/Survival.**

LEAVES The foliage from trees that produce the tree's food through a process called photosynthesis. Leaves are not naturally green—they may be red, yellow, or orange—but they look green because of the high presence of chlorophyll used to make food. Once fall arrives and the colder weather stops this food production, leaves often change color because of losing their chlorophyll and eventually fall to the ground, returning to the soil as nutrients. These downed leaves can be very noisy when hunters, deer, or small animals, such as squirrels, approach the hunter's deer stand. They can announce a deer's presence with their noise. **See Autumn/Canopy/ Chlorophyll/Food/Frost/Leaf Drop/Noise/Photosynthesis.**

LEVER ACTION A mechanism found in rifles that utilize a "cocking lever" for spent bullet extraction and injection of an unused cartridge. **See Autoloader/**

Lever Action

Bolt Action/Double-Barreled/Firearms/Rifle/Pump Action/Side by Side.

LICK A mineral lick, natural mineral lick, or salt lick. A place where whitetail and other animals go to acquire needed minerals for body and antler growth. **See Antlers/Baiting/Ethics/Fair Chase/Minerals/Nutrition/Ossification.**

LICKING BRANCH See **Overhanging Branch**.

LIFE CYCLE/LIFE SPAN The entire process or stages of a deer (or any living thing) going through its life—from breeding to conception, birth, infancy, growing up, being an adult, and eventually dying. See **Birth/Breeding/Fawn/Maturity/Rut**.

LIGHT PATTERNS In white-tailed deer, the amount of sunlight that their eyes receive. It is the governing factor for antler development or growth. Light patterns also appear to cue the whitetail as to the proper time for breeding in the fall. This ensures the fawns will be born when available nutrients for growth are plentiful. See **Antlers/Camouflage/Eyes/ Ossification/Photoperiodism/Ultra-Violet/Vision**.

LINE OF FIRE The area from directly in front of your gun barrel or arrowhead proceeding toward the actual target where the bullet or arrow impacts. Anything within this pathway will be struck, whether intended or not, so always be sure of your intended target and that the shooting path is clear to that target. See **Back Stop/Safety/ Shooting Lane**.

LINE OF SIGHT Looking down the sights of a gun, through the scope, over the gun barrel, and so on. This is a straight line from your eye to its target. However, since a bullet or an arrow begins dropping immediately because of the effect of gravity, it will not follow your line of sight over any considerable distance. The path or trajectory of an arrow or bullet traveling over the distance between its exit from the bow or firearm to its objective may be arched as the hunter raises it above the line of sight. See **Accuracy/Rifling/Sighting In/Trajectory/Zeroing-In**.

LIP CURL See **Flehmen**.

LIPOGENESIS The building up of fat in the body by eating more food than the body requires for its daily functioning. Whitetails instinctively eat more than they need to purposely build up fat reserves that allow them to survive the winter when food is scarce. Hunters field dressing a deer often note the amount of fat that they must remove during that process. Copious amounts of fat indicate that the whitetails are finding ample amounts of food to eat and that the land is able to sustain their numbers. See **Carrying Capacity/Die-Off/Herd Size/Overbrowse/Starvation/Winterkill**.

LIVE WEIGHT The weight of a deer "on the hoof." Adult white-tailed does can weigh from 80 pounds to close to 200 pounds in the northern climates. White-tailed bucks can weigh from 90 pounds to over 400 pounds As a general rule, the male of the whitetail species weighs more than the female in any latitudinal area. A field-dressed deer weighs about two-thirds of its live weight. See **Body Weight/Dressed Weight/Field Dressing/Hog Dressed**.

LIVER An organ in the body of mammals that looks dark-brownish red, is very large, and is responsible for changing sugars in the blood to glycogen and storing it until needed. A hit to the liver is a fatal wound for a whitetail. Evidence of a liver hit is the presence of dark red, almost black-looking blood. **See Blood/Blood-Trailing Dogs/Flukes/Liver Fluke/Parasites.**

LIVER FLUKE A white, worm-like parasite observed in or on a deer's liver. They are not harmful in low numbers, but excessive amounts can cause anemia in the whitetail and make them lethargic. Deer pass the flukes out as cysts, which are ingested by land snails or slugs. The slugs are then ingested by the deer and gravitate to the liver, which starts the process all over again. **See Diseases/Hunting Maladies/Microorganism/Parasites.**

LOCKING OF ANTLERS A sparring match between two bucks of somewhat equal strength and social order as a test for who is higher on the dominance scale. If neither backs down, then a ferocious battle may ensue where the bucks' antlers become entwined and "locked together." Bucks have perished because their antlers became hopelessly entangled when fighting. They often struggle to the point of exhaustion. When one deer dies, the other will drag his body around and violently try to dislodge it, succumbing to further exhaustion and his own death. Both deer are highly vulnerable to predators at this time. **See Alpha Buck/Dominance/Fighting/Flailing/Hierarchy/Sparring.**

LOG BOOK See Hunting Log.

LONGBOW The straight-limbed bow is the forerunner of the recurve bow and its latest off-spring. the compound bow. A favorite of archers during prior generations, the longbow is regaining adherents or fans through its nostalgic use as "traditional archery." **See Archery/Bow and Arrow/Compound Bow/Crossbow/Recurve Bow.**

LONGITUDE The east-west directional imaginary vertical lines running from the North Pole to the South Pole that are used, in conjunction wiht the lines or degrees of latitude, to locate one's position on Earth and/or on a map. Zero degrees longitude runs through Greenwich, England, whereas the International Date line in the Pacific Ocean is designated as 180 degrees. **See Compass/Global Positioning System/Latitude/Navigation.**

LUNAR INFLUENCE The effect of the moon. The moon has a strong effect upon this planet, influencing tides, animal movement, and breeding cycles. The wise hunter will always be aware of the moon's phases. A good rule to hunt by is this: Always be in your stand whenever the moon is visible during daylight hours, as deer tend to be more active when the moon is visible. A lunar month is 29.5 days long, the time it takes for the moon to revolve around our Earth. **See Autumnal Equinox/Crepuscular Activity/Full Moon/Harvest Moon/Hunter's Moon/Moon/New Moon/Quarter Moon Phase/ Vernal Equinox/Waning Moon/Waxing Moon.**

LURES/DEER LURE Ways to attract deer using food or sex.

A. Food. Acorns, apples, beechnuts, clover, alfalfa, and any of over one hundred plants, forbs, and so on that deer find attractive to eat. Whatever food item is most nutritious and desriable at the moment could lure deer in when they are ready to feed. Several artificial food scent lures have been manufactured as food attractants.

B. Sex. Obviously, the most perfect sexual attractant to a buck during the rut is an estrous doe. Multiple does nearing estrus would come in a close second. Sexual scents composed of female pheromones collected from the urinary tract of a doe in sexual heat (estrus) are sold commercially. These lures are used to attract bucks to a hunter's area during the rut. The buck is focusing upon finding the source of those pheromones quickly. Some scent manufacturers substitute or mix bovine (cow) or sheep pheromones in their lures, claiming them to be chemically the same. **See Attractant Scent/Estrus/Flehmen/Pheromones/Scents/Urine.**

LUTENIZING HORMONE A hormone released by the pituitary gland in the buck's brain—initiated by photoperiodism—that is needed to trigger production of testosterone (male sex hormone) in the buck's testicles. This increased level of testosterone then initiates antler production. **See Antlers/Light Patterns/Photoperiodism/Rut.**

LYME DISEASE Traditionally, a tick-borne disease transmitted to humans by the bite (sucking blood) of the Ixodes tick. In recent reports, up to one-fourth of the new cases of Lyme disease were transmitted by other bloodsucking insects, such as mosquitoes and black flies. This situation obviously bears watching.

It is generally accepted that the tick must be attached to the body for about 24 hours in order to transmit the disease. An early symptom of Lyme disease is a red bull's-eye-shaped rash (a ringlike configuration with red borders and a colorless center) at the site of the bite. Untreated, the late symptoms can be flu-like fever; swollen, painful, and achy joints; headache, stiff neck, fatigue, muscle ache; enlarged lymph nodes.

This debilitating disease, with its cardiac, arthritic, and neurological (nerve) symptoms, can be successfully treated with antibiotics, if caught early enough before the debilitating, later symptoms show up. The diagnosis of Lyme disease is usually not made by blood tests alone. It depends upon a combination of symptoms and two or more positive blood tests

A USDA-approved vaccine purportedly prevents infection from Lyme disease, but long-term field results from actual hunters have not yet come forth. No one actually knows any side effects of the vaccine nor its long-term results. That does not mean that there are not any! The old-standby prevention method is to use a tick spray containing DEET (n,n-diethyl-m-tolumide), applied to one's clothing (not directly to the skin) before going outdoors. Tuck in pant legs, keep your neck covered, and wear gloves, to cover any places where ticks may get at bare skin. During the hunting season, ticks will vacate their former host (tour deer) when they sense that it is cooling off (i.e. the deer is no longer living), so be aware of their possible presence while you are skinning your deer. Upon returning to your cabin or vehicle, immediately examine your body and remove any ticks. **See Arthropods/Health/Hunting Maladies/Ixodes Tick/Parasite/Safety/Tick.**

M

MADSTONE See Bezoar Stone.

MAGAZINES See Whitetail Magazines.

MAIN BEAM The longest antler from which other points project. One main beam is on each side of the buck's head. Other than the browtines, the next point off the main beam is the G-2, followed by the G-3, and so on. **See Antlers/Bifurcate/Boone and Crockett Club/Browtine/Drop Tine/Mass/Pope & Young/Scoring/Spread/ Sticker Point/Symmetry.**

MALE SEX HORMONE See Testosterone.

MALNUTRITION A situation that occurs when a whitetail cannot get enough to eat, either through poor food quality or lack of availability. Whitetails instinctively will seek out the most nutritous food available. However, sometimes, as in winter, all they are doing is stuffing their stomachs, not supplying their bodies with anything of value for energy, fat building, or body growth. **See Die-Off/Mortality/Overbrowse/ Predators/Starvation/Winterkill.**

MANAGED HUNT A white-tailed deer hunt offered by professional guides for less than the very best animals. These are mature deer but not trophy class. The hunter knows this before-hand and accepts this as a condition of the hunt. Managed hunts are obviously less expensive than trophy hunts. **See Baiting/Controlled Hunt/Deer Fence/Fair Chase/Fence/Game Farm Buck/Guided Hunt/High Fence Hunting/Land Management/Quality Deer Management/Sportsmanship/Trophy Hunt.**

MAPS Topographical maps of the hunting area. Combined with quality aerial photographs, these maps canhelp you begin your pre-scouting efforts begin right at your kitchen table. Potential travel corridors for deer can almost jump off the page at you if you know how to look for

Maps

them. Having your best potential spots mapped out before you even start physically scouting an area can save you days of trekking. **See Aerial Photographs/Bureau of Land Management/Orienteering/Orthophotoquad/Scouting/Survival/Topographical Map/United States Geological Service.**

MARROW See Bone Marrow.

MASK See Face Mask.

MASS/ANTLER MASS The length and thickness of the tine and main beams of whitetail antlers. The score of a rack with a thick, heavy bulk of antler all the way to the tips rapidly increases in both Boone and Crockett Club and Pope & Young scoring systems. Normally the main beams decrease in circumference from the base to the tips. A heavily palmated rack (broad, like moose antlers) with even mass on both antlers could make up for short tine lengths during the scoring process of the rack. **See Antlers/Boone and Crockett Club/Drop Tine/Forkhorn/G-1/G-2/Green Score/Main Beam/Net Score/Nontypical/Palmated Rack/Pope & Young/Scoring.**

Mass

MAST The nut crop from certain trees, such as oak, beech, pecan, and hickory that are favored as food by the white-tailed deer. During your pre-season scouting activities, it is a good idea to take along your binoculars and glass up into the canopy of the white and red oak trees. Note and/or mark those trees with a heavy nut crop and hang your stand nearby in September or early October, when the deer will be tripping over themselves to get at the falling nuts to fatten up for the months ahead. **See Acorn/Beechnuts/Food/Frost/Fungus/Hardwoods/Mushrooms/Nuts/Oaks/Pine Cones/Soft Mast.**

MATING See Breeding.

MATERNAL GROUP A group of females with the same bloodline or lineage, such as a matriarchal doe, her daughters, and her granddaughters. **See Fawns/Lead Doe/Twins.**

MATRIARCHAL DOE See Lead Doe.

MATURE BUCK A large or sexually mature buck deer (three and one-half to five and one-half years old). Generally accepted signs that a mature buck is using the area as his home base or core area are large rubs on large saplings or trees, deep gouges in rubs made by the burrs or browtines of a large antlers and tracks approximately two and one-quarter inches or longer in a scrape or under a licking branch. **See Overhanging Branch/Rub/Scrape/Tracks.**

MEATPOLE See Buck Pole.

MECHANICAL BROADHEADS Hunting arrow points built to fly like field or practice points because of reduced friction. Thee have less tendency to plane or veer off as untuned broadheads can. Mechanical broadheads have sharp blades that open on impact with their target to slice and cause hemorrhaging. **See Arrowheads/Arrow Speed/Arrow Weight/Broadheads/Equipment/Feathers/Helical Fletching/Hemorrhaging.**

MECHANICAL RELEASE A hand-held device that attaches to a bowstring at the arrow nocking point, either directly to the string by a nocking loop, or some other device. It is used by the archer to draw the bowstring back, hold it for aiming , and then release the arrow when the shot is taken. A mechanical release is perceived to provide more consistent and accurate shots than finger shooting. **See Anchor Point/Archery/Finger Release/Nocking Loop/Nocking Point/Release.**

MELANISTIC The unusually dark, often black, coloration of the skin or coat of an animal. **See Albino/Pelage/Piebald.**

MELATONIN A hormone released by the pineal gland in the brain that causes the pituitary gland to release the lutenizing hormone, which in turn triggers testosterone production. **See Eyes/Lutenizing Hormone/Pineal Gland/Pituitary Gland/Rut/Testosterone.**

MENTAL PREPARATION/MENTAL STATE Deer hunters' attitude, aptitude, and mental conditioning in their quest to pursue the white-tailed deer. Spouses often refer to this state as one of "obsession," but deer hunters know it to be their passion for the hunt. Basically, the term relates to any activity that hunters use to prepare for the upcoming season, often starting in the summer months, well before the actual big-game hunting season officially begins. anti-hunters also refer to this state of mind as being "murderous," but true hunters will not be deterred by their illogical arguments. **See Bambi Syndrome/Buck Fever.**

METABOLISM/METABOLIC RATE The normal functioning of the body, involving food consumption, digestion, energy exertion, waste elimination, and so on. Whitetails slow down their metabolism during the harsh months of winter, often surviving off fat reserves accumulated during the fall of the year. During winter, food is scarce and obtained at a great cost of energy, often more than is produced by the food. **See Die-Off/Winterkill/Yarding.**

METATARSAL GLANDS A gland located on the outer side of each hind leg, usually represented by a darkish tuft of hair. Hunters, deer biologists, and scientists do not yet fully understand the significance of this gland in the world of the white-tailed deer. **See Breeding/Freshening/Glands/Hind Legs/Hocks/Nasal Gland/Scent Scrape.**

MICROORGANISMS Very small bacteria, algae, viruses, and so on that exist in a deer's digestive system and other organs. Some are disease-causing bacteria or viruses that are too small to see with the naked eye but are nevertheless deadly to the white-tailed deer and to humans. Often they can only be truly identified under a microscope. Some are vital to living, such as those necessary for digestion, for the breaking down of vegetative matter in the four stomachs of the deer. **See Diseases/ Flukes/Liver Flukes/Lyme Disease/Parasites/Stomach/Ticks.**

MIDDAY HUNTING The hours from 10 A.M. to 2 P.M. are often considered nonproductive times to be afield, because supposedly deer are not moving then. That is not the case, as we now know that deer do not stay bedded all the time, but often get up, snack, relieve themselves, and/or move to another area. Particularly during the rut, a white-tailed buck is constantly on the move—even during these hours—while he is searching for does ready to breed. Likewise, savvy hunters will not get out of their stands to go back to the cabin or vehicle for lunch or a smoke. Many novice hunters do just that, and many a spooked deer has fallen to the sustained effort of wise hunters who stay in their stands and let less experienced "woods walkers' drive deer to them. The lesson is to stay in your stand as long as possible so that when your deer comes by, you will be there to claim it. **See Estrus/Rut.**

MIGRATION Moving from one region to another. The white-tailed deer does not migrate in the same sense as do elk, caribou and other ruminants. If the snow gets too deep, deer will bunch up in a particular area, known as a "deer yard." This traditionally used area might have a fir tree overstory that provides some heat retention, some food, and protection from predators. The deer often walk the trails to keep the snow beaten down; which in turn allows increased mobility and some wind protection. **See Carrying Capacity/Overbrowsing/Yarding.**

MINERALS Nutrients necessary to humans and other plants and animals, including the white-tailed deer. Deer require a certain amount of minerals in order to grow and function though their life cycle. Bucks, in particular, require a continuous supply of calcium and phosphorous for their antler production. They obtain these minerals from eating plants that grew in mineral-rich soil. They also temporarily "borrow" needed minerals from their own bones in order to produce their antlers. The minerals are replaced in the bones during other times of the year through normal feeding. Areas of the country with poor soil minerals usually produce bucks with smaller racks. Likewise, nursing does need mineral replacement in their bodies as they pass these vital elements along to their fawns. **See Antlers/Baiting/Ethics/Fair Chase/Minerals/**

Natural Mineral Lick/ Nutrition/Ossification/Phosphorous.

MINERAL LICK An area where certain minerals such as sulfur, salt, and phosphorous are brought to the surface naturally by springs or seepage or are artificially placed there by humans. These concentrated deposits of necessary minerals are often visited by whitetails and other animals to consume as a needed element in the growth of their bodies, bones, and antlers. **See Antlers/Baiting/Ethics/Fair Chase/Minerals/ Natural Mineral Lick/Nutrition/Ossification/Poaching/Salt Lick/Sportsmanship.**

MOCK RUB Rubs created by hunters. Mock rubs can draw, stop, and distract a buck. Some hunters wear hip-high rubber boots and rubber gloves to avoid putting their scent into the area and then take a large wood rasp and recreate several rubs strategically placed on trees near their stand site. Some hunters even put a drop or two of pre-orbital gland scent on the rub for authenticity. **See Breeding/Prerut/Rub/Rut/Scent.**

MOCK SCRAPE Scrapes made by hunters. Wearing rubber boots and gloves, the hunter finds an appropriate spot (in a semi-open area where deer naturally travel and can see and smell it) and uses a stick to paw away the leaves and forest litter, forming an oval and looking much like a real scrape. Into this fake scrape is poured deer urine or any quality lure. Don't skimp on the lure, as you want the earth to reek with urine smell. Some hunters place their scent canisters in the center of the mock scrape, thus assuring it is refreshed when they are hunting over it. Purposefully made just before serious breeding scrapes appear, mock scrapes can be deadly. Since the dominant buck in an area usually makes the first scrapes, any new scrape is usually checked by him, just to see who this new intruder is. **See Breeding/Freshening/Rub/Scents/Scrape.**

MOLARS The teeth located in the back of the mouth that are customarily used for grinding food. Biologists use the number of molars and the degree of their wear as an indicator of age for a whitetail. These are the teeth deer use in chewing their cud, and they are often worn down with age as deer ingest sand and grit with their food. **See Aging of Deer/Cud/Graze/Incisors/Teeth.**

MOON Earth's natural satellite. Phases of the moon, in particular the second full moon after the fall equinox (September 23), appear to trigger the breeding cycle of deer. Early observations of hunters noted that just after the "hunter's moon" occurred, the whitetail started to change its normal routine and enter into a breeding period that made bucks more visible and thus easier to hunt. Although this "hunter's moon" or full moon occurs at different times within the autumn season (due to the moon's rotation around the Earth of 29.5 days per month), it does so on a predictable basis each year. the rut will thus always occur during one of three times: early in the season, late in the season, or in the middle of the breeding cycle—in that order. The next three years will follow that same pattern. Records show that 1999 was an early rut season—beginning at the October full-

PHASES OF THE MOON

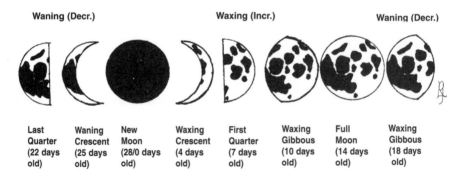

Waning (Decr.)			Waxing (Incr.)				Waning (Decr.)
Last Quarter (22 days old)	Waning Crescent (25 days old)	New Moon (28/0 days old)	Waxing Crescent (4 days old)	First Quarter (7 days old)	Waxing Gibbous (10 days old)	Full Moon (14 days old)	Waxing Gibbous (18 days old)

moon phase (October 24) and peaking during the following new-moon phase (November 8), following which buck activity began to decrease. A "second rut" increase in activity occurred approximately 28 days later, when does not already bred came into estrus again and maturing yearling does first came into heat. **See Diurnal Activities/Full Moon/Harvest Moon/Hunter's Moon/Lunar Influence/New Moon/Quarter Moon Phases/Waning Moon/Waxing Moon.**

MORNING The first hours of huntable daylight. On opening day of the deer hunting season, this is the prime time to hunt the whitetail. Deer are returning to their bedding area after a night of feeding. Together with the evening hours, when deer head to the fields for food, morning is an opportune time to hunt deer. However, many novice hunters only hunt in the morning and evening hours of the day, often missing deer movement at midday. **See Escape Route/Mid-Day Hunting/Opening Day/ Travel Corridor.**

MORTALITY The death rate. Fawn survival rates, are usually only 50 to 60 percent in their first month of life. If they have eluded predators, disease, abandonment (rare), farm machinery, malnutrition, and so on, then they have a good chance of living. Their survival really depends upon their mother's experience and prior success at fawn raising.

Breeding bucks have been known to exhaust their body reserves to the point of being unable to survive the winter because of a lack of body fat and insufficient food available. Accidents with cars or trucks take a considerable toll of the whitetail's population, also. However, because of their high birth rate and a decreasing number of hunters, the whitetail population is currently on the rise. Nature's way of controlling overcrowded numbers is for disease to set in and make a dramatic downward crash in the population. Unfortunately, this is usually after significant damage has been done to the environment through overbrowsing. **See Die-Off/Epizootic Hemorrhaging Disease/Fawns/Malnutrition/Overbrowse/Predators/Survival/ Winterkill.**

MOSSYBACK/"OL'MOSSY HORN" Affectionate references to a multi-tined monarch buck that is occasionally seen and has often eluded a group of hunters. Sometimes a deer's reputation lives on long after the deer does. Hunters' tales of seeing him often change him into a phantom of the woods or "ghost buck." **See Alpha Buck/Boone and Crockett Club/Cheater Points/Drop tine/Genetics/Net Score/Nontypical/Pope & Young/Sticker Point/Trophy/Wallhanger.**

MOUNT Taking an animal's skin, antlers, hooves, and tail, and having a taxidermist make a lifelike reproduction of that animal. Most whitetail mounts are of antlered bucks, but doe mounts are not unheard of, nor are full-body mounts. **See Antlers/Boone and Crockett Club/Drying Period/Green Score/Net Score/Pope & Young/Taxidermy/Trophy/Wallhanger.**

MOVEMENT Moving or changing position. The white-tailed deer is driven to movement by the same four factors that affect humans: food, water, cover, and sex. Increased deer movement (e.g., feeding) occurs just ahead of an advancing storm front, especially late in the year. At the peak of a storm, whitetails will move very little, as they are conserving energy.

For hunters, movement while on stand is their worst enemy, as deer readily detect any movement by a hunter. In particular, bowhunters must make slow and deliberate movements from their tree stand perch.

Hunters also will be confronted by nagging questions such as, "Where have all the deer gone?" "Should I stay at this stand, where I have not seen a deer all day, or should I move somewhere else?" Conventional wisdom states that if you know that a big buck is in the area, stay put! The longer you wait at one spot, the better the chance of seeing that deer. Obviously, there are exceptions to every rule, but don't be too hasty to give up on your stand site. **See Barometric Pressure/Buck Fever/Eyes/Foul Weather/Fronts/Patience/Silhouette/Vision/Weather/Yarding.**

MUSHROOM A meaty fungus found growing in the moist, darker parts of the forest floor, which usually has a "cap" over its thick stem. Mushrooms do not produce their own food, but rather redirect the decaying nutrients from other organic materials, such as wood. Whitetails find these soft mast delectable and will eagerly consume them. **See Biomass/Food/Soft Mast.**

MUSK/MUSKY ODOR A strong, pungent odor that emanates from a buck's tarsal glands on his hind legs. He deposits this personalized identification odor into his scrape by urinating over these glands, letting their odor be deposited into the scrape and thus identifying him and advertising his dominance and breeding status. Hunters can readily smell this odor in a scrape that is actively being worked. **See Glands/Kairomone/Metatarsal Gland/Nose/Rut/Scent Checking/Scrape/Tarsal Gland.**

MUTUAL GROOMING See Grooming.

Muzzleloader

MUZZLELOADER   Sometimes referred to as a "front-end stuffer," any firearm charged and loaded by "ramming" loose powder or powder pellets followed by a patch (used as a gas seal) and then a round or conical projectile (bullet) down the barrel from the muzzle end and tamping lightly with a ramrod. A muzzleloading rifle is highly accurate and effective in harvesting deer. Usually, a special muzzleloading season is set aside for exclusive use of these primitive weapons. **See Black Powder/ Firearms/Foot Pounds of Energy/Gunpowder/Guns/Knock Down Power/ Pyrodex.**

MUZZLE VELOCITY   The speed—measured in feet per second—at which a bullet or slug leaves the barrel of a firearm. The higher the muzzle velocity, usually the larger the powder charge behind it and the greater the knock-down power of the bullet and the further the distance it will travel. **See Ammunition/Bullet/Calibre/Knock Down Power/Pistol/Rifle/Shotgun.**

NASAL GLANDS Found just inside the nose of the whitetail. Biologists do not yet know their precise function; however, they suspect that these glands are used in some sort of chemical communication between whitetails. Whitetails have been observed apparently applying nasal gland secretions onto licking branches. **See Flehmen/Forehead Gland/Glands/Nose/Overhanging Branch/Pre-Orbital Gland/Scent/Scent Checking/Tarsal Gland.**

NATIONAL RIFLE ASSOCIATION (NRA) The foremost gun-owners organization that is charged with preserving our right to possess firearms as guaranteed by the Constitution of the United States of America. Organized in 1878 by Teddy Roosevelt, it has become the steadfast advocate for firearm safety and ownership under the Second Amendment. Without its strong membership numbers, financial resources, and thus voting clout, the American deer hunting fraternity might not be around today. **See White-tailed Deer Organizations.**

NATURAL SELECTION Originally a concept about the evolution of a species as proposed by Charles Darwin. It holds that naturally occurring events (in addition to those imposed by humans) prevent some individuals or groups of organisms from surviving and passing their unique characteristics along to future generations. **See Body Size/Breeding/Harvesting Does/Spikes.**

NAVIGATION A method of determining one's position or course. Hunters can use a variety of tolls for navigation.

    A. Maps. Contour lines on maps connect areas of like elevation. It is a universally accepted practice that "North" is always located at the top of the map. Used in conjunction with a compass and/or GPS unit, maps can be highly informative to hunters. They show gullies, ravines, funnels, and other bottlenecks. They indicate the location of swamps and other wet areas as well as cliffs, hills, mountains, and other barriers.

    B. Compass. These hand-held devices determine direction by means of a magnetic needle turning freely on a pivot and pointing to magnetic north. It generally allows hunters to enter an unknown area and then, by reversing their direction 180 degrees, to return to roughly the same area that they started from.

    C. GPS unit. This hand-held electronic device allows hunters to leave and return to their vehicle, camp, tree stand, or downed deer, with precise accuracy. Using a triangulation method with signals from three or more satellites overhead, hunters are able to know just where they are at all times.

    D. Two-Way Radios. These vocal communication devices allow hunters to stay in contact with each other within the range limitations of the radios. They are often used to warn other hunters of deer coming their way, to arrange to meet for lunch, to advise buddies that one has successfully gotten a deer, and so on.

See Aerial Photographs/Bureau of Land Management/Compass/Contour Lines/Global Positioning Satellite/Orienteering/Orthophotoquad/Survival/Topographical Maps/United States Geological Service.

NET SCORE The final score or measure of deer's antlers (tine lengths, girth, and so on) after deductions have been made for categories like drop tines or dissymmetry. See Boone and Crockett Club/Drying Period/Genetics/Grand Slam of Deer/Green Score/Mass/Nontypical/Pope & Young/Scoring/Spread/Symmetry/Trophy/Typical.

NEW MOON The Moon, when its reflected surface is facing the Sun. Thus, it is not seen on Earth. It looks as if there

Two-Way Radio for Navigation

is no moon in the night sky; however, close examination reveals a darkened object. See Full Moon/Harvest Moon/Hunter's Moon/Lunar Influence/Moon/Rut/Solstice/Waning Moon/ Waxing Moon.

NICHE An area where a creature finds its place to live or fill a void. See Core Area/Cover/Home Range/Security.

NIGHT VISION Optical equipment that enhances one's ability to see clearly after the sun has set and darkness becomes the law of the night. They can be used for night scouting, counting numbers and size of a deer herd, or finding one's way back to camp or a vehicle. They are unethical to use for actual hunting or shooting of game. See Binoculars/Binocular Vision/Ethics/Glassing/Jacking/Optics/Poaching/Spotting Scope.

"NO-SEE-UMS" See Black Flies.

NOCK Located on the rear end of an arrow, a double-pronged plastic device that fits around the bowstring, snugging the arrow to it until the arrow is released into flight. See Anchor Point/Archery/Nocking Loop.

NOCKING LOOP A string release cord or metal loop attached to a bowstring directly behind the arrow rather than under it. It is used with a release aid and has many distinct advantages over finger release or direct release contact on the bowstring:

A. The string or metal loop placed directly behind your arrow will make bow tuning easier because of the consistent and uniform contact between the arrow, the string, and the release

B. This uniform, direct pull, and lack of arrow contact prevents the arrow from being knocked off the string at full draw

C. The arrow will not be knocked off your string when you do not take the shot and let the string down because it does not push against the arrow's nock in any way.

D. The string or metal loop will position your peep sight into proper alignment.

E. Since mechanical releases can wear out the bowstring where they repeatedly attach to it, it is much easier to replace a string or metal nocking loop than it is to replace the whole string.
See Accessories/Archery/Bow Hunting/Equipment/Finger Release/Mechanical Release/Nocking Point/Release/String Loop.

NOCKING POINT The area of the bowstring server specifically wound and wrapped to accept the arrow's double-prong nock. It is this point that archers bring back to their cheek when drawing the bowstring back. **See Anchor Point/Archery/Bow and Arrow/Finger Release/Mechanical Release/Nocking Loop/String Loop.**

NOCTURNAL Active at night. Old bucks are like wise old men. They did not get to be old by being stupid. Bucks learn early in life that does and their fawns make good sentinels for danger. They usually let does and fawns enter the food sources first, hanging back and waiting for any signs of danger. Because they arrive later and leave earlier than the does and fawns, this means that hunters have fewer daylight hours in which to see a buck. If bucks won't come to you, just maybe wise hunters have to go to them! You can have a reasonable chance at tagging a buck soon after they rise from their daytime bed in the evening or right before they bed down in the morning. These are limited windows of opportunity! The closer you hunt to a buck's bedding area, the more likely he is to realize that you are hunting him. To spook him in his own sanctuary will cause him to clear out of the area entirely. You can get close, but you cannot invade. Locating your stand somewhere between the feeding areas and the buck's bedding area is the best strategy. The first two hours of the morning and the last two hours of the evening are the most productive sighting and hunting times.

Remember, the smart bucks become more nocturnal as a result of their first human contact. Thus, the best time to get that wise, old Mossy Back is at the very beginning of the season when he has not been too pressured by other deer hunters or small game hunters. **See Barometer/Crepuscular/Diurnal Activity/Lunar Influence/Moon/Pressure/Time of Day.**

NOISE A sound in the woods not made by the hunter that brings information that is beneficial to the hunt, such as incoming deer, another hunter approaching, or alarmed birds and animals. To deer and other animals, these sounds are normal and accepted. However, any noise made by hunters will immediately alert every animal around, especially deer, who will avoid the area that the noise came from. Prudent hunters will

Nontypical Rack

have checked all of their equipment for squeaks, or loose parts before the hunt and not find out about them during the hunt. **See Calls/Climber Stand/Ladder Stand/ Leaves/Permanent Stand/Portable Stand/Sounds in the Deer Woods/Trail/ Tree Steps/Wind.**

NONTYPICAL (ANTLERS) Non-similar or unevenly built antlers that are usually the result of genetics or of an injury either to the buck's antler itself while growing (in velvet) or to his body. An injury generally produces abnormal growth and is retained and duplicated for at least another year, sometimes permanently. Researchers tend to think that an injury to a buck's leg on one side of the body results in a weight compensating adjustment in the size or diversification of points or mass in the opposite side antler. **See Antlers/Boone and Crockett Club/Browtine/Drop Tine/ Genetics/Pope & Young/ Rack/Scoring/Sticker Point/Typical/Velvet.**

NOR'EASTER Strong winds and intense, unsettled, stormy weather that comes into the northeastern part of the country from off the Atlantic Ocean. This section of the United States usually receives its weather from the western parts of the country; however, a low front stationed out in the Atlantic can bring unsettled weather from off the coast into this region. Thus, Nor'easters are usually associated with bad weather. **See Air Currents/Barometer/Cross Wind/Foul Weather/Inclement Weather/ Prevailing Winds/Thermals/Upwind/Weather/Wind/Wind Chill/Zephyr.**

NOSE A deer's foremost sensory organ. It is used to trail other deer, identify fawns, seek out food, test for receptivity of breeding status—in short, in almost everything a deer does. A deer often licks its nose in order to increase its sensitivity of smell. Besides helping to locate and identify danger, a whitetail's nose helps it to specifically identify individual deer and to locate food and determine its edibility. A buck also uses its nose to trail and identify a doe's breeding status and receptivity. **See Estrus/Flehmen/Human Odor/Hygiene/Musk/Scent/ Scent Checking/Smell/Urine.**

Nose

NOSE BOT/NASAL BOT Larvae of the common bot fly, which has laid its eggs on the nose of a whitetail. When the deer licks its nose, which it does many times during the day, in order to keep its nose moist and sensitive to odors, the deer ingests the eggs. Upon hatching, the larvae travel to the nasal area of the deer and are then sneezed out, where they develop into mature flies, mate, and start the process all over again. **See Diseases/Parasites.**

NRA See National Rifle Association.

NURSING Does providing milk for their fawns, even after they have started to eat green grass and other foliage. A nursing fawn will approach the forward part of its mother's rear leg and thrust its muzzle toward the lactating teats. With this head thrusting mannerism, it nurses or drinks milk from its mother. With a single fawn, the lactating doe may lift her leg for the short span of nursing; however, nursing twins are often so rambunctious in their nursing thrusts that the dam must stay four-legged solid in her stance just to prevent from being knocked over. **See Afterbirth/Baby Teeth/Blat/Colostrum/Dispersal/Fawn/Gestation/Lactation/Milk Teeth/ Placenta/Twins.**

NUT The seed-bearing fruit of certain hardwood trees, such as oak and beech, which are favorite foods of the wild turkey and the white-tailed deer. Whitetails prefer white oak acorn nuts above all other food and will travel miles to dine beneath an oak with dropping acorns. **See Acorn/Beechnut/Deciduous Forest/Food/Hard- woods/Mast/Oak/Pine/Turkey.**

NUTRITION The act or process of being fed, sum of the processes of taking in food, digesting it and using its components for energy, body (cell) parts replacement, and then eliminating waste. **See Alfalfa/Basal Metabolic Rate/Biomass/Browse Line/Food Plot/Forage/Forbs/Green-Up/Habitat/Overbrowse/Quality Deer Management/Starvation/Yarding.**

OAKS/OAK GROVE Trees that produce a mast crop of acorns. The white oak acorn is the absolute favorite food of the whitetail. Deer will travel miles to an oak tree whose acorns are falling. The white oak does not faithfully produce acorns every year. Their productive output can be greatly enhanced when fertilizer is placed around the oak's dripline—roughly a circle on the ground the diameter of the oak's canopy of leaves. **See Acorn/Beechnuts/Binoculars/Deciduous/Food/Mast/Nuts.**

ODOCOILEUS VIRGINIANUS The official, scientific name of the eastern white-tailed deer; also known as the Virginia whitetail, because it was first observed in Virginia by early colonists. It is the dominant deer in North America and ranges from the equator to 60 degrees north latitude (the tree-line in Canada). Seventeen sub-species of white-tailed deer (family Cervidae, species *Odocoileus virginianus*) are located within the United States and Canada. The whitetail is the evolutionary cousin of another species of the Cervidae family—the western mule deer, *Odocoileus hemionus*. **See Subspecies/White-tailed Deer.**

ODOR See Scent.

OFF-SEASON Any time other than the official, regular deer hunting season. Any off-season time is useful to scout deer, but be careful not to overly intrude upon them or you will alert them to your presence and possible intent thus causing them to modify their home range or movement patterns. Be advised that it is not wise to carry a firearm in the deer woods during the off-season as a game warden could accuse you of poaching or hunting out of season. **See Ethics/Fair Chase/Game Warden/ Poaching.**

OLFACTORY Having to do with the sense of smell. White-tailed deer are highly dependent upon their sense of smell for their survival (nutrition, safety, communication, and breeding). **See Communication/Scents/Smell.**

OMASUM The third in line of a whitetail's four stomachs, as is typical of a ruminant. Some digestion and nutrient absorption take place here. **See Abomasum/Cud/ Digestion/Reticulum/Rumen/Ruminant/Stomach.**

ONE-SHOT KILL Cleanly and humanely dispatching a deer with only one shot, as all hunters prefer to do. This is often referred to as "one and out." **See Ethics/Fair Chase/Shot Placement.**

OPENING DAY The first day of firearms season,which can have a traumatic effect upon most deer. The pre-dawn slamming of vehicle doors, the sounds of numerous human voices, and metal clicking together, the smells of humans all tend to change undisturbed deer into alerted deer very quickly. Deer will quickly react to these intrusions and move to get away from them. The key to success on opening morning is to have done your pre-scouting early enough, to have already discovered where deer go when disturbed and then position yourself to intercept them before they reach that sanctuary. Of course, you will not choose a spot where the wind will blow your scent across the escape route, and you will not walk on or cross the escape route, thus leaving your scent. You wear your rubber boots and do not touch any limbs, or plants on your way in. Last, but not least, you choose a spot where you have a good visual vantage point and a clear view of the direction that you expect deer to come from. **See Escape Route/Morning/Pressure.**

OPTICS The science of light and vision. For most deer hunters, the best tool for aiming at a deer is a scope. Scopes not only magnify images, but they also gather existing light, making it easier to shoot accurately in low-light conditions. The most popular rifle scopes, because rifles shoot over longer distances, are in the 3-9X variable power range. If you hunt with a shotgun where cover is heavier and shorter shots are usual, 1-4X power is ideal.

Optics

Every hunter needs quality binoculars because the deer that you do not see are the deer that you do not bring home. Hunting binoculars should be lightweight and durable. For most hunting conditions, an 8X32 model is the ideal choice. Those hunters needing to do long-range glassing should consider 10X40 models. Rubber-armored, roof-prism models usually provide good durability. The standard rule is to buy the best binoculars that you can afford.

Spotting scopes are handy on the gun range and essential for hunters who spot and stalk. They are more powerful than binoculars, they gather more light, and are usually steadied by a tripod. Spotting scopes allow you to see much farther, much better. **See Binoculars/Equipment/Laser Sight/Night Vision/Range Finder/Scope.**

ORCHARD Planted fruit trees, often abandoned from previous homesteads or farms, that provide a delicious and attractive source of sweet, ripe fruit that deer cannot resist. If you find a fruit tree or orchard of trees with ripe fruit ready to fall, you can be sure that now is the time to set up a stand nearby as the deer will soon discover the fallen fruit. **See Apple/Browse/Deer Sign/Feeding Areas/Fields/Food/Forage/Fruit/Overbrowse/Pears/Persimmons/Terrain.**

O

ORGANIZATIONS See White-tailed Deer Organizations.

ORIENTEERING This term is sometimes used by hunters as a synonym for map reading and wilderness navigation skills. All hunters should know how to get into and back out of the woods without becoming lost or disoriented. These skills are needed to return to one's vehicles at the end of the hunt. Hunters should know how to use a compass, GPS unit, aerial photographs, and topographical maps, to they are familiar with and can navigate around the land they hunt. **See Bureau of Land Management/Compass/Contour Lines/Global Positioning Satellite/Navigation/Scouting/Terrain/Topographical Maps/United States Geological Service.**

ORPHAN A fawn that seems to be without a mother. Newborn whitetail fawns are purposely left alone for long periods of time for their own safety and protection from predators. The doe is nearby but out of sight. She will react to protect her fawn from harm in some instances. All too often humans find a fawn in a field and wrongly assume that it has been abandoned. More likely than not, that is not the case and the fawn should be left alone, not even touched. **See Camouflage/Doe/Fawn/Predator/Survival.**

ORTHOPHOTOQUADS "Maps" that are viewed through stereoscopic eye pieces, and provide a three-dimensional (3-D) view of the land, thus allowing the observer to discern various types of crops, vegetation, foliage, and other aspects of land cover. They are useful to hunters in that they can assist them in their pre-scouting activities. **See Aerial Photographs/Bureau of Land Management/Contour Lines/Maps/Navigation/Scouting/Survival/Terrain/Topographical Maps.**

OSSIFICATION Turning to bone. As antlers finish growing, they begin to harden. The velvet's supply of blood is shut down. This turning to bone then proceeds from the inside out. It is at this stage of antler development that a buck starts to rub trees, fence posts, or brush so as to rub off the now drying velvet. Researchers tell us that this process is controlled by light patterns (photoperiodism) so that all bucks lose their velvet during the same period within a couple of weeks of each other. **See Antlers/Light Patterns/Photoperiodism/Rubbing/Sheds/Velvet.**

OUTFITTERS Professional guides. These are more prevalent out in the West and in the Canadian provinces, where hunters that are unfamiliar with the area, often hire an outfitter to take them into an area that might provide an opportunity to take a trophy whitetail. Some governmental entities require that nonresidents hire an outfitter. Once a hunter arrives at an outfitter's home or office, the outfitter is generally expected to make arrangements for all aspects of the hunt, including sleeping, food, transportation, trophy and meat follow-up. **See Controlled Hunt/Fair Chase/Game Farm Buck/Guides/Guided Hunts/High Fence Hunting/Managed Hunt/Pack Train/Sportsmanship.**

OUTLINE In hunting terms, the contour, silhouette, or shape of an animal or a hunter being contrasted or profiled against a background of lighter shades. **See Eyes/Movement/Silhouette/Skyline/Vision.**

OVARIES The female reproductive body parts that produce and release one or more eggs (ova) on a specific cycle. The eggs are sometimes fertilized by male sperm and result in a fetus. **See Breeding/Doe/Fawn/Gestation/Hormones/Rut.**

Overbrowse

OVERBROWSE The treeline that has been nipped above the reach of most of the herd. The white-tailed deer, if left unchecked, will quickly overpopulate the carrying capacity of the land. In order to get at any available food, deer will even stand on their hind legs to get at leaves and twigs. Once the grasses, forbs, brush, and reachable leaves are gone, the land is definitely stressed from its deer-supporting activities. Massive die-off then occurs. **See Browse Line/Carrying Capacity/Die-off/Food/Forage/Habitat/Land Management/Starvation/Winterkill.**

Overhanging Branch

OVERHANGING BRANCH At an active primary scrape, there is usually a limb that juts out about five feet above the scrape. A buck chews, licks, rubs its pre-orbital glands on it as he leaves his mark or notification of his presence. Other deer, investigating the scrape and its "licking branch" will be able to identify which buck "worked" the scrape last, and will deduce his virility and breeding status. **See Facial Rubbing/Forehead Gland/Nasal Gland/Pre-Orbital Gland/Primary Scrape/ Scrape.**

OVERSTORY See Canopy.

OVER-UNDER SHOTGUN A double barreled shotgun or rifle-shotgun combination with barrels arranged one over the other, instead of side by side. **See Double Barreled/Recoil/Shotgun/Side by Side.**

OVULATION The time during the breeding cycle when the ovaries of a female release a ripe egg for reception of the male sperm and thus fertilization and the start of a new member of that species. Sometimes, actions of the male of the species are needed to stimulate this egg release; other times, he must be present and able to copulate or breed the female. The white-tailed buck is able to determine about when the doe is able to breed, and thus stays close by her, fending off all other males who wish to pass on their genes to her. The white-tailed buck will breed a doe several times over the period that he perceives her to be fertile or ready to ovulate. **See Breeding/ Ejaculation/Estrus/Flehmen/Rut/Vulva.**

PAC BOOTS/PACS A hunting boot with rubber bottoms and leather tops. They usually have replaceable felt liners and are used for cold weather hunting. **See Clothing/ Footwear/Rubber Boots.**

PACK HORSE/PACK TRAIN Mules, horses, ATVs, or trucks that guides or outfitters use to take their client and supplies into the hunting area and out again. **See Guides/ Outfitters.**

PALATABLE Able to be consumed, that tastes good, is edible, and so on. **See Aging Meat/Gamey Taste/Popiteal Gland/Venison.**

PALMATED RACK Rare whitetail antlers that are "moose-like" that is, their distal portions are broad, flat, and lobed. **See Antlers/Genetics/Green Score/Main Beam/Mass/Net Score/Photoperiodism/Symmetry/Testosterone/Velvet.**

PANTING Breathing heavily in order to expel heat and thus cool down. When chased during warm weather or engaging in sparring matches for dominance or even outright fighting, whitetails will pant to acquire the needed levels of oxygen, in order to return to normal breathing rates. **See Fight/Radiation/Sparring/Tending.**

PARASITES Organisms that live off of a host (for nourishment, protection, and reproduction) Like any living organism, deer have their share of parasites deer parasites include the following:

    Blot Fly. Flies that infest a deer's nasal passage and hatch eggs, causing irritation and even brain damage and causing the deer to stop eating.

    Liver Fluke. A white, worm-like parasite observed in or on a deer's liver. Excessive amounts can cause anemia in whitetails and make them lethargic.

    Tapeworm. An internal, or intestinal, worm that consumes food directly from a deer's digestion tract. The existence of tapeworms is a sign of overcrowding and overbrowsing that has led to deer grazing in cow pastures.

    Dog Tick/Wood Tick. The larger of the two kinds of ticks found on the whitetailed deer. Hunters often observe this six-legged parasite on the outer coat of a deer; particularly as the deer is hanging on a deer pole. The tick's visibility indicates that it has recognized that its host is no longer alive and it is vacating the dead animal in order to find a new, warm-blooded host that will serve its nutritional needs.

    Deer Tick. A six legged, blood-sucking insect, about the size of a sesame seed, that attaches itself to a deer's body, eyelids, or soft tissues, gorging itself on blood. This tick also feeds on field mice and its bite is the prime carrier for Lyme disease in humans.

    See Anthrax/Arthropods/Fluke/Health/Hygiene/Lyme Disease/Pathogens/Ticks.

PARTURITION The formal name for "giving birth." See **Birth/Breeding/Copulation/Doe/Estrus/Fawn/Fetus/Nursing/Ovaries.**

PARTY PERMIT See **Doe Permit.**

PATH/DEER PATH Well-used trails in the woods, hedgerows, and along creek bottoms that deer frequently use because they lead directly to a feeding or bedding area and are close to escape cover, thus affording an element of security. See **Buck Trail/Corridor/Deer Run/Deer Sign/Edge/Path/Tracks/Trail/Travel Corridor.**

PATHOGENS Disease-causing organisms, whether viruses, bacteria, or spirochetes. See **Epizootic Hemorrhaging Disease/Die-Off/Diseases/Lyme Disease/Parasites.**

Path

PATIENCE The ability to wait quietly. If deer hunting teaches the hunter anything, it is patience. Waiting on stand for hours at a time on a daily basis is a true test of one's mettle. Remember, you cannot shoot a deer if you are not out in the woods. Even when the moment of truth arrives and that big buck appears, a simple mistake on your part can dish up a big bowl of humility. Learning to stay calm and endure long hours of empty watchfulness, while still maintaining your optimism that the great "horned" stag will come any minute now, is the mark of a true hunter! See **Buck Fever/Movement.**

PATTERNED/PATTERNING The way white-tailed deer often notice the repetitious habits of their human pursuers, getting to know the hunter's entry and exit points. If an old buck has you figured out, you are not going to see him. The best way to hunt this buck is to vary your entry means and never let him know that he is being hunted. See **Learned Behavior.**

PAUNCH See **Rumen.**

PAUNCH SHOT Also called a "gut shot" not immediately fatal wound to the stomach or intestinal area. This shot in a nonvital zone causes a lingering death and suffering for a deer. A paunch shot should never be taken on purpose. If it does accidentally occur, the hunter should wait at least three hours before taking up the gut-shot deer's trail, rather than continuing to push it mercilessly. See **Blood Trail/Followup/Shot Placement/Wounded Game.**

PAWING(S) Not to be confused with scrapes, disturbed areas of ground that indicate that something—turkeys, deer, squirrels—has worked over the ground cover or leaves to find acorns, nuts, or fruit. Turkey pawings are usually small, scattered around because of flock activity, but generally pointing in the direction of travel. Deer pawings are larger in size and more pronounced. Bachelor buck groups working an area can tear it up thoroughly. Pawings are usually found around mast-bearing trees and grainfields. **See Acorn/Mast/Scrape/Squirrel/Turkey.**

PEAK OF RUT In the United States, between November and January. Following the peak, the testosterone level in a buck's testes decreases and the buck goes through a physiological, hormonal, and attitudinal change, becoming more docile. **See Rut/Start of Rut.**

PEARS A favorite food of white-tailed deer, which will eat just about anything. They are particularly fond of apples, pears, persimmons, and other available fruit. Whitetails have been known to travel miles from their core area (home range), when pears start falling from the trees. **See Apples/Baiting/Food/Fruit/Orchards/ Persimmons.**

PECKING ORDER **See Hierarchy.**

Pedicle

PEDICLE The area on a buck's head where his antlers will grow from. The male hormone—testosterone—causes button antlers to grow, slowly at first, but increasing rapidly during the summer. Once testosterone starts to decrease in production, the antler's base at the pedicle begins to disintegrate, and by February or March, the bucks will cast their antlers (sheds). The pedicle area on the buck's skull quickly heals, bringing closure to that year's antler production. But within a few weeks, the antler buttons begin to form again, and the buck goes through another hormonal, physiological, behavioral, and sexual experience. **See Adrenal Glands/Antlers/Casts/ Pituitary Gland/Rack/Sheds/Testes/Testosterone/Velvet.**

PEEP SIGHT A hole or circle in a rear sight closest to the shooting eye that allows hunters to accurately aim the firearm or archery equipment. On a bow, the peep sight is usually embedded within the bowstring and lines up with the shooting eye when the bow is drawn. **See Accessories/Archery/Buckhorn Sight/Gun Sight/Optics/ Shot Placement.**

PELAGE The hairy covering of a mammal. It often enhances the animal's ability to blend in with its surrounding, such as the white spots on a fawn or the subtle contrasts of a whitetail. **See Albino/Camouflage/Piebald/Summer Coat/Winter Coat.**

PELLETS/DEER PELLETS See Droppings.

PENIS The male breeding organ that inserts into the female vaginal area at breeding time and delivers the sperm for reproduction. **See Breeding/ Ejaculation/Hypogonadism/ Prerut/Rut/Testes/Testosterone/ Vulva.**

PERIPHERAL VISION Side vision. In relationship to humans, deer have much larger eyes and are much better equipped for night vision. Due to the location of their eyes on the top and sides of their heads, deer also have better side or peripheral vision. **See Color Blind/Eyes/Rod Cells/Vision.**

PERMANENT STAND A tree stand, ladder stand, or platform that is left in place over the years, more or less attached to a tree. These stands are most often made of wood and use tarps, boards, or camouflage materials to prevent a hunter from being

Permanent stand with rungs between trees.

spotted by a deer. See **Climber/Fall Restraining Device/Harness/Ladder Stand/Noise/Portable Stand/Stands/Tree Stand/Tree Steps.**

PERMISSION TO HUNT A necessary condition before you can hunt on private property. Posted signs mean "Stay off or you might be arrested and charged with trespassing." Check the name on the mailbox or the county extension office's plat maps for the landowner's name. Remember to always be respectful of farmers' time. While they will be courteous to you and usually chat, to them time is money. If the sun is shining, they must make hay. That's their living. Always have permission to hunt on someone's land! See **Crop Damage/Food/Fruit Trees/Landowner.**

PERSIMMON A sweet, plum-like fruit, that once ripe, will attract deer from far and wide. Once fall's first frosts have come, there is no better place to erect a stand than near a persimmon tree with its falling fruit. Deer will appear continuously until the last of this sweet fruit has fallen. See **Apples/Berries/Crab Apple/Deciduous/ Edge/Food/Fruit/Mast/Orchards/Soft Mast.**

PHEROMONES Sexual, chemical communicators. Although visual and vocal signals are used by deer in the wild, scent making is one of their most effective means of communication. During the rut, a buck's hormonal and sexual reproduction systems are at their peak. Sexual chemicals called pheromones (composed of steroids and fatty acids), coming from an estrous doe's urinary tract, stimulate a buck's limbic, or pleasure-seeking, portion of the brain. This limbic system is responsible for stimulating the buck's active sexual drives and expressions. The doe's sexual pheromones carried on the air currents communicate her readiness to breed.

Once a buck discovers estrous pheromones in the air, he will almost give up eating and all his normal, everyday activities, just to seek out the source of that delectable odor, the doe in heat. Sexually frustrated because the doe is not receptive to his mounting and breeding her, a buck will make scrapes and rubs, strengthening his neck muscles by beating on brush and small saplings. This action usually occurs during the prerut or false rut of mid-October. This "false rut" serves to break up the bucks' bachelor groups, as sexually frustrated bucks become less tolerant of each other's presence and become more belligerent toward each other, often engaging in sparring matches upon encountering another buck of near equal size, rack, or age. A buck running across the middle of a field during midday (if it is not being chased by dogs) is a good indication that he has been aroused by the pheromones of an estrous doe. See **Allomone/Automobile-Deer Accidents/Communication/Flehmen/Kairomone/Lures/Pheromone/Scents/Sparring/Urine.**

PHOSPHORUS One of the necessary nutrients found in the soil that contributes to bone and antler growth in whitetails. See **Antlers/Nutrients/Sodium.**

PHOTOPERIODISM The length of the day that an animal is exposed to sunlight. The diminishing ratio of daylight to dark is usually associated with the deer breeding cycle—the rut. The amount of daylight striking a deer's eyes affects the pituitary gland, setting off its secretions that in turn affect other hormonal glands (e.g., adrenaline, testes). Nature uses this stimulus to initiate the breeding cycle of the white-tailed deer. **See Adrenal Glands/Antlers/Mass/Ossification/Pineal Gland/Rut/ Solunar Tables/Testes/Testosterone.**

PHOTOSYNTHESIS The act of deciduous tree leaves producing food for the tree, carbon from carbon dioxide in the atmosphere and oxygen and hydrogen from water drawn up from the soil are mixed with chlorophyll as a catalyst to produce sugars that the tree stores in its roots and consumes as energy to grow. Once a frost occurs, and photosynthesis stops, the leaves of a deciduous tree turn to their real color, no longer green. **See Autumn/Chlorophyll/Deciduous/Leaf Drop.**

PIEBALD Spotted hair color caused by a mixture of pigmented and nonpigmented hair. Piebald deer will have normal color eyes, ears, and lips. They are not true albinos. Most piebald deer have a calico look to them, that is, a mixture of tans, browns, and patches of white. **See Albino/Melanistic/Pelage/Pink-Eyed Deer.**

PINK-EYED DEER A true albino of any fauna species has pink eyes, as well as a white coat. **See Albino/Melanistic/Pelage/Piebald.**

PINEAL GLAND A gland the size of a pea, located deep within a deer's brain, that once stimulated by an increasing amount of sunlight admitted through the buck's eyes (usually around April/May), causes decreased hormonal production of melanin in the bloodstream. Once the melanin is low enough to affect his testes, an increase of testosterone occurs. **See Adrenal Glands/Glands/Lutenizing Hormone/Melanin/ Photoperiodism/Pituitary Gland/Rut/Testes/Testosterone.**

PISTOL A handgun, either a revolver or clip-loaded. Some hunters actually bring down whitetails with handguns. **See Ammunition/Ballistics/Caliber/Firearm/ Foot Pounds of Energy/Guns/Handgun/Knock Down Power.**

PITUITARY GLAND A small endocrine organ located within the brain, often referred to as the "master gland" which controls or stimulates secretions of other glands. It controls the timing or onset of the rut in whitetails, after a noticeable decrease in sunlight coming through the deer's eyes and/or the appearance of the full moons in the fall. **See Adrenal Gland/Albino/Day Light/Glands/Lutenizing Hormone/ Melanistic/Photoperiodism/Prerut/Rut/Testes/Testosterone.**

PLACENTA The tissues and organs that internally feed and sustain a fetus within a maternal mammal. It is expelled after the birth, hence it is also called the "afterbirth." It is usually eaten by the doe so as to return vital minerals, vitamins, and nutrients to her system and to discourage leaving any scent around to attract predators. **See Afterbirth/Amniotic Fluid/Birth/Doe/Fawn/Nursing/Predator/Twins.**

PLANNING Any anticipatory action taking by hunters that prepares them for their next hunting trip. It can range from daydreaming, to making lists, to purchasing equipment or supplies, to packing them. **See Aerial Photographs/Hunting Log/ Maps/Preparation/Topographical Maps.**

PLAT MAPS County property ownership maps, which usually can be purchased at the county extension office or the farm bureau. They identify the landowner's name and are also used to locate areas on farms that offer a mixture of wooded cover and crops. These fascts show you where deer are most likely to feed, bed down, and travel (i.e., travel routes and escape routes). **See Aerial Photographs/Escape Route/ Planning/Topographical Maps.**

PLAY FIGHTING Often observed by hunters scouting before the season, this form of "locking antlers" between two male whitetails helps establish the dominance order of the males as to their breeding hierarchy and social rank. **See Dominance/Fighting/Sparring.**

POACHING The illegal killing of deer, often at night, whether during the hunting season or not. Poachers kill to gain a trophy set of antlers (often to sell), to secure food to sell to the market (venison is elite fare in fancy restaurants), or simply to obtain a thrill just for shooting. The usual method is to shine a light on a field at night. The light mesmerizes the deer, if shone in their eyes, and the poacher then shoots them right between the red reflections of their two eyes. **See Attitude/Baiting/Bambi Syndrome/Ethics/Game Warden/Herd Balance/Jacklighting/One Shot Kill/ Sportsmanship.**

POINTS/ANTLER POINTS The tines or long, bone-like spikes projecting from a male whitetail's head. The sum of their combined lengths and girths, less any deductions for oddities, provides a ranking system for judging whitetail antlers. **See Antlers/Beam/Bifurcate/Boone and Crockett Club/Eastern Count/G-1/G-2/Main Beam/Pope & Young/Rack/Spike/Tine/Trophy/Western Count.**

POPE, SAXTON An early archer, who along with his partner, Art Young, helped establish many of the standards we use today in bowhunting the white-tailed deer. His name, along with Young's, are used in the title of the Pope and Young Club, which keeps bowhunting records of annual trophy kills. **See Fred Bear/Pope & Young/Art Young.**

POPE & YOUNG CLUB An orgnization that maintains an archery record book with measurements of antler mass (length and girth) for trophy animals exceeding a certain size. To be entered in the Pope & Young record book, a "typical" whitetail must score at least 125 points, while a "nontypical" rack must score 155. **See Antlers/Boone and Crockett Club/Browtine/Drop Tine/Drying Period/Fair Chase/Grand Slam of Deer/Green Score/Main Beam/Mass/Net Score/Nontypical/Rack/Scoring/ Spread/Sticker Point/Symmetry/Trophy/Typical.**

POPITEAL GLAND A small, peanut-sized gland located in the fatty deposits of the front part of a whitetail's hind legs. Care should be given to remove these grayish colored glands so as to prevent the meat from being tainted and tasting bad. **See Field Dressing/Gamey Taste/Glands/Hind Legs/Hocks/Palatable/Venison.**

POPULATION The number of white-tailed deer in the United States—approximately twenty to twenty-one million. That is the same number or more that were present at the time of the early settlers. **See Balanced Herd/Herd Size/Quality Deer Management.**

PORTABLE STAND Any tree stand, ladder stand, or tripod, that is easily put up or taken down, at least on a seasonal basis (that is, is not left afield for future years' use). Once installed, it is recommended you take a few minutes to clip away any nearby limbs or branches that would be in the way of shooting your deer. Drag up some brush and strategically place it around you so as to add that final touch of realism and camouflage your new stand. **See Climber/Fall Restraining Device/Harness/Ladder Stand/ Noise/Portable Stand/ Stands/Tree Stand/Tree Steps.**

POSTRUT See Late Rut.

POSTED SIGNS Signs that mean "Stay off or you might be arrested and charged with trespassing." The owner's name must be on the signs so that gives you additional information to work with. Often just a simple request to hunt the land will result in permission from farmers, but if they refuse, remember that it is their land and they must have a reason for denying you permission. You must respect their wishes. Do not ever go down the road, pull off to the side, and sneak onto their land. That is a sure way to have them call the sheriff on you.

Land posted for many years can become deer sanctuaries harboring a good population of mature deer. If you cannot hunt a particular piece of posted property, then seek permission to hunt on neighboring property and hunt as close to the posted property's borders as you can. **See Landowner/ Ethics/Permission to Hunt.**

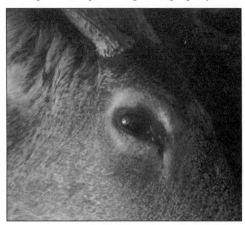

PREORBITAL GLANDS Glands located near the inside corner of the eyes of a white-tailed deer that it rubs onto a licking branch, to communicate to other deer who owns it. **See Eyes/Glands/Nasal Gland/Over-hanging Branch.**

PRERUT In the northern United

Preorbital Gland

States, a period beginning in mid-October and producing a high level of activity for twenty-four to forty-eight hours. The mature bucks start to act "goofy," while they start to look around for the first doe who has come into estrus. Then the prerut abruptly ends. Bucks have suddenly become alerted to the upcoming breeding season by encountering the estrous pheromone of a few mature does in heat. Some of these does are not willing to breed yet but serve to excite every buck in the area as to what is to come. The observant hunter, who is out in the woods, will see bucks chasing down every doe they see, just to stick their nose between her hind legs to check her status or receptivity to breed. This is the best time for rattling a buck, as he is looking for the possibility of two bucks fighting over a doe in heat. While they are busy fighting for the right to breed her, he hopes to slip in and get to her first. Also called "preliminary rut," "false rut," or "first rut." **See Automobile-Deer Accidents/Chase Phase/ False Rut/Flehmen/Grunting/Late Rut/Mock Rub/Primary Rut/Rut.**

PRESCOUTING   Like scouting, but in the off-season, before one gets serious about finding, focusing upon, and hunting a specific white-tailed buck. **See Planning/Preparation/Scouting.**

PREDATOR/PREDATION   Any animal, including humans, that prey on another species. To escape animals trying to kill and eat them, deer browse quickly and then move to bedding areas to regurgitate or chew their cud, further digest their food through their four-chambered stomach. The whitetail's short browsing period, followed by bedding in secluded areas, permits the deer the best overall chances for survival. The natural predators of deer are black bears, cougars, bobcats, coyotes, domestic dogs, wolves, and humans. **See Balanced Herd/Bears/Canine Carnivor/Cougar/Coyote/Die-Off/Dogs/Feral Dogs/Fox/Prey/Winterkill/Wolf.**

PREFERENTIAL FOODS   Those foodstuffs that would be eaten by the whitetail before all others, such as those that provide energy or fat reserves or protein and minerals for building muscles, bones, and antlers. This is opposed to those nutritiously deficient foodstuffs that just provide fill for the whitetails' stomachs in winter but none of the above-mentioned nutritive benefits. **See Acorns/Alfalfa/Apples/ Carbohydrates/Clover/Energy/Fruits/Mushrooms/Nuts/Nutrition/Over-browse/Understory.**

PRELIMINARY RUT **See Prerut.**

PREPARATION Going into the woods prepared to address any situation. However, to carry all possible equipment to address every possible situation would require hunters to drive their hunting vehicles right up to the tree stand. Instead hunters might take along two articles (a) their brains, the best survival item, and (b) a backpack or fanny pack containing a few essential items. **See Accessories/Backpack/Beginner's Luck/Benchrest/Fanny Pack/First Aid Kit/Hypothermia/Hunting Log/ Planning.**

PRESERVE A wildlife area that prohibits hunting or trapping of animals. This private or state-owned sanctuary provides safety for wildlife, helps reduce hunting-season stress, and serves as a source for wildlife translocation if needed. **See Game Farm/High Fence Hunting/Managed Hunt.**

PRESSURE Forces that influence deer.

> **A. Air.** Barometric pressure has an effect on the activities of the white-tailed deer. A falling barometer signals the onset of a change in weather, if not a storm (low front) coming in. Deer tend to eat heavily prior to a severe change in the weather. They also feed heavily during the night after a storm has passed through. A rising barometer indicates good weather coming, and deer act accordingly. **See Barometer/Foul Weather/Frost/Inclement Weather/Nocturnal/Storms/Temperature/Warm Weather/Weather/Wind.**

> **B. Deer. See Stress**.

> **C. Hunter.** Pressure from hunters ensures that old bucks do not remain in a relaxed state for very long. Without the rut and its many distractions, bucks are primarily concerned with staying alive. Two factors in the autumnal months greatly affect their lives. First is the intrusion from small game hunters and early-season bowhunters. Bucks will not tolerate any human interference in their world. If they sense that they are being hunted, mature bucks stay out of sight, at least until the rut forces them to adjust their thinking patterns. Second is the buck's rising testosterone level which gives early impetus to his avoidance of other deer. This is when the bachelor groups break up and a buck starts staking out his breeding territory. Here he will make rubs to advertise his presence, usually establish rub lines, start to make scrapes at random, and possibly later establish active breeding scrape lines.

The pre-season scouting done by many hunters, looking for just these signs of a buck's activity in an area is what often turns a buck that has survived one or more hunting seasons into an increasingly nocturnal animal. After wind, hunting pressure is the second worst enemy of the deer hunter. Other hunters unwittingly teach deer how to avoid humans. Wise hunters limit their intrusions into a buck's breeding area so as not to disturb him at this time.

Even does are affected by hunter intrusion. Once a mature doe has experienced hunters, she becomes even more difficult to hunt because her home range is often less than one thousand acres and she is acutely familiar with it. In addition, because she almost always has other deer around her, many more eyes are watching to protect the deer herd. **See Buck Fever/Doe Harvest/Eye Contact/Hunter Pressure/Opening Day.**

> **D. Anti-Hunters.** Anti-hunters often put as much pressure on deer as hunters do. These are the uninformed or naive part of the human population that have not taken the time to learn that hunters are the only really effective management tool for controlling deer herd size and preventing more deer-automobile collisions, crop and ornamental shrub depredation, and so on. By attributing human characteristics to deer, they are trying to protect deer from hunters, but the overall result for the deer herd is an increase in starvation, automobile deaths, disease, and predation. **See Bambi Syndrome/Ethics/Poaching/Posted Signs.**

PREVAILING WINDS The most commonly occurring direction of the wind or air currents for your area. In most of the United States, we talk about the westerlies, ranging from the northwest to the southwest as the most often occurring wind direction. Knowing the prevailing direction of the wind is important to hunters in placing a stand, as they would not want the winds blowing from the stand toward a deer trail, their shooting lane, or any direction that they expect the deer to come from. Hunters should check the wind occasionally to detect any convection currents that may betray them. **See Barometer/Convection Currents/Cross Wind/Downwind/Foul Weather/Thermals/Upwind/Wind.**

PREY A source of food to a predator, that is, any potential victim lower on the food chain. Prey animals usually have eyes on the sides of their head, while predators have foreward-looking, binocular vision for spotting and focusing on their prey. **See Bears/Binocular Vision/Carnivore/Eyes/Food/Food Chain/Herbivore/Predator/Vision.**

PRIMARY RUT Approximately 28 days after the prerut peak, the actual main breeding time of the white-tailed deer. A week to ten days before the onset of the primary rut is the most aggressive time for bucks. They are frustrated at not being able to breed every doe in sight and will engage in serious territorial fights for breeding right. In the northern United States, the primary rut usually starts between November 1 and 30. It will vary depending on when the rutting moon (second full moon after the autumnal equinox) falls and how many rut suppressants exist.

It is a frenzied time that continues into the period when bucks match up with does in heat (estrus) and extensive and frenzied breeding takes place. Breeding activity experiences a slight decline after one to two weeks, as more and more does are bred and bucks are roaming farther afield to find unbred but receptive does. Any unbred doe will come back into heat (estrus) and be receptive to a buck's advance approximately 28 days later. The breeding activity peaks for about two weeks during the primary rut, as it is then that most of the does in any herd come into estrus and are actively bred. **See Breeding/Chase Phase/Estrus/Hierarchy/Late Rut/Prerut/Rut/Secondary Rut/Testosterone.**

PRIMARY SCRAPE Largest of the pawed-up areas that a buck uses for advertising his presence, his dominance, and breeding status. These are usually four inches in diameter or larger. Primary scrapes are usually made in areas off the trails that does usually use and in an area where the buck feels very secure. Observant hunters can usually fins a line of secondary scrapes that are formed nearer to doe trails but lead off in a direction that points toward the primary scrape. These active scrapes are always freshly worked to the bare earth; dark, muddy, and smelling musky from buck urine; occasionally surrounded by rubs and deer droppings; and always clear of any leaves, twigs, or forest debris. Most times, the buck will leave his hoof print in the center of the scrape. Of vital importance to identifying a primary scrape is the presence of an overhanging or licking branch. An active primary scrape will always have one. During the primary rut, many scrapes are temporarily abandoned for a several reasons. Mostly, it is because with so many does coming into estrus all at once, a buck has no need to wait at a scrape hoping to find a willing doe. Once you find a primary scrape, set up your stand downwind and hunt it there! **See Boundary Scrape/Overhanging Branch/Rut/Scent Checking/Scrape/Secondary Scrape/Testosterone/Urine.**

PROTEIN All animals require protein, a "building block of life." Food intake with less than 16 percent of protein does not provide the materials needed for maximum natural growth of body size and antler mass in whitetails. Deer will always instinctively seek out the most nutritious foods available to them, including those with an appropriate level of protein. **See Alfalfa/Clover/Food/Food Plot/Nuts.**

PUBLIC LAND County, state, or federal lands that are public property and usually heavily hunted. To be successful on public land, hunters must get there before the arrival of all the other hunters and work their way back into the more remote and interior areas where the deer will flee to when the other hunters arrive. Then they can let the other hunters drive the deer to them. **See Bureau of Land Management/Permission to Hunt/Posted Signs.**

PUMP ACTION In a rifle or a shotgun, a method of ejecting a spent shell, injecting a fresh cartridge, and cocking the mechanism for its next firing. In this popular firearm action, the forearm pump is usually located at the foreword half of the firearm and under the barrel. Sliding forward the forearm and subsequently pulling it back completes the motion. **See Autoloader/Double Action/Double Barreled/Front Loader/Lever Action/Shotgun/Side-by-Side.**

PUSH Also called a drive or deer drive, a hunting technique where hunters move through an area of cover that might house deer in the hopes of getting a shot at them or having them move past a waiting stander or watcher. **See Drive/Standers.**

PYRODEX A form of propellant used in muzzleloaders, in-line frontloaders, and so on. **See Black Powder/Foot Pounds of Energy/Gun Powder/Knock Down Power/Muzzleloader.**

QUALITY DEER MANAGEMENT(QDM) A movement of farmers, landowners, and hunters to improve the quality of deer herds and/or hunting experiences. Rapidly making headway and gaining adherents, QDM advocates reducing the number of antlerless deer to well below the land's carrying capacity and for allowing younger bucks to grow up and demonstrate their antler growth potential before shooting them. Over 600 of the nation's leading deer biologists and managers and approximately 9,400 hunters, landowners, and farmers are members (as of June 2000) of the Quality Deer Management Association (QDMA), a nonprofit educational organization dedicated to ethical hunting and sound deer management. Describing itself as the leading educational organization on improving the quality of deer and deer hunting, QDMA helps hunters increase their knowledge about food plots, habitat management, deer research, deer management, antler growth, and data collection. The most respected organization within its field, QDMA produces quality research findings in its quarterly journals, educational books, videos, and workshops and seminars. You can contact QDMA at

> **Quality Deer Management Association**
> **P. O. Box 227**
> **Watkinsville, GA 30677**
> **1-800-209-DEER**

See Balanced Herd/Buck-Doe Ratio/Carrying Capacity/Controlled Hunt/ Doe Harvest/Food/Food Plot/Habitat/Land Management/Nutrition/White-tailed Deer Organizations.

QUARTER MOON PHASES When the moon is directly overhead or underfoot (on the opposite side of Earth) at sunrise or sunset. **See Circadian/Lunar Influence/Moon.**

QUIVER A bow-hunting accessory that should hold your arrows firmly enough so that they do not fall out when you are walking through the brush or woods or rattle when you shoot. Rattling arrows make a bow noisy, and a loose quiver just resonates the sound of loose arrows even more. Many hunters prefer to take their quivers off their bow once they are in their stand and hang it nearby for easy arrow access. **See Accessories/Archery/Arrows/Bow and Arrow/Equipment/Safety(Hunter).**

QUARTERING SHOT When deer angle away or towards hunters. Whether with a bow or firearm, this shot at whitetails is effective in securing a mortal hit. It is *not* a broadside nor head-on shot.

Quartering Shot

R

RACK The hard, bony, multi-tined antlers of the white-tailed deer. **See Antlers/Beam/Bifur-cate/Browtine/Drop Tine/Eye-tine/G-1/G-2/Main Beam/Non-typical/Spread/Sticker Point/Symmetry/Trophy/Typical/Velvet.**

RADIATION Normal body heat that is lost to the outside environment. The longer, hollow guard hairs of a whitetail's winter coat and the fuzzy furlike hair near its body provide for almost no loss of body heat to its environment, allowing it to sleep in the snow and not melt it. During the hot summer months, the shorter outside guard hairs and paucity of the wool-like

Rack

underhair allow the whitetail to radiate a large amount of heat from its body, to keep it relatively cool. **See Conduction/Guard Hair/Hair/Summer Coat/Winter Coat.**

RADIOS Two-way communication devices that are very useful to the hunter. They are often used to alert hunting partners of deer coming their way, of a change in your hunting location or time of leaving your stand, or for asking for help with your downed deer. Some hunting partners whittle the time away by checking in every hour on the hour so as to reinforce their staying in their own stand longer. Radios are also useful for keeping in touch with each other as you and your partner move into your stands in the dark. They certainly provide additional safety for the deer hunter and added confidence that help could be on the way if necessary. **See Equipment/ Safety/Survival.**

RADIO TELEMETRY/TRACKING COLLAR A signal-emitting collar placed on a captured deer by scientists who then follow its movements, developing data on travel patterns that has added greatly to our understanding of the white-tailed deer. **See Buck-Doe Ratio/Herd Size/Predation.**

RAIN Wet weather conditions that affect the whitetail's daily pattern. Deer browse and move over their woodland trails during light, gentle rains, but during drenching downpours they will seek cover. After rain, when the woodland leaves are moist and pliable, is a good time to stalk-hunt as opposed to stand-hunt. Leaves and forest twigs are less likely to break or crackle underfoot. Remember that because the wet forest floor makes the deer quieter in their travels, deer sounds may also escape the hunter's ears. **See Foul Weather/Freezing/Hypothermia/Ice/Inclement Weather/Safety/Sleet/Snow/Survival/Weather/Wind.**

RANGE FINDER A hand-held optical device, whether mechanical or electrically powered, that assists hunters in judging the distance to an outlying stump, a specific tree, or even a deer. Knowing the actual distance to a target increases the chances of making an accurate and effective shot. **See Binoculars/Equipment/Laser/Optics.**

RANK The position a specific buck or doe holds within the social hierarchy of its herd. A higher dominance level in the social order holds a corresponding higher rank. **See Alpha Buck/Bachelor Buck Groups/Dominance/Hierarchy/Lead Doe.**

RATTLE BOX/BAG A device used to simulate the sound of two bucks sparring with their antlers or actually fighting. Its cadence or sequence of action is important for calling in a buck who thinks that two males are fighting over an estrous doe. The buck comes to investigate and hopes to steal the supposed doe away while the two combatants are too busy with each other to notice his theft. **See Antlers/Rattling/Sparring.**

RATTLING/RATTLING ANTLERS The clanging together by a hunter of synthetic or real deer antlers meant to simulate the sound of two bucks sparring for dominance or breeding rights or actually fighting over a doe already in or soon to be in estrus. Subdued rattling during the prerut will create an immediate response from bucks who are frustrated from not finding a willing doe to copulate with. Making your rattling calls sound submissive will draw the interest and aggression of all bucks, especially the dominant bucks, who realize that all they have to do is show up and aggressively snort-wheeze, and younger, less mature deer will run off.

Rattling is often accompanied by the clashing of brush, the raking of leaves, a grunt or two from a grunt

Rattling

tube, and the stomping of feet on the ground the idea is to provide an aural (sound) image in a buck's mind of two bucks fighting. The newly interested buck comes in, usually to steal away the doe presumably being fought over or possibly to take on the victor and establish his dominance.

Hunters are usually advised to bang the antlers together at three to four different times during each morning hunt. The actual sequence is the hunter's choice. Some hunters give a violent clashing of the antlers after they have let the woods settle down in the morning. This loud burst is supposed to get the deer's attention and announce that the're bucks in the area. (I personally do not use or recommend this disturbance at this time of the morning, because I wish my deer to be in as natural a state as possible.)

An alternative is to tickle the antlers together about one hour after sunrise. That sound will carry well and pique the interest of any nearby deer. If, after an hour has passed, nothing satisfactory results from the first antler contacts and you want to see what is out there, this is a time to intensify your efforts with a good clashing of the antlers. Usually an hour after the second sequence, a hunter can produce some intense rattling, to try to bring in any nearby buck.

The most important tip to remember about rattling is that at any time a buck might come rushing in. Anticipate that and be prepared to shoot the investigating buck. **See Antlers/Communication/Grunt/Rattling Box/Scents/Sounds in the Deer Woods/ Sparring.**

RAVINE Usually a washed-out area that runs somewhat up and down a hillside. Ravines are tough to hunt because of the swirling eddies of wind (which disperse scent) usually produced in them. **See Draw/Funnel/Gully/Hollow/Saddle/ Terrain.**

READING SIGN Observing indications that an area is home to deer during pre-season scouts, still-hunts, or off-season wanders through a potential hunting area. There are many deer signs or indicators, such as those listed below in the See section. **See Beds/Browse Line/Deer Sign/Droppings/Overbrowse/Rub/Scat/Signpost/Trail.**

RECIPES Methods of cooking venison. Venison was once reserved solely for royalty to hunt and consume. It is still meat "fit for a king," the hunter! A general viewpoint on venison cuts is "The closer to the ground, the more flavorful the meat." This is because the muscle tissue is leaner and contains more connective tissue. Since it is doing more work (transporting the deer around) than the upper body muscles. Chefs and other good cooks use the guideline that all tender cuts are cooked rare (overcooking makes them tough), while all tough cuts of meat should be cooked well-done. Cooking meat until it's well done usually takes a little longer and often uses moisture to prevent it from drying out and becoming difficult to chew. A good way to assess the readiness of these tougher pieces is to test with a fork for tenderness. Venison cuts include roasts, chops, steaks, shanks, sausage, deer hamburger, and stew meat. **See Aging Meat/Back Straps/Fat/Field Dressing/Gamey Taste/Jerky/Tenderloins/Venison.**

RECOIL The kickback of a gun firing a bullet. Every time hunters send out a projectile, whether it is an arrow or a bullet, they are experiencing Isaac Newton's third law of physics: "For every action, there is an equal and opposite reaction." Recoil is what the shooter feels when the originally stationary projectile (the arrow or bullet) pushes back and off from the base that it is launched from. A general rule of recoil is that the larger the powder charge and/or bullet size, the lighter the firearm frame and the less absorbent the material between the bullet and the shooter, the larger the recoil or kickback of the firearm. Firearm shooters use porting at the firearm's barrel end, specialized recoil pads at the shoulder stock, and a myriad of other devices to lessen the "kick," or punishment from a powerful bullet. **See Accuracy/Knock Down Power.**

RECORD BOOK A record kept by several outdoor organizations to keep track of trophy white-tailed deer antler mass, spread, tine length, and so on. Each group proposes its own measuring system, establishes a minimum net score for entry, and ranks the racks accordingly. **See Boone and Crockett Club/Pope & Young/Safari Club International.**

RECTUM The terminal end of the intestine from the sigmoid flexure to the anus. In layman's terms, this is the posterior end where the deer eliminates its solid waste, usually in pellet form. **See Anus/Droppings/Field Dressing/Internal Organs/ Urine.**

RECURVE BOW A bow midway between the longbow of olden times and the newer compound bow. The recurve has forward bent ends at both limbs that increase speed because of its reflexive action. **See Archery/Bow and Arrow/Compound Bow/ Longbow.**

REGENERATION The revegetation of an area after it has been extensively logged, clear-cut, or had a major fire. Whether from seeds, rhizomes, or roots lying dormant in the soil or from seeds dropped by birds, carried by the wind, passed through animals, or planted by squirrels, an understory of low vegetation starts the process once again. The annual or yearly plants take root first, followed by perennials (bushes). Then come the initial fast-growing trees followed by hardier trees, ultimately leading to a climax forest. All of these are a natural progression of Mother Nature's cycle for keeping her nakedness covered. **See Annuals/Clear-Cut/Overbrowse/Shrubs/ Understory.**

REGURGITATE The bringing back up of partially chewed grasses and/or browse in a ball-like form, a bolus, that a deer has previously quickly ingested and stored in the first of its four stomachs. Later, when the deer has bedded down in secure cover, safe from predators, it can bring back up this cud, and then completely chew it for proper digestion. If a whitetail is alerted to something or senses danger, this regurgitative process stops and a "fight or flight" decision has to be made. **See Abomasum/ Bolus/Cud/Omasum/Reticulum/Rumen/Ruminate/Stomach.**

Release

RELEASE(S) The means by which archers set an arrow free from their control. They can use their fingers to hold the bowstring or one of the many mechanical releases available. **See Archery/Finger Release/Mechanical Release/Nocking Loop/ Nocking Point/String Loop.**

REPELLENT Any odor, sound, visual material, or anything else that repels or drives away a pest or prey animal. Hunters usually do not want to drive away whitetails but rather attract them. Hunters sometimes unwittedly repel a whitetail because they have used a dominant buck lure that scares lesser bucks and intimidated does away from the area, or rattled deer antlers too aggressively. Sometimes even using a skunk cover scent will indicate to the deer that something spooked the "skunk" that they smell and cause the deer to avoid the area. **See Allomone/Attractant Scent/Kairomone/ Lures/Scents.**

REST Any mechanical device that holds an arrow in place while shooting or that holds a firearm in position for steadiness during the shot. **See Accuracy/Archery/ Bipod/Shooting Sticks.**

RETICULUM The second of four stomachs in a ruminant. After a whitetail has hastily eaten enough to fill its rumen, or first stomach, it retires to chew its cud or regurgitated balls of digestive matter. Once worked over more thoroughly by its teeth, the cud then is swallowed, bypassing the rumen and going directly to the reticulum for further digestion. Bezoar stones, also called "madstones," are sometimes found in the reticulum of the white-tailed deer **See Abomasum/Bezoar Stone/Bolus/Cud/Omasum/ Regurgitation/Rumen/Ruminate/Stomach.**

RETINA The surface area on the inside of a deer's eyes. The whitetail has a rather large set of eyes for its body size. Biologists also tell us that the cells in a deer's retina are largely rods, which function best at near dark conditions and are better for detecting movement rather than color. But rest assured that deer do see some color. Scientists are just beginning to verify that whitetails are able to identify some color hues, particularly in the yellow-blue spectra. That is one of the main reasons that the whitetail feeds and is active at night during the new moon phase when little light is reflected from the moon. **See Eyes/Peripheral Vision/Poachers/Rod Cells/ Security/Vision.**

RETREAT An area of security that a whitetail retires to when threatened. **See Buck Trail/Cover/Edge/Escape Route/Safety Zone/Security/Travel Corridor.**

RIDGE A flat area along a hillside, where deer can easily walk on level ground without being silhouetted or skylined. **See Bench/Outline/Silhouette/Skyline/Terrain/Travel Corridor.**

Rifle

RIFLE A long-barreled firearm, that usually has rifling in its barrel. It is used for longer range shooting than a shotgun, is generally more accurate, and has more knockdown power because of the projecticle's increased velocity. **See Ammunition/Ballistics/Bullet/Caliber/Firearms/Foot Pounds of Energy/Guns/Handgun/Hydrostatic Shock/Kinetic Energy.**

RIFLED SLUG A shotgun slug with angled fins or "rifling" that will impart some spin on the projectile after it leaves the smooth bore of older-style shotguns. The newer style shotguns with rifling in their barrels are better adapted to using saboted shells, not rifled slugs (because the rifling in the barrel counteracts the fins on the slugs). **See Accuracy/Ammunition/Ballistics/Brenneke Slug/Foster Slug/Rifling/Shotgun/Slug.**

RIFLING The lands and grooves in a gun barrel that causes a bullet to spin or rotate in flight, thus increasing its accuracy. **See Accuracy/Firearms/Gun/Shot Placement.**

RIGOR MORTIS The "stiffening up" of a dead deer's legs, jaw, and generally any moveable part of its body as tendons lose their flexibility after a certain amount of time. **See Field Dressing/Follow-Up/Stiffen Up.**

RITUALS Deer hunting traditions. Examples range from smearing deer blood on the face of a first-time successful hunter to cutting the shirttail off of a hunter who missed his or her shot at a buck. **See Deer Camp.**

ROAD KILL Dead deer or other animals lying on or near the side of the road, having been hit by cars or heavy trucks. Hitting a deer can cause substantial damage to an automobile. Predators, such as foxes and hawks can often be observed attempting to consume dead deer by the roadway. Many state and county road crews make routine dead deer pick-ups, particularly during the prerut chase phase, when deer movement becomes more noticeable and deer-vehicle crashes occur. **See Automobile-Deer Accidents/Carrion/Chase Period/Mortality/Predator/Rut.**

ROD CELLS One of two types of cells in a deer's eyes. Rod cells are for night vision and motion detection, whereas cone cells are for color perception. **See Eyes/Retina in Deer's Eyes/Security/Vision.**

RUB/RUB LINE/RUB TREE Part of the white-tailed deer's complex communication system. Rubs usually start appearing during the first two weeks of September in most states. The primary reason bucks make rubs is to establish a visual and scent signpost for does and other bucks to see. This marks their core area or home range. Just prior to the rut, bucks are feeling the effects of an increased level of testosterone in their bodies. At this point they start marking their breeding territories with rubs by raking (rubbing) their antlers against the trunks of trees, saplings, and even bushes to expose the bare inner part (usually lighter in color) of the trunk. As he rubs a tree, the buck leaves scent from his forehead glands, a sexual stimulant to does. The buck will often sniff and then lick his own rub seemingly receiving pleasure from ingesting this glandular scent. Rubs are usually a vertical swatch about a foot in length. This signpost advertises his presence to does and warns other bucks away. Bucks coming down a trail and encountering some fresh rubs will often investigate them so as to try to identify who made them. Does interpret the rubs as sexual signposts.

Keeping track of rubs from year to year is a good idea as deer tend to use the same areas. In September, start checking old rubs or rub lines for signs that the old mature buck from last year survived and is once again using this territory as his own turf.

The usual rule of thumb is the bigger the rub, the bigger the deer. However, this cannot always be counted on as huge bucks have been observed totally demolishing small saplings or bushes. Big bucks do leave some telltale gouge marks (from the points of his antlers) on their rubs. All you can safely say about a rub is that it was made by a buck deer and more than likely indicates his previous line of travel. Several rubs over a prescribed area are called a rub line and usually indicate a buck's preferred travel route. Most often, the rubs were made over several trips by the buck and not all

Rubbing

at once. Hunting along a rub line can be productive, as the buck may continue to use it as his travel route, particularly while checking scrapes. Rub lines can reveal a repeated pattern of travel by bucks. Bucks often rub the same tree year after year, sometimes even killing it by girdling it.

Fake rubs can be utilized to position any deer investigating it so that the hunter can make a clean shot. With a rock, or your knife scrape the bark from the side of a sapling or two facing the direction that you expect the deer to approach from. Smearing a little forehead gland scent on this fake rub adds to its attractiveness. **See Alpha Buck/Deer Sign/Forehead Glands/Mock Rub/Mock Scrape/Scent/Signpost/Velvet.**

RUB URINATION After making a scrape, a buck will often step into the middle of the scrape, and urinate on the tarsal glands located on the inside hocks of his rear legs, letting their (i.e., his) scent flow into the scrape. This both advertises his presence and his readiness for breeding and displays his dominance over other bucks. **See Hock/Rut/Scrape/Tarsal Gland/Urinate.**

RUBBER BOOTS Any outer footgear made of rubber that hunters use to keep their feet warm and dry in wet or cold weather. These may be placed over boots or worn with felt liners or heavy socks. Rubber boots are an excellent means of keeping human scent off the ground as hunter walk to their stands. **See Clothing/Footwear/Foul Weather/Inclement Weather/Pacs/Scent.**

RUMEN The first and largest of the whitetail's four stomachs. Everything that the whitetail eats first goes into its rumen, sometimes referred to as its paunch. After a deer has consumed about eight to ten quarts of vegetative materials, it will retire to a safe spot and regurgitate clumps or balls of this partially fermented material in order to more thoroughly chew it up. This is referred to as "chewing its cud." **See Abomasum/Cud/Omasum/Reticulum/Ruminant/Stomachs.**

RUMINANT Cud chewer, category of animals that have multichambered stomachs. (The whitetail has a four-chambered stomach.) **See Abomasum/Cud/Omasum/Regurgitate/Reticulum/Rumen/Ruminate/Stomach.**

RUMINATE Also known as "chewing its cud." Being ruminants, deer consume a lot of food quickly, in order to spend the least amount of time exposed to potential predators, and then retreat to the safety of heavier cover. All this newly eaten material is held in its first of four stomachs. While resting in their daytime beds, deer will regurgitate mouthful-size balls of hastily chewed food and thoroughly chew it for proper digestion. **See Cud/Regurgitate/Ruminant/Stomach.**

RUN/RUNWAY See Deer Run.

RUT The breeding season. The rut drastically changes bucks' normal daily activities. Instinctively, bucks know that prior to this time, they must pack on weight for the upcoming rigors of the rutting season. With a higher than normal amount of testosterone streaming through their bodies, bucks seldom eat. They bed down far less than normal and usually spend most of their time making and checking scrapes, seeking out soon-to-come-into-estrous does, "tending" and breeding with receptive does, and chasing off other bucks. This is often hunters' best time to find their buck, as the bucks no longer think first of survival but only of breeding. They are most vulnerable at this time.

Without the rut and its many distractions, a buck is primarily concerned with only one thing—staying alive. During the prerut stage, where a buck's testosterone level has risen, his neck has swollen, and he has shunned the acquaintance of other bachelor-group bucks, he prepares himself for active breeding.

In the northern portion of the whitetail's range, the breeding period occurs at a somewhat predictable time each year, although evidence is showing this to be a three-year cycle. The rut usually lasts about forty days. Regardless of the temperature—be it warm or cold—the rut will occur at the proper time. This is nature's way of assuring that fawns will be born at a time of nutritious food in the spring and that they can grow up enough to survive the upcoming rigors of winter.

When the buck-to-doe ratio is balanced or equal (generally three does to one buck is realistic), buck competition will be intense, as several bucks will compete for the receptivity of any doe coming into estrus. If you use calls immediately before and

Buck in rut

immediately after the peak of the rut—when estrous does are few—mature bucks will regularly approach your calls.

These are the four main periods of the whitetail rut or breeding cycle:

1. The prerut which becomes noticeable in September and usually peaks around October 15. During this period, bucks show more interest in does. The does themselves are not interested in this increased attention yet!

2. The seeking/chase phase which has two component parts. First comes the scrape-making period. Bucks have worked themselves into an excited sexual frenzy by false fighting with bushes and small trees (which strengthens their neck muscles for sparring with opponents for breeding dominance) and by actively making scrapes. The bucks are priming themselves for action and to begin looking for does. This becomes a time of intense and continual deer movement. As the does start being chased, all deer, but especially bucks, will become highly visible, noisy, and apparently will have discarded their normally secretive nature.

Next is the **chase period** which occurs at the very end of the scraping period and just prior to does entering into estrus—usually during the week prior to peak breeding.

This is the time to use a doe decoy (two are even better) with a good doe-in-heat urine scent on a cotton ball (which holds the scent longer) set in back of the decoy. Bucks tend to rush up to any doe they see, especially one who smells right. The urine will hold the buck's attention for a long time and allow you to get the perfect angle for a shot. Decoys that are easily visible at field edges, on logging roads, in clear-cuts or natural woods openings are all good bets. The greater distance and the more directions that your decoy is visible from the more bucks it will attract.

The chase phase is also a prime time to use rattles and/or grunts to call a buck. When a buck hears what he thinks is another buck tending a doe, or two bucks actually fighting over a ready-to-breed doe, he will readily come to investigate, hoping to take over the actual breeding privilege.

3. The main rut or breeding period, which is the peak of the breeding period. This day-and-night breeding orgy usually lasts from five to seven days. Approximately three-quarters of the mature does are bred. The date does not vary by more than a couple of days each year.

4. The post-rut or late breeding period which occurs twenty-eight days after the peak or start of the primary rut, when any unbred does come into heat (estrus) again. Bucks are on the move to discover these does and change their status to "bred." By this time, after sparring, actually fighting, defending their breeding territory, chasing off rivals,, and mating with many does multiple times, the white-tailed bucks have depleted a lot of their body fat reserves. When the breeding season is finally over and the onset of real winter is close, they must try to replenish their fat reserves or they may not survive the winter months. **See Breeding/Chase Phase/Copulation/Estrus/ False Rut/Late Rut/Prerut/Primary Rut/Rub/Scrape/Testosterone.**

RUT SUPPRESSANTS Six known conditions that have a negative effect upon the intensity of the daytime activity patterns of rutting deer. Singly, they are detrimental to rutting activities, but in combination, their cumulative effect can make a rut become totally nocturnal.

A. Weather. Whitetails move when the barometer is moving. Active changes in the weather, whether it is deteriorating or improving, cause deer to begin feeding, breeding during the rut, or moving to sheltering areas. Extremely heavy, prolonged rain or snow will severely dampen rutting activities.

B. Temperature. In the northern whitetail range, excessively warm temperatures will rapidly diminish rutting activities. If daytime temperatures fall above a buck's "comfort zone" (twenty to fifty-five degrees), the heat will curtail his activities. Likewise, temperatures below twenty degrees also tend to slow down breeding activities. The rather large-bodied whitetails (see Bergmann's Rule) of the Canadian provinces reportedly have a lower comfort range, while the more southern whitetails (possibly a different subspecies) have shorter hair and higher heat tolerance for their comfort range. Outside their comfort zone, whitetails appear inclined to move very little on their own, unless the barometer is falling thus indicating an approaching storm front.

C. Human Pressure. Some state deer biologists establish their main hunting seasons to fall right after the rut or breeding season has occurred. This is usually so that most of the does can be bred, and more specifically, so that there are enough bucks around to do the necessary breeding of all the does. The rut usually occurs during the archery season, which does not attract as many hunters as gun season. The increased number of hunters afield during firearm season quickly tells the whitetail to move under the cover of darkness for security's sake. Since whitetails are not used to a lot of human activity in their living area, a noticeable increase will change their daytime activities in a dramatic way.

D. Skewed Doe-to-Buck Ratio. Areas with a ratio greater than three adult does to one buck will have fewer daytime rutting activities (chasing, scraping, breeding and so on) than areas with a lower ratio, which will demonstrate outstanding daytime (i.e., visible) rutting activities. It is a generally accepted premise that the vast majority of bucks harvested during any deer season will be inexperienced yearling bucks, whose own attempts at breeding will be diminished by the presence of older bucks. However, should there be a dramatic decrease in the more experienced, dominant bucks that do the actual breeding, the intensity of daytime rutting activities will be noticeably lower. **See Buck-to-Doe Ratio/Testosterone.**

E. Food Sources. Rutting bucks will follow the does. Does will go to the best available food sources. Thus, if your area has poor-quality food or even a lack of nourishing food, you will not see rutting activities there.

F. Baiting. Baiting is a controversial topic among hunters. Approximately half the states recognize it as a legal hunting method. The existence of bait piles or mechanical feeders on a neighboring property will invariably attract and hold deer there, often instead of on the property that you are hunting. Where baiting is legal, the old adage is true: "He who has the bigger bait pile, wins!" **See Breeding/Copulation/ False Rut/Fat/Hunter's Moon/Late Rut/Prerut/Pressure/Seasons/Tempera- ture/Testosterone/Weather.**

RUTTING MOON See Hunter's Moon.

SABOT/SABOT SLUG A rather recent entry of shotgun ammunition. For increased accuracy, its designers modeled it on an artillery format. Sabots are usually smaller in diameter, more aerodynamically designed, and wrapped in a two-piece plastic casing that falls away after the slug exits from the barrel. They are especially effective in shotguns with rifled barrels, because the plastic sleeves grab the rifling and impart a stabilizing spin to the whole projectile. A sabot's real advantage comes into play downrange, where its imparted spin and nose-heavy format keep it stable and more accurate. These slugs often retain more knockdown power at increased dis-

Sabot Slug

tances (beyond 100 yards) than do other full-bore slugs, such as Brenneke or Foster. **See Ammunition/Brenneke Slug/Foster Slug/Rifled Slug/Shotgun/Slug.**

SADDLE A dip or lower elevation of a hilltop that makes an easier route of travel to the other side of the hill. Deer often will travel this "path of least resistance" because they feel secure that they will not be silhouetted or skylined. Sometimes a saddle is referred to as a "funnel." **See Draw/Funnel/Gully/Hollows/Ravine/Terrain/ Topographical Map.**

SAFARI CLUB INTERNATIONAL One of the record-keeping organizations that tracks the biggest and best of animal species, including the white-tailed deer. Unlike some of the other record-keeping groups, it does recognize white-tailed bucks based upon the region that they come from. Minimum entry scores for typical racks are 125 and around 131 for nontypical racks. **See Boone and Crockett Club/Pope & Young/White-tailed Deer Organizations.**

SAFETY(DEER) Being safe from danger. Whitetails use all of their senses for one of their two functions in life (a) breeding and perpetuating the species and (b) survival. Only in rare cases will they let down their guard and disregard their own safety. One example is a lovesick buck pursuing a doe in heat (estrus). Sensing danger of any sort sends deer into flight toward any thicket or cover that they can put between the source of danger and itself. **See Cover/Edge/Escape Route/Fight or Flight/Predator/Safety Zone.**

SAFETY(HUNTER) Being safe from injury. Safe hunting should always be the number one concern of any hunter. All safety equipment should be given the "twice over" before going into the field. In particular, any piece of equipment or safety device used with tree stands should be checked, rechecked, and rechecked again. The following topics are particularly important for all safety-minded hunters to pay attention to. **See Back Stop/Blaze Orange/Eye Contact/Fall Restraining Device/First Aid Kit/Flashlight/Foul Weather/Hypothermia/Survival/Tree Stands.**

A. Blaze Orange/Fluorescent Orange/Hunter Orange. Humans can see this bright, fluorescent orange color for a long distance in the deer woods. Worn for safety, it helps identify that a human is present.

B. Harnesses. Full body harnesses are the safest and best. They keep you upright if you should fall out of your tree, thus allowing you to orient yourself without being suffocated and passing out.

C. Permanent Tree Stands. Never assume that because you recently replaced a board or "It's not that old" that everything on a permanent tree stand will hold up in the dark on opening morning. Extreme cold and windy days can severely loosen or even fracture nails and/or screws. You are banking your life or your mobility on this assumption! Check the stand a couple of weeks before the season opens. Don't take a chance opening morning in the dark. Use a safety rope or harness while climbing up the stand. The extra assurance of safety that it provides you greatly offsets any inconvenience of undoing and refastening it as you move up in elevation.

D. Portable Tree Stands. Pre-season practice with your portable tree stand can avert a major accident. It also can allow you to eliminate any noisy parts. After all the pieces of your portable stand have been looked over for flaws, hang the stand a couple of feet off the ground, put on the gear that you normally use, climb aboard, and then go through every possible movement and contortion that might occur during the actual season. Bounce a little on it to check its grip, stand near the edges. (Does it tip?) Lean fully out on the harness belt. (Does it inspire confidence?) Come to a full draw, then shift your weight again. These actions should disclose any noises, flaws, or areas that need attention.

E. Tree Steps. Never assume that last year's holes are okay for this year's tree steps. Those holes used last year could have loosened their grip or extreme cold weather could have taken the strength out of the metal. It is best to use new holes in the tree or put new screws in if you did not take last year's out. Sometimes a tree step with a larger biting head is all that is needed. Painting white or glow paint (that shows when hit with a flashlight beam) on the tops of your tree steps can provide that extra assurance of where the next step down is.

F. Weather. Howling gale force winds that rock your tree stand, lightning, or driving sheets of rain are generally unwise to hunt in. Besides, under those condition, the deer are usually holding up, trying to stay warm or dry themselves. Deer movement will be limited. Use common sense as to whether you should be out in that kind of weather, and if it is unsafe or dangerous, think safety first!

SAFETY ZONE Places where state hunting regulations do not allow for any hunting. Examples include established wildlife preserves, areas within five hundred feet of a road or a building. It is in safe areas like these that the whitetail can live and reach maturity, if not old age. **See Core Area/Cover/Edge/Home Range/Safety(Deer)/Security.**

SALIVA/SALIVARY GLANDS In whitetail glands located on the top of its mouth, as opposed to in humans, whose glands are located under the tongue. Whitetails often appear to be slobbery, with copious amounts of saliva dribbling out of their mouths. A buck chewing on a licking branch over his newly worked scrape leaves scent information in his saliva as to who he is and his level of dominance. **See Bolus/Chemical Signpost/Communication/Cud/Digestion/Drool/Overhanging Branch.**

SALT BLOCK/SALT LICK:
    A. Natural. A place where salts or minerals collect on a hillside such as a wet spot. Deer seek out these naturally occurring elements to ingest them because their body needs them for proper nutrition, and antler growth.
    B. Man-made. Salt blocks, mineral blocks, or commercial powders of deer attractant chemicals placed by hunters for deer, in order to increase the health of the herd, promote antler growth, or attract deer closer for a shot at them. Caution: In some states, it is illegal to hunt over a salt lick. Be sure to check the game laws in the area that you hunt. **See Antlers/Baiting/Ethics/Fair Chase/Minerals/Natural Mineral Lick/Nutrition/Ossification/Poaching/Sportsmanship.**

SANCTUARY Any safe area that disturbed deer will head for if they feel threatened in any way. It is usually the thickest, most impenetrable cover in the area and where intrusion by humans has been minimal. The deer knows that it will be safe in this area, because no human scent has ever been detected there. **See Bedding Area/Core Area/Cover/Escape Route/Safety.**

SCAT The dung or solid waste of an animal eliminated to the ground. **See Droppings/Fecal Droppings/Spoor.**

SCENTS The variety of smells deer give off that indicate their breeding status, their fears, or their direction of travel and the odors hunters give off that can betray their presence to the deer.
    A. Deer. When startled, deer emit an alarm scent from the interdigital glands between their toes. Thus, when other deer walk the same trail and smell those fear-inducing scents, they too become more wary. Fecal droppings, pheromonal deposits, urinary deposits, and other scent markings are common over the whitetail's trails. The almost-ready-to-breed doe begins to give off scent signals a day or two before actually entering estrus. These signals are picked up by any buck around her and the chase phase begins.

Scents

Hunters use various deer-luring scents, such as attractant/food, curiosity, masking, or sexual in their pursuit of the white-tailed deer **See Aromatic/Attractant/ Glands/Interdigital Gland/Metatarsal Gland/Mock Rub/Mock Scrape/ Nasal Gland/Scent Checking/Urine.**
    B. Human. Deer are occasionally exposed to human scent but possess the normal predator-to-prey aversion to it. Whitetails in agricultural areas are used to smelling the oil, diesel fuel, and tire scents. from farm equipment, but even they do not get accustomed to having human scent on the ground near them. Human scent wafting

through the air, on the brush around them, or on the ground, puts deer into the alert mode.

For this reason, hunters must keep themselves as clean as possible. Shower with a scent-free, antibacterial soap in the morning after you have eaten breakfast (pay special attention to making sure that your hair is clean). Even your teeth and mouth should be attended to as they too give off an odor that can alarm deer. At the very least, wipe yourself down in the morning with odor-free wipes (Scent-free baby wipes work well). The point here is to remove as much of the bacteria-causing odor sources from your body.

Likewise, savvy hunters will keep their tree stand area as scent-free as possible. Wear gloves when climbing to keep scent off the steps of a fixed-position stand. Never leave your climbing stand overnight at the base of the tree, as it will broadcast your scent through the night.

Your hunting clothes should also be as free of any odor as possible. All of your personal hygiene will be for naught if your clothing gives you away. Do not wear your hunting clothes while filling up the gas tank, while eating bacon and eggs (or anything else) for breakfast, or in any other situation where your hunting outfit is likely to absorb odors. In fact, the best place to put your hunting togs when you are not wearing them is in a new plastic bag containing some of the leaves and maybe even a little dirt native to the area where you are hunting. This outfit is best left outside to air out the night before and put on or carried up the hill with you while moving to your stand. The use of a carbon-activated, scent-absorbing suit under your outer garments (e.g., a Scent-Lok suit) will do wonders in containing your odor during the day.

In the morning, while trekking to your stand (especially if it is uphill) try not to exert so much effort that you perspire. Human sweat becomes a fertile medium for odor-causing bacteria to flourish in. It is a waste product that smells bad and that deer associate as belonging to a human! If you will have to exert much effort going to your stand, dress lightly in layers, carry your heavy outer garments with you in a pack, and put them on after you have arrived at your stand.

Some hunters use cover-up scents that try to mask a human's odor, such as skunk odor, red fox urine, raccoon urine. Most of these will effectively overpower your own scent, especially if you have taken precautions to be as clean as possible yourself. However, remember that a skunk has given off its essence as an alarm or used it defensively. Doesn't it make sense that deer would associate an alarmed skunk with danger?

In the morning, any scent that you give off is rising with the morning thermals. This makes your elevated stand much more effective, as your scent will be lifted above the deer returning to their bedding area. You can be surrounded by deer in the morning hours and not be detected. However, this is not the case in the evening, when the thermals are flowing downhill and your scent is likewise descending. A deer downhill or downwind of you will quickly become alarmed, and possibly stomp its front leg, snort, and then flee, thus alerting other deer to a possible threat. Other deer will then avoid your area, because of that alarm snort and possible alarm scent laid down by the alerted deer's stomping. Whenever hunters use scents, they must place their stand so that their own scent blows away from the direction that they expect the deer to approach from. Hunters are often advised not to hunt a stand unless the wind is right, that is, not blowing from the hunter to the likely deer approach route. **See Air Current/Chlorophyll/Cross Wind/Downwind/Flehmen/Hygiene/Kairomone/Overhanging Branch/Pheromone/Scent Checking.**

SCENT BOMB The laying of a deer lure, whether a food, sexual, or curiosity lure all around your stand. The lure can take many forms, such as sticks dipped in a gel-like lure and then stuck into the ground, 35mm film canisters stuffed with clean cotton with liquid lure poured on it, or drag ropes or scent wicks hung all around your stand. The main idea is to saturate your area with the scent that you are using. **See Attractants/Estrus/Lures/Prerut/Rut/Scent Checking/Scent Hanger/Scent Drag/Scent Post/Sex.**

Scent Checking

SCENT CHECKING Deer check their environment for evidence of danger, food, and sex. White-tailed deer use their noses and sense of smell as their primary defense. Deer often travel with their noses into the wind, thus being alert to any danger before it reaches them. The observant hunter will often see them looking over their shoulders if the wind is coming from that direction. Coming upon a deer trail, scrape, or rub, deer will smell it just to see who most recently traveled that way. Bucks often scent check for does that are coming into estrus, through the process called flehmen. They are actually smelling estrous pheromones in the doe's urine on the ground. The bucks roll their lips/nose back, trapping the urine scent to determine the degree of the doe's readiness to breed.

If a hunter sees a deer put its nose in the air and then start looking around, that deer has caught a whiff of danger and will soon try to identify the hunter's location. **See Flehmen/ Kairomone/Mock Rub/Nasal Gland/Overhanging Branch/Rub/Rub Line/Scent Hanger/Scent Post/Scrape/Tarsal Gland.**

SCENT DRAG A clean rag saturated with deer lure tied with string to a hunter's boot, so as to create a scent line leading close to the stand. Any buck crossing the hunter's trail will notice and hopefully follow the scent back to the hunter. The rag is often then attached to a branch within shooting range of the stand as a further attractant to the buck. **See Lures/Scents/Scent Bomb/Scent Hanger/Scent Post.**

SCENT HANGER Any deer lure that is hung on a nearby tree or branch for the purpose of attracting deer to come closer to a hunter's stand. **See Scent/Scent Bomb/Scent Post.**

SCENT MARKING The act of an animal placing its personal odor on a particular spot, such as a buck placing his scent on an overhanging branch or a rub. **See Downwind/ Flehmen/Kairomone/Mock Rub/Nasal Gland/Overhanging Branch/Rub Line/Scent Hanger/Scent Post/Scrape/Tarsal Gland.**

SCENT POST Also called a "scent bomb" or a "scent hanger," a deer-luring strategy that involves placing one or more (sometimes as many as four to six) scent bottles or wads of fresh cotton soaked in lure in a semicircle around a hunter's stand. A nearby deer picks up the scent drifting on the air currents and follows it back to its source. Scent posts are an excellent tool for holding a deer's attention while the hunter draws his bow or raises his firearm undetected. **See Allomone/Communication/ Downwind/Flehmen/Kairomone/Overhanging Branch/Rub Line/Scent.**

SCENT TRAILS One of several hunter strategies using deer scent. It is based upon the concept that when one deer smells where another deer has walked, it tends to follow that other deer's trail. Hunters use a drag rag, a boot pad, or an actual tarsal gland soaked in deer urine and dragged on the ground behind them as they go to their stand. The hunters (wearing rubber boots and gloves to negate their own scent) lay a trail, usually beginning one hundred to three hundred yards from the stand, and bypassing the stand, never leading directly to it. On the way into your stand area, the scent trail must usually be refreshed on the rag or boot pad every twenty-five to forty yards. This keeps the following deer's interest because weakening scent seems to indicate that the "deer" being followed was going the opposite direction.

A properly laid scent trail will often allow hunters to see deer that they would not normally see because they were out of sight or range when they first discovered the scent trail and began following it. The idea behind this technique is to position a deer following the scent trail for the hunter to get a good shot. **See Scents.**

SCOPE An optical instrument. For a majority of hunting situations, a variable power (e.g., 3-9X) scope should be set at the lower settings (i.e., 3X or 4X). These settings provide an expanded field of vision and allow for more light-gathering capabilities during prime early morning or late evening hunting periods than higher settings. Lower settings also allow hunters to more easily scan the immediate area to pick up game animals moving or hidden from the naked eye. The scope's magnification settings can be increased when needed for longer distances. **See Binoculars/ Equipment/Laser/Optics/Range Finder.**

SCORING For antlers, the act of adding up the number of inches for each main beam then adding the lengths of each tine over an inch long, measuring the girth of the main beams at their pedicles and so on. All this adds up to a green or gross score before any reductions are taken off and before the required drying period has elapsed. After being measured again once the rack has dried, the final or net score will determine the rack's entry into the record book or not. **See Antlers/Boone and Crockett Club/Drop Tine/Drying Period/G-1/G-2/Green Score/Main Beam/Net Score/Nontypical/ Pope & Young Spread/Trophy/Typical.**

SCOUTING Examining an area for deer sign and the presence of deer.

A. Pre-Season. Using county plat maps, aerial photographs, topographical maps, driving country roads looking for names on mailboxes, talking to residents, and glassing the fields from the roadside are all valid ways of starting to discover where deer might be located. Sometimes one of your own relatives will own property nearby and will know how to contact a property owner so that permission can be obtained to hunt.

Where there are oaks (and acorns), look for squirrels to find where deer will be feeding. Food plot scouting can easily be done glassing from a pickup truck, as deer living in farming or ranching communities pay little attention to a pickup. If you learn a buck's pattern during the late summer and early fall, the very best time to take him is at the earliest legal opportunity. As the breeding season starts, most bucks totally change their normal routines and patterns. **See Aerial Photographs/Bedding/ Bench/Contour Lines/Deer Sign/Dewclaws/Droppings/Habitat/Maps/Mast/ Orthophotoquad/Ridge/Spoor/Topographical Maps/Tracks.**

B. During the Season. Most of your fall scouting that occurs during the hunting season should be from a distance, with a minimum of invasive activity so as not to spook the deer from your hunting area. It is best to do it at midday, when active deer travel is at a minimum. Scouting has importance at this time, as conditions often change during the season. For example, acorns drop and will attract deer to that area; the weather starts to drastically change. Leaves drop, and there is less canopy cover for the hunter. Food access and sources change, and deer tend to travel in more edge and thicker cover because of the increasing proximity to humans invading their world. **See Binoculars/Cover/Edge/Food/Glassing/Security.**

C. Post-Season. Scouting during the winter, after the hunting season has ended allows you to use aerial photographs and topographical maps. **See Aerial Photographs/Contour Lines/Cover/Global Positioning System/Maps/Navigation/Orienteering/Orthophotoquad/Terrain/Topographical Maps.**

SCRAPES Circular or oblong pawed-out areas anywhere from one foot to four or more feet in diameter. Wildlife researchers and serious hunters delineate three types of scrapes: (a) boundary (or border scrapes), (b) primary scrapes, and (c) secondary scrapes. It was once thought that bucks instinctively know that the best place to meet a doe is over or near a scrape. Supposedly that was their main reason for their making one. The latest thinking is that scrapes are more a dominance display of stature, strength, and prime rank in the social hierarchy. All bucks know their rank in this dominance hierarchy and know which buck last freshened a scrape. Scrapes have been recently described as being a buck's normal method to "carpet bomb" the area with his scent.

Bucks prefer to make scrapes on flat ground. The buck clears the area with his front hooves and then urinates in it. Often he will urinate over his back hocks, letting the urine run over his tarsal glands, adding their scent to his urine. This scent picture identifies the scrape as his and displays his readiness to breed. However, remember that scrapes are used by all deer (both sexes and all levels of the deer pecking order) to communicate with each other.

An active primary scrape, will also usually have a licking branch over it, which the buck has chewed or thrashed with his antlers and rubbed with the pre-orbital glands located at his eyes along with the nasal and forehead glands. The buck will also often lick this branch, testing his own scent and working himself up into a sexual frenzy. This action usually occurs in middle to late October as bucks are seriously gearing up for the primary rut. They are on the move, making rub lines, forming scrapes, looking for does, and checking them to determine if and when they are ready to breed.

Hunting active scrapes at this time can be very effective and successful. A mature buck will often check his scrapes as often as he can. Two elements are key for successfully hunting a buck along his scrape line. First, try to keep the woods as fresh as possible. Too much evidence of a hunter's presence in the woods will alert the buck that he is being pursued. This might cause him to become completely nocturnal or he just might vacate the area totally. So try not to walk on the deer trails, thus leaving your scent and alarming the buck or does that he is pursuing. Give known bedding areas a wide berth for the same reasons.

Look for fresh (active) scrapes located away from the field edges. Field edge scrapes were either randomly made and never revisited or were made by young copy-catting bucks who haven't figured out yet why they are feeling the urges that they are experiencing. Scrapes on field edges are not worth hunting. You have to get back into the timber and find the actively used scrapes. Hunting near a scrape in a thicket or under forest canopy cover during the chase phase of the rut can be productive. However, some hunters will spend their time hunting near open-cover scrapes made by small bucks at night. They will not see a big buck there, and probably not even its small-racked maker, as sixty to eighty percent of all scrapes are made at night. In fact, most scrapes are worked or freshened at night.

There is no better way of identifying a scrape's degree of activity than either picking up some of the moist dirt with a rubber glove covered hand or bending right down over the scrape and smelling the pungent odor of urine and scent gland. Does and other bucks will "freshen" this scrape also, but the point is, it is being used and that means that its maker will be checking it. The activity level of a scrape can be determined by the number and size of tracks in the scrape. The buck wants it used so that

Scrape Making

he can identify a doe who is advertising that she is ready to mate. Such a scrape offers a good hope of seeing the buck visiting it during daylight (shootable) hours.

The majority of scrapes made by bucks are pawed out in areas that are frequented by heavy doe activity during late October. It is believed that many secondary scrapes are made to lure does into the buck's core scraping area, which is usually located in a private, secure sanctuary. A new scrape opened up in November will be infinitely more active than the October or secondary scrapes. **See Boundary Scrape/ Flehmen/Freshening/Mock Scrape/Musk/Overhanging Branch/Primary Scrape/ Rut/Scent/Scent Checking/Secondary Scrape.**

SCRAPE HUNTING GUIDELINES Tips for effective hunting near scrapes.
    A. Never walk right up to a scrape and start poking around in it. If you must closely examine it, do so with a stick or better yet, with rubber gloves on so that you do not contaminate it with your scent and scare the buck away. Do not stay at the scrape any longer than you have to.
    B. Avoid setting up too close to a scrape. Always be downwind of it, more than fifteen yards but less than twenty-five yards away. Remember, a buck will often scent check his scrape by circling downwind of it. Total odor and visual camouflage are absolutely essential to the bowhunter. Gun hunters can set up between fifty and seventy yards away, depending on the thickness of the cover. Again, the setup must be downwind.
    C. Add tarsal gland, buck lure, or doe-in-heat scent to entice the buck to come in for a closer examination of his scrape and its false visitor. **See Freshening/ Hind Legs/Hocks/Metatarsal Gland/Overhanging Branch/Primary Scrape/ Scent Checking/Scrape/Secondary Scrape/Terrain.**

SCRAPE LINE Several scrapes made together that form a line of direction, usually toward the primary scrape. This collection of smaller, lesser used scrapes is generally believed to be made to lure or direct a doe toward a buck's primary scrape area, which is located in a secure or safe area where he is waiting. A scrape line is usually found in bottlenecks, funnels, and along trails. It is the primary scrape that gets most of the buck's attention. He will keep it clear of debris, yet full of his scent (an indication of his superior breeding status). However, those secondary scrapes that indicate the scrape line are often quickly made, erratic in shape, and often contain a few leaves and twigs. They are not used as often as the primary scrapes and may be freshened only about once or twice a week. Remember watchingsecondary scrapes is not as productive as watching a primary scrape. **See Boundary Scrape/Freshening/Hind Legs/Hocks/Metatarsal Gland/Mock Scrape/Overhanging Branch/Primary Scrape/Secondary Scrape/Terrain.**

SCROTUM The skinlike sack that houses a buck's testicles, or sperm-producing organs. The scrotum hangs beneath the buck, adjacent to his penis. The main purpose of its hanging below the buck's body is to dissipate the normal body heat that would weaken or kill off the sperm. **See Hypogonadism/Penis/Photoperiodism/Testes/Testosterone.**

SEASONS Periods for deer hunting set by the wildlife agencies of each state, usually in the fall of the year around the time of the rut. Often the archery hunting season occurs during the peak of the rut, just after the does have been bred. With so many bucks being culled out of the herd during the firearms season, those that are left will breed the remaining does who come into the second or late estrus. If the dominant buck is killed or other, more mature bucks have been taken, the younger, inexperienced bucks will get their chance to pass on their genes.

To serious deer hunters, there are only two seasons: deer hunting and the rest of the year. However, rather than limit themselves to just the few weeks of hunting season, true hunters can divide that "other season" into hunting-related activities:

A. Scouting Season. The best time to scout deer is right after the hunting season has ended, when there is fresh snow on the ground. This gives hunters an idea of what deer survived the hunting season.

B. Shed Hunting Season. Usually early springtime, when most of the snow is gone and greenup starts, cast antlers are readily observable. You will have to time your search carefully though, as sheds are quickly consumed by mice, porcupines, and squirrels. **See Antlers/Autumn/Leaf Drop/Pedicles/Rack/Sheds.**

SEBACEOUS GLANDS The basic oil glands located in the skin around hair follicles. They emit a fatty substance called sebum, which is a fatty lubricant. **See Glands.**

SECOND RUT See Late Rut.

SECONDARY SCRAPE These pawed-up, rough-looking circles of earth are made with more frequency than primary scrapes, but they receive far less attention from the buck who made them. Secondary scrapes are mostly three feet in diameter or smaller, and sometimes erratic in shape. They often contain leaves or twigs, but usually do not have a licking branch over them. They are generally made close together and often form what is known as a "scrape line," which points toward the safe area where the buck has actively worked on his primary scrape. Rarely revisited by the buck who made it, secondary scrapes are not primary scrapes and thus are not as productive to hunt over.

Immature bucks do not start making scrapes until mid- to late October. This is instinctual but probably also an observed and learned behavior from more mature bucks. Big, mature bucks start making scrapes in September; however, some of the experts tell us that the dominant bucks work their scrapes year round. The licking branch over the primary scrape is heavily worked during the year as a scent depository or advertisement. The actual pawing of the ground is displayed most often in the fall. Bucks not making active breeding scrapes yet. **See Overhanging Branch/Primary Scrape/ Rut/Scrape Line.**

SECURITY The safety every whitetail seeks safety as a prime requirement for survival, sometimes even before food and sex. Being a prey animal, the whitetail is basically skittish and will not expose itself to danger once it has been identified or sometimes just perceived. **See Core Area/Corridor/Cover/Doubling Back/Habitat/ Home Range/Nocturnal/ Deer Run/Senses of Deer/Sixth Sense/Travel Corridor/Transition Zone.**

SEDENTARY Staying at home or settling down in the same area. Young bucks (one or two years old) will often be forced to disperse out of their mother's core area, mainly to promote the dilution of the gene pool. Female whitetails are more likely to remain in their mother's home range, sharing it with her in an extended female group called a "matriarchal group" with the oldest doe as the leader. **See Dispersal/Doe/Home Range/Inbreeding/Lead Doe/Matriarchal Group.**

Seeking

SEEKING PHASE A time of intense and continual deer movement. Prior to this phase, bucks have worked themselves into sexual frenzy by faux fighting bushes and small trees (this strengthens their neck muscles for sparring with opponents for breeding dominance) and by actively making scrapes. The bucks have primed themselves for action and to begin looking for does. As the does start being chased, all deer, but especially bucks, become highly visible and noisy and seem to discard their normally secretive nature. **See Breeding/Chase Phase/Late Rut/Prerut/Rut.**

SEEP A spot where ground water oozes slowly to the surface, forming a damp area and sometimes an actual pool of water. In drier areas, it is used as a watering hole for wildlife. **See Water.**

SELECTIVE HARVEST A quality deer management practice used when biologists, deer researchers, and/or landowners desire to reduce an overabundance of one sex of the whitetail. They may mandate that only one sex be harvested and not the other so as to bring a more proper buck-to-doe ratio about and provide for a healthier herd. **See Buck-to-Doe Ratio/Carrying Capacity/Doe License/Doe Permit/Harvesting**

Does/High Fence Hunting/Quality Deer Management/Skewed Ratio/Spikes.

SENSES OF DEER For deer, in order of importance: smell, eyesight, hearing, touch and taste, and even a "sixth" sense (a deer's reaction to things that just do not seem right to it). During high winds or heavy, driving rains or snows, a deer's senses are greatly diminished. Deer behave nervously when they are unable to smell, hear, or see everything around them. They feel vulnerable to predators and act accordingly. Often deer will keep on the move, relying mainly upon their vision to detect any danger ahead of them. **See Eyes/Hearing/Nose/Smell/Sounds/Vision.**

SERVER A wrapped portion of the bowstring that contains the nocking point, where the hunter's fingers hold or a mechanical release attaches. **See Nocking Loop/ Nocking Point/Releases.**

SEXUAL MATURITY When an animal is capable of successfully engaging in the act of procreation. A white-tailed buck is capable of breeding at approximately a year and a half. A doe fawn, either born early in the summer and coming into estrus late in the breeding season (early winter) is also capable of being bred. **See Breeding/Buck/Copulation/ Doe/Ejaculation/Fawn/ Gestation.**

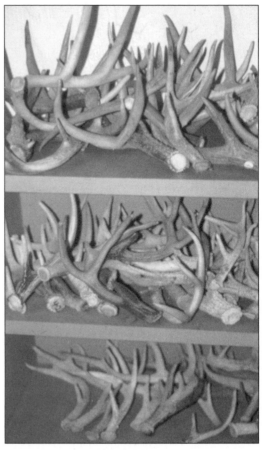

SHADOWS A hunter's best friend. Never set up with the sun shining in your face. Usually the north side of a tree will allow you to keep in some part of the trunk's shadow all day long. To take maximum advantage of shadows during the day, try to place your stand in a tree with multiple trunks or two or more trees growing close together. **See Camouflage/ Crepuscular/Eyes/Vision.**

SHED(S) A loose antler usually found on the ground. By late January, early February, most

Shed Antlers

bucks have lost their antlers. Their attachment at the pedicle is severely weakened and could fall off while walking. Finding a matched set of antlers is a rarity. Finding a single shed antler is usually a good sign that a buck survived the hunting season and will be around for the next season. Shed antlers do not just litter the forest floor but are consumed by mice, squirrels, porcupines, and so on for their mineral content. **See Adrenal Gland/Antlers/Horn/Net Score/Nontypical/Pedicle/Photoperiodism/Scouting/Testosterone/Typical.**

SHOCK How a bullet kills. The stored or kinetic energy of a bullet traveling at a high speed transfers destructive shock waves to surrounding tissue, resulting in severe damage. The animal actually dies of traumatic shock, not necessarily of blood loss. **See Bullet/Foot Pounds of Energy/Knock Down Power/Hydrostatic Shock.**

SHOOTING LANE(S) Narrow corridors for shooting opportunities. Long before leaf drop, it is wise for bowhunters to clear away leaves, tree branches, and any other objects, especially small, dead tree limbs, that may block the chance to shoot at a deer. In fact, the best time to clear shooting lanes is in late winter or early spring before new growth starts. Time spent preparing open shooting lanes is time well spent by hunters. Clear lanes early—way before the season starts, and not just before opening day—as the deer must get accustomed to these changes in their environment. They do notice them!

Keep shot opportunity corridors relatively narrow but adequate for your own shooting capabilities. Never make a lane so wide that it disrupts the deer's natural environment and thus make them avoid the area altogether. It is better to have several shooting opportunity corridors radiating off in several directions than one wide single lane. **See Back Stop/Line of Fire/Stands/Trimming.**

SHOOTING PRESSURE The intense drive some hunters feel to bring home a deer. As a result, they will not use common sense or exhibit basic, good sportsmanlike hunting skills. The basic rule still is, If you are not absolutely sure of your target—and what is behind it—do not pull the trigger! Whitetail hunters should be able to stay calm, take their time, not feel pressured to shoot, but make the shot count. **See Buck Fever/Sound Shot.**

SHOOTING STICKS One or two rods, usually three to five feet in length, that are held upright under a gun to reduce movement and stabilize the firearm. Handy in open areas where natural gun rests are scarce. By propping your rifle, shotgun, or pistol upon these two sticks, your aim can be steadier for long distance shots. **See Accuracy/Bipod/Rest/Shot Placement.**

SHOT GROUPING See Grouping.

SHOT PLACEMENT Placing a projectile where it can do the most damage to the life-sustaining organs of the deer. An arrow or a bullet is just a chunk of irritating metal if

Shooting sticks will help assure one's shot placement.

it does not strike a vital area that mortally wounds the deer.

Newly alerted deer usually crouch, in order to spring forward, or turn to the side, rather than dive or leap up when an arrow is launched at them. Shooting two to three inches lower on a nervous or alert animal, rather than at the normal, center heart spot as you would on a calm, unsuspecting deer, will usually tag it. **See Accuracy/After the Shot/Back Stop/Benchrest/Blood Trail/Downed Deer/ Going Away Shot/Hair/Instinctive Shooter/Wounded Game.**

SHOT SHOW The annual Shooting, Hunting, and Outdoor Trade Show held for all who are involved in the outdoor sporting life. One can expect to see most of the big names in deer hunting there, and other commercial ventures.

SHOTGUN Any form of relatively short-ranged, smooth-bored, long firearm that projects a lead slug. It can come in several different gauges, such as 10, 12, 16, 20, 28, and .410 for single slugs or use several different variants of buckshot: 00, 000, and so on. **See Ammunition/Buckshot/Caliber/Firearms/Foot Pounds of Energy/ Gauge/Guns/Handloading/Slug.**

SHRUB A vegetative plant ranging in size between a bush (low to the ground) and a tree (growing skyward and towering over the forest floor. Shrubs are useful as a source of browse for whitetails. Household ornamental shrubs, when eaten by deer, cause homeowners anxiety and animosity directed toward whitetails. **See Brush/Food/ Tree.**

SIBLINGS A brother or sister. Does usually have twins, but triplets are occasionally observed. **See Fawns/Lead Doe/Twins.**

S

SIDE-BY-SIDE A double-barreled shotgun with barrels placed alongside each other. By using 00 (double aught) or 000 (triple aught) buckshot shells, hunters give themselves a reasonable chance of bringing down the quarry. **See Buckshot/Double Barreled/Rifle/Shotgun.**

SIGHT See Vision.

SIGHTING-IN Simple testing of a firearm's accuracy to assure that you have the best opportunity for a clean kill. After you have traveled any great distance or sent your firearm through a transport system not entirely under your control, upon arriving at your destination, you should retest or zero in that firearm so as to make sure that it shoots where you zeroed it in. **See Accuracy/Benchrest/Shot Placement/Zeroing In.**

SIGHTS See Gun Sight.

SIGN See Deer Sign.

SIGNPOST/SIGNPOST RUB Part of the white-tailed deer's complex communication system. They usually start appearing during the first two weeks of September in most states. The primary reason bucks make rubs is to establish a visual and scent signpost for does and other bucks to see and smell their dominance level and be put on notice that this is their area. Rubs mark a buck's core area or home range. However, it has been observed that several bucks will sometimes take over and use another buck's rub—depositing their own scent—and thus, expressing their own dominance. **See Aromatic/ Core Area/Deer Sign/Dominance/Glands/Home Range/Rub/Scent/Scrape/ Trails.**

SILHOUETTE The act of being outlined against a lighter background and thus standing out as a blob or an unnatural looking feature in a deer's environment. Tree stand hunters are often silhouetted against the sky when they do not have enough branches or leaves to break up their form. Even in a ground blind, hunters need to break up their form so as to not be identified as danger by the deer. The purpose of camouflage, whether it is dappled or contrasting colors or even the leaflike ghillie suit with pieces of artificial vegetation dangling from it, is to break up a hunter's silhouette and reduce the possibility of being identified as danger. **See Back Cover/Bench/Color Blind/ Ghillie Suit/Light Patterns/Outline/Predator/Retina/Security/Vision.**

SINEW See Tendon.

SINGLE SHOT (FIREARM) Any firearm that chambers only one round, and does not have a magazine, tube feed, or other means of injecting another round, short of manually breaking open the breech and inserting a new bullet. **See Ammunition/ Autoloader/Rifle/Shotgun.**

SINGLETON A single fawn. A doe usually gives birth the first year to one fawn. Thereafter, she is most likely to produce twins and occasionally triplets. **See Birth/Does/Fawn/Gestation/Triplets/Twins.**

SIXTH SENSE A feeling of apprehension or being ill-at-ease about something that is about to happen. Humans refer to this feeling as intuition or extra sensory perception. Whitetails seem to display a sixth sense of their own when for no readily apparent reason, they discover hunters by looking up into the tree at them, mysteriously turn and walk away, or avoid an area altogether after having used it reliably on a daily basis. This avoidance of their fate is unexplainable in human terms and thus attributed to an extra "something." **See Senses of Deer/Security/Sleep.**

SKEWED RATIO Too many does per buck in a herd. The ideal number of bucks to does is one to one. Three does to each buck is considered a good ratio. However, beyond that with five or more does to one buck, the ratio is considered skewed and will result in an intense rut with many buck fights, lasting longer than usual. **See Balanced Herd/Buck-to-Doe Ratio/Die-Off/Doe Harvest/Herd Size/Winterkill.**

SKINNING The act of removing the hide from a deer carcass. If the hide is to be mounted by a taxidermist, care must be exercised in removing the skin around the eyes, nose, and pedicles. Be sure not to cut too far up the deer's neck when field dressing it, as the taxidermist may not be able to repair the cut. **See Aging Meat/Caping/Field Dressing.**

SKUNK/SKUNK ESSENCE The scent of a skunk (allomone) that gives it an advantage and sends the message, "Stay away from me, I will spray you and make you smell bad." Used by deer hunters to hide or cover up their own scent, it sometimes causes deer to come and investigate what caused the skunk to spray. **See Allomone/Communication/Cover Scent/Kairomone/Scent.**

SKYLINE(D) The act of being outlined against the sky, thus being identified as a source of danger to the whitetail. Tree stand hunters are prone to this if their outline is not broken up by tree branches, limbs, or leaves. Still-hunters walking along a ridge could easily be viewed against the sky by a deer on a bench below the hunter. **See Back Cover/Light Patterns/Outline/Peripheral Vision/Vision.**

Skylined

SLEEP A state of rest. Whitetails seldom completely sleep, although hunters have shared stories of sneaking up upon a resting and seemingly asleep deer. While deer have been observed taking "cat naps" of short duration, they tend to be ever-vigilant and often keep their eyes half open and their ears twitching and listening for signs of danger. **See Diurnal/Security.**

SLEET Frozen or partially frozen rain that generally makes hunters uncomfortable. One advantage of sleet is its scent suppression, which reduces hunters' chances of being detected. When sleet lasts for only a short time, deer will continue their normal routine. If, however, sleet falls for a long time or is preceded by or followed by other inclement weather, whitetails will hunker themselves down into a more protected area. **See Foul Weather/Freezing/Hypothermia/Ice/Inclement Weather/ Rain/Snow/Temperature/Weather/Wind.**

SLUG A form of solid lead projectile fired out of a shotgun; sometimes referred to as a "pumpkin ball." There are several styles, including finned Foster slugs for nonrifled barrels and plastic-jacketed sabots for rifled barrels. **See Brenneke/Firearm/Foot Pounds of Energy/Foster/Gauge/Knock Down Power/Sabot/Shotgun.**

SMELL A sense that white-tailed deer, and especially bucks, rely heavily on. A deer may question and even investigate something that it thinks it sees but does not yet recognize as danger, but it will never stay around long when its brain alerts it to possible danger via smell. Deer constantly use the wind as an aid in their direction of travel, scent checking for danger in the direction that the wind is coming from. The observant hunter will often notice deer licking their noses with their tongues, a means of enhancing their olfactory (nose) sensing abilities. Under ideal conditions (e.g., medium humidity, a slight breeze), whitetails can smell a hunter up to 150 yards away. **See Allomone/ Communication/Human Odor/Kairomone/Scent/Scent Checking.**

SNORT The most prevalent deer sound encountered by the novice hunter. A deer's alerting or alarm snort is made by loudly exhaling air through its nose and may be intended to get the suspected danger to move and then be identified. Both bucks and does may snort in order to alert other deer that they have scented a predator. While detecting a hunter's scent, a deer will snort but may not necessarily know the hunter's exact location. Upon hearing a snort alarm, a hunter should freeze in place until the deer calms down and feels safe. When a deer bounds off because it has identified a source of danger, a hunter will often hear multiple snorts with each bound. **See Aggressive Snort/Alarm Posture/Alarm Snort/Blow/Communication/Foot Stomp/Sounds.**

SNORT WHEEZE A buck sound, usually accompanied by a snort that issues an aggressive challenge to another buck. The hairs on his neck and back will be erect, and his ears will be laid back. Hearing this sound means that there could soon be two highly aggressive bucks sparring and ultimately clashing antlers. Get ready for some fast and furious action! **See Alarm Posture/Alarm Snort/Blow/Communication/Sounds in the Deer Woods.**

SNOW Weather conditions that can be excellent for hunters. A light covering (more than a dusting) of snow makes it easy to see where deer have recently traveled. Tracking deer or following a blood trail is easier if there is a snow cover. Heavy snowfall can be a burden to hunters without snowshoes, as they must exert a lot of energy to travel in deep snow. White-tailed deer must also exert extra energy and consume precious body fat in order to move around. **See Crust/Foul Weather/Freeze/Frost/Ice/Inclement Weather/Temperature/Tracks/Trails/Weather/Yarding.**

SNOWMOBILE A tracked vehicle, specifically made to travel on top of snow, which has opened up the snowy wilderness to hunters. Their ability to get into, and just as importantly to get back out of, areas where deep snow would have previously prevented them from going has made snow country whitetails more vulnerable. Snowmobiles also benefit deer and other wildlife in that their weight helps pack the snow down to a more manageable depth for easier travel that expends less energy. **See All-Terrain Vehicle/Migration/Snow/Wilderness/Winter.**

SOCIAL CALL(S) Specific sounds whitetails make that calm other deer, reaffirms their presence to others, and help to identify just who is around. Nursing does often emit reassuring sounds to their fawns. Bucks use a social grunt when they are together in summer bachelor groups as they learn to identify each other by sound. If one loses track of another, it will grunt softly to let the other bucks know his whereabouts. This stimulates a buck to investigate so as to identify who made the grunt. **See Body Language/Calls/Communication/Contact Call/Deer Blow/Sounds/Vocalization.**

SOCIAL GROOMING See Grooming.

SOCIAL ORDER See Hierarchy.

SOCIAL STRESS See Stress.

SOFT MAST Usually the seed-bearing fleshy fruits such as apples, grapes, pears, and persimmons. Soft mast can also include the seed-bearing parts of various berries, forbs, fungi, and grasses. **See Apples/Crab Apple/Deciduous/Food/Frost/Grapes/Hardwoods/Mast/Oaks/Pawing/Pears/Persimmon.**

SOFTWOODS Any tree not considered a hardwood, such as most conifers, firs, pines, poplars, and so on. **See Cover/Forest/Hardwoods/Terrain.**

SOIL CONSERVATION SERVICE A county service, usually at or near the county seat, that can provide good quality aerial photographs, plat maps, and orthophotoquads. **See Aerial Photographs/Aerial Survey/Land Management/Orthophotoquads.**

SOLSTICES The longest and shortest day of the year. The summer solstice is the longest day of the year (June 22), while the winter solstice is the shortest day of the year (December 22). Interestingly, the timing of the whitetail's breeding season and its fawn dropping season correspond rather closely to these times of maximum and minimum daylight hours. Timing in breeding helps the perpetuate the whitetail as a species. Since a buck can only breed a few weeks out of the year (the rut), it is critical that fertile does are easily detected by him at that time. **See Autumnal Equinox/Equinox/Full Moon/Lunar Influence/Moon/New Moon/Winter Solstice.**

SOLUNAR TABLES A series of predictions as to when the rut will begin, peak, and reoccur. These tables are usually based upon the effects of the Sun, and movement and phases of the Moon, but are also tempered by weather conditions. (Dark, overcast skies appear to neutralize the moon's triggering effect, thereby delaying the onset of the rut.)

The Sun signals to deer that the breeding season is coming. The noticeable decrease in the amount of sunlight (photoperiodism) that enters a deer's eye triggers the pineal gland to react. This occurs at the autumn equinox (September 23) and starts the chemical, physical, and emotional changes in a deer's body.

The moon thus sets the date when the breeding cycle will actually occur. The bright light of the second full moon after the equinox and the darkness of the following new moon seem to trigger or synchronize the rut. **See Glands/Hunter's Moon/Moon/ Photoperiodism/Pineal Gland/Rut.**

SOUND SHOT Shooting at a noise. Deer hunters should be alert to every noise and sound that they hear in the whitetail woods. They owe it to themselves to attempt to identify and make some sense out of all that they hear. One of the cardinal rules of hunting is to first identify your target before you shoot. Firing a bow or a firearm at just a sound in the woods can only lead to a mishap. Never, never, shoot at a noise! The life you save may be another human being, even a family member. **See Buck Fever/Hunter Maladies.**

SOUNDS IN THE DEER WOODS Sounds in the woods that hunters should be aware of and use to thier advantage while hunting. The following sounds are some of the more common ones hunters should be familiar with.

    A. Antler Rattling. Rattling real or synthetic antlers, or antler bags, can bring a rutting buck to your gun or bow. Driven by his sexual urge, a buck will be attracted to the sounds of two other "bucks" fighting or sparring. Using artificial vocalizations, such as from a grunt tube, reality to the desired mental image that you are trying to create in the buck's mind. Adding estrus or dominant buck scent to the scenario often places the buck in the most advantageous spot for a clean shot, particularly for bowhunters. **See Antlers/Sparring.**

    B. Bird Alarm. Blue jays and crows are most raucous and noisy when they spot a intruder in their immediate area. Once the alarm has sounded, it is best to move on quietly or sit down, let the woods quiet down, and hope that the alarmist soon moves away.

C. Buck Walk. "Crunch, crunch, crunch"—pause—"crunch, crunch, crunch" is a very distinct sound that is easily identified as a buck walking but only after you have heard it several times. Be careful to learn the difference between this and a squirrel's scampering in the woods. Until you do, you will be fooled many times, although the heightened state of alertness keeps you ready for when a real buck comes. **See Gait/Trot.**

D. Foot Stomp. A deer will raise its front leg, then forcefully stomp it down on the ground, hoping to startle the suspected danger into moving and thus being identified. Other deer in the near vicinity will feel this stomp and become alerted also. In performing this stomp, the deer also deposits an alarm scent from the interdigital glands between its hooves onto the ground, which will forewarn any other passing deer that danger was identified at this spot. This sound may sometimes be accompanied by a deer snort call.

E. Doe/Fawn Walk. Usually more dainty than a buck, does and their fawns seem to glide through the woods. A mature doe can, however, walk very stiffly, announcing her presence and trying to get the source of her concern to move and identify itself. This sounds is similar to that of a foot stomp but with less instensity and the frequency of a stilted walking pace.

F. Squirrel Alarm. When disturbed, squirrels direct raucous barking and chattering at the source of their disturbance. This chattering often alerts other animals to the presence of danger.

G. Stand Noises. Squeaks, groans, metal-against-metal grating noises should all be eliminated before the stand is put up.

H. Water. Creeks will help mask the noise of a hunter's entry or exit. Whether you slowly and carefully walk in the creek or use a canoe to gain access to an isolated area, the sound of running water will cover any noice you make. **See Body Language/Calls/Contact Call/Ears/Noise/Portable Tree Stand/Stands.**

SOYBEANS A highly nutritious and desirable food for deer, planted by farmers as a cash crop. Deer often prefer this food source over other food sources like mast crops, when it is available. **See Crop Damage/Feeding Area/Fields/Food/Food Plot.**

SPARRING Also called "play fighting." During late summer and early fall, when their antlers have hardened, two bucks often engage their antlers and shove each other in a test for future position during the breeding period. Dominance is usually quickly established by the stronger or more fit of the two bucks. If both deer are evenly matched, a fight could break out. The deer scouter can also see "bush sparring," when an individual buck rakes a small sapling or brush in order to strengthen his neck muscles for future real sparring matches against another buck. Hunters can raise a young buck's curiosity by imitating bush sparring with a set of antlers. **See Agonistic Behavior/ Aggression/Alpha Buck/Bachelor Buck Groups/Dominance/Fighting/Flailing/ Hierarchy/Locking of Antlers.**

Sparring

SPIKE A buck deer with a single tine growing out of each pedicle. Spikes are often considered inferior animals, but in reality these small racks occur because of poor nutrition or late birth. See **Age of Deer/Alpha Buck/Bachelor Buck Groups/Dominance/Harvesting Spikes.**

SPINE SHOT A shot to the spine or backbone that runs along the top of a deer's back. The spine encases the main nerves or spinal cord that leads from the brain to the rest of the deer's body. Struck in the spine by a bullet or an arrow, a deer will usually drop immediately and be paralyzed below where the arrow or bullet hit. While

Spike

deadly, a spine shot is a low percentage shot to intentionally try for. See **Shot Placement/Wounded Game.**

SPLAY/SPLAYED A life-threatening situation that occurs when whitetails attempt to walk on ice and fall with their back legs spread out ("splayed"), thus tearing muscle, dislocating hips, and generally rendering the deer crippled. Deer do not recover from this catastrophic injury and become predator bait. See **Hind Legs/Predator.**

SPLAYED TRACK Tracks that spread out or are exceptionally wide, often associated with a heavy-bodied deer. See **Artiodactyla/Cloven Hooves/Dewclaws/Hoof/ Toes/Tracks/Trail.**

SPOOKED Alarmed, a deer's nervous reaction to an unidentified noise or sighting, usually resulting in flight or at the very least, a quick vacating of the immediate area. Once alarmed, a deer generally will head for its escape cover (a steep, wooded ridge; a thick stand of low pines, or cedar swamp, for example.) A buck will usually remember an area that he was alarmed in, and will not soon head back that way. After he has calmed down, he will probably be very cautious or wary of that area for some time. **See Adrenal Gland/Alarm Snort/Alert Snort/Escape Route/Fight or Flight/Flag/Flight/Foot Stomp/Head Bob/Instinct.**

SPOOR A track, trail, or any sign of an animal being pursued as game. For the whitetail, this could include hoof prints, dewclaw marks, upturned leaves characteristic of a trail, droppings, urination, blood trail, rubs, and scrapes. **See Deer Sign/Droppings/Fecal Droppings/Feet/Habitat/Hooves/Scat Tracks/Trail.**

SPORTSMANSHIP A term that entails many factors and meanings for ethical deer hunters. They exhibit a genuine respect for the wildlife they pursue. They view hunting as a personal challenge wherein they will follow the game laws to the letter. They respect the rights of a landowner and other hunters' stands or hunting areas. They abide by the expectations of fair chase, not engaging in deer jacking or using a vehicle to chase or drive deer. They do not cut or damage farmers' fences. They use the best equipment that they can afford, which helps to assure a clean, quick kill. They find their arrow and then doggedly pursue a wounded animal until it is recovered. All of the above and more constitute good sportsmanship by ethical deer hunters. **See Attitude/Blood Trailing Dogs/Deer Fence/Deer Search, Inc./Downed Deer/Ethics/Fair Chase/Follow-Up/Game Warden/Glassing/Guided Hunt/ Wounded Game.**

SPOTLIGHTING/SPOTTING Shining light into a deer's eyes at night to temporarily spellbind it. Poachers, unethical "horn hunters," and other nonsportsmen, will then shoot the deer between its glowing eyes, often taking the "trophy" antlers and leaving the carcass behind. **See Baiting/Ethics/Eyes/Game Warden/Glassing/Jack Lighting/Jacking/Poaching/Sportsmanship.**

SPOTTING SCOPE An optical device used for assessing target shot placement at the range or for locating a whitetail out in the wilds for stalking or even long-range shooting. **See Binoculars/Jacklighting/Poaching/Scope/spotlighting.**

SPREAD The width of antlers. Antlers can be visually measured against the width of the buck's ears (from tip to tip this distance averages fifteen inches). A rack exceeding that gauge is usually considered trophy size. The spread of a set of antler's is also a factor in several of the record book measures. **See Antlers/Boone and Crockett Club/ Genes/Green Score/Main Beam/Net Score/Nontypical/Pope & Young/ Rack/Scoring/Trophy/Typical.**

SPRING EQUINOX See **Vernal Equinox.**

STAG The great-antlered male of the white-tailed deer family of *Cervidae*, a buck deer. See **Antlers/Buck/Cervidae/Forkhorn/Spike/Trophy/Whitetail.**

STAGING AREA A section of deer travel routes just above a feeding area, where deer seem to gather to see what other deer are coming, who is already in the feeding area, and if any danger is present. Once satisfied that all is well, deer move out of the staging area and into the food plot. See **Back Tracking/Feeding Area/Habitat/Stand Placement/Terrain.**

STALKING Sometimes referred to as still-hunting, one of the most nerve-wracking, yet satisfying deer hunting tactics. It involves sneaking up on deer that you have previously spotted and getting close enough for a good clean shot. Stalking can be thought of as being part of a stillhunter's repertoire. It is most often associated with mule deer hunting but is not unheard of in hunting whitetails. From a ridge or other high vantage view point, without silhouetting yourself against the skyline, you thoroughly glass an area through good binoculars or a spotting scope, looking for deer. You may have to visit several ridges before you actually spot the deer that you want to stalk. Once you have chosen the trophy, you must carefully think out and plan your every move to place yourself in an advantageous position to shoot your nonalerted quarry. You absolutely must take into consideration the wind direction, your position, the deer's position, the lay of the terrain, and all available cover between you and the deer that you are stalking.

The ideal habitat for stalking deer is agricultural land where the vegetation is belt-high and thick (but not so thick that you cannot move through it quietly). The advantage of a human's erect spine over the deer's horizontal spine really pays off here. In a world of vertical objects (trees, brush, or corn), you look for deer by spotting their flat (horizontal) backs showing above and in contrast to the vegetation or their raised heads. The stalking hunter can constantly scan the habitat for deer, while the deer are relatively blind while their heads are down.

If you are stalking game during inclement weather and you begin to sweat, either stop and remove a few layers of clothing, or better yet, slow your pace by one-half so that you do not perspire and later get chilled. See **Clothing/Foul Weather/Inclement Weather/Layers/Optics/Snow/Still-Hunting/Weather.**

STAMP/STAMPING See **Foot Stomp.**

STANDS/STANDHUNTING/STAND PLACEMENT An apparatus used to hunt deer. The best time to standhunt is when deer are moving, usually just before sunset when the deer are traveling to their feeding areas or just before sunup as they travel to their bedding area. Other good opportunities are any time during the rut, when bucks are especially active all day, and during the firearms season when hunters keep deer running from cover to cover. Whether you use a tree stand or ladderstand, a ground blind, or just sit up against a tree, try to choose a spot that breaks up your silhouette yet offers you clear shooting lanes. The best option is to set your stand in the center of a single tree with three or more vertical trunks, or three to five trees closely adjacent to each other. Sit downwind of the deer with your back to the sun, which puts it in the deer's eyes, not yours.

After choosing a likely area to watch, the key to successful standhunting is being comfortable and staying put so that the deer comes to you. Be weight and noise conscious, but take along those extra items that will keep you comfortable on stand, for example, a hot thermos of tea, soup, or coffee (too aromatic for my personal likes); extra warm clothing, including socks and mittens; toilet paper and a capped urine bottle for scent control. Bring your lunch. It is widely believed that most hunters leave their stands too early and thus miss out on the deer that were coming in their direction. While you

Stand

stay put, others who are moving about to go for lunch or to take a noontime nap just might move deer in your direction.

Choose stand sites based on the nature of the terrain, deer entrance and exit routes, and wind conditions. Some hunters watch fields before the season starts and locate their desired quarry. After patterning their buck's entry and/or exit point, hunters return the next afternoon, follow the faint trail back into the woods, and set up a tree stand ten to twenty yards off the trail. The next huntable evening, hunters wait for their buck. If they see the buck elsewhere or on a different trail, the next afternoon they move the tree stand closer and then hunt. By repeating this procedure nightly, and of course not spooking the buck in the process, hunters can eventually home in on the buck's bed-to-feed route.

Hunting fifteen to twenty or more feet up a tree allows your scent stream to flow over the heads of most deer. It also puts you well above the deer's normal line of vision. A fundamental rule says to always set up downwind of where you expect deer to come from.

Getting into your desired hunting area without being seen, heard, or smelled is of optimal importance. You must consider how you will get to your stand in the pre-dawn darkness. It is best to be in your stand long before it is light enough to see and before any other hunter is out moving about. It is very advantageous to be in your stand, let the woods quiet down and return to normal, and then utilize those other hunters' entry into the area to drive the deer toward you. Consider a travel route that will be quiet and easy. Deer will not come around you if they know that you are there. However, once the woods fall silent again, any alerted deer will have forgotten that crunching of leaves or broken twig.

Going in, try not to cross any deer trails, as your scent will readily give your presence away. Using a small flashlight in the morning to guide your way in is generally okay. You should check with conservation officials as to its legality though. Putting a morning stand up in the darkness requires one to be as quiet as possible. The clanking of metal, the clinking of chains, could alert every deer in the feeding area below you. Even getting into your stand requires the utmost care and quiet.

Getting out of your morning stand also requires the utmost care and quiet. Most bowhunters get down too early, assuming that "Nothing else is coming through, so I might as well get some breakfast." During the rut, when a deer could appear at any time during the day, you should be prepared and equipped to stay all day in your stand. You cannot really stay too long!

You might even want to go in a week or two before the season during midday (wearing rubber boots and gloves so as not to leave your scent around) and quietly remove fallen branches, rake away leaves, and discreetly mark a trail. Just as important is when and how you leave your stand. Then, too, you must be quiet, and unnoticed and leave as little scent around you as possible. Try to place your stand where the deer will be out of sight not long after they pass. This will give you an opportunity to get down and sneak away from your stand without unduly alerting them to your presence.

Have available with you more tree steps than you think you will need. It pays not to cut yourself short here as they are useful for extra handholds on windy days or equipment holders. In placing the tree steps onto the tree, never place them so far apart that you will have to stretch between them. With heavier clothing and insulated boots, steps that were easy in the summer become more difficult to reach. Some of the new "climbing sticks" are worth looking at as some have shielded step guards and are easily attached to a tree. Be careful, though, because putting up two, three, or four sections of these climbing sticks can be noisy.

Always use your safety harness when climbing, sitting, standing, or descending to prevent an accidental fall. Get into it immediately and stay in it. If you slip it is better to have the safety harness catch you and hang awhile than it is to fall all the way to the ground and break a bone or even be killed. The following are some of the more commong types of stands.

A. Ground Blind. Hunters often place branches and brush or camouflaged mesh near a trail, water source, or scrape in hopes of ambushing a deer.

B. Ladder Stand. These are the least portable, heaviest stands, but they are very stable and comfortable. Placing the ladder stand so that the hunter's outline is concealed by branches allows for a very effective setup. Because of their stability, ladder stands are the ideal choice for older or disabled hunters.

C. Tree Stand. This stand puts you and your scent above the deer and generally offers a better view of the woods. Folding tree stands and most portable self-climbers are easiest to set up. Always check the nuts and bolts well before the season starts for cracks, stress, or wear and replace any worn parts. Permanent tree stands should be checked yearly for safety and broken or weakened parts. Don't forget to always use a safety harness while going up, staying in, and coming down a tree stand. **See Blind/Climbing Stand/Fall Restraining Device/Harness/ Permanent Stand/Portable Stand/Strap-On Stand/Tree Steps.**

STANDER/DRIVE STANDER One of the hunters stationed at the end of a deer drive that hopes to see a fleeing whitetail, trying to keep ahead of the hounds, drivers, or pushers. The waiting hunter may be located directly in front of or to the side of the drivers, thus attempting to seal off the whitetail's escape route. **See Drive/Escape Route/Hounds.**

START OF THE RUT Generally occurs around the second full moon after the autumnal equinox. It is a time when the bucks, already highly energized by testosterone, start to breed the does, who have just come into estrous. **See Equinox/False Rut/ First Rut/Hunter's Moon/Moon/Peak of Rut/Prerut/Rut/Rut Suppressants/ Testosterone.**

STARVATION Dying from lack of food. More deer die from starvation in winter than during any other season. When snow covers the ground for long periods of time, edible vegetation becomes increasingly difficult to find. As a survival technique, the whitetail lowers its metabolism during the winter by moving around less over its trails. When the deer herd grows too large for the food supply, starvation will inevitably pare out the weakest and the smallest. **See Browse/Carrying Capacity/Die-Off/Food Plot/ Habitat/Land Management/Nutrition/Overbrowse/Winterkill/Yarding.**

STATE LAND Public land, owned by the state, that is available for all residents to hunt on. **See Landowners/Permission to Hunt/Posted Signs/Public Land.**

STERNUM The "chest bone." The bottommost area of cartilage or bone connected to the ribs in a deer's chest. **See Field Dressing/Internal Organs.**

STICKER POINTS Also known as "drop points," these irregular antler points that grow or curve downward on a buck's rack. While impressive looking, they move the rack's score over into the nontypical ranking system. **See Boone and Crockett Club/Drop Tine/Genes/Green Score/Net Score/ Nontypical/Pope & Young/ Rack/Scoring/ Trophy/Typical.**

Sticker Points

STIFFEN UP The rigid seizing up of the body joints after a deer has been dead about an hour, rigor mortis. This term is often used in the debate by hunters as to how long one should wait after a shot, allow the deer to lie down and stiffen up, before going to get it. Suggestions range from twenty minutes to one hour. **See Field Dressing/Follow-Up/Rigor Mortis.**

STILL-HUNTING Sometimes referred to as "stalking," a technique that involves moving quietly through the woods in search of deer. It is called "still-hunting" because you spend most of your time standing still. It has often been said that you still-hunt ninety percent with your eyes, and ten percent with your feet. Still-hunters take several quiet steps and stop blending into the shadows between two or more trees, always breaking up their silhouette, and scan the area carefully for deer. Then, they use their binoculars to meticulously comb the area for antlers; a flick of the ear; the black, glassy orb of an eye; a white throat patch; or the horizontal tan or brown line of a deer's back in an otherwise vertical world. Finally, once they are convinced that no deer are in sight, they take several more, absolutely quiet steps into the next set of shadows, in order to gain a new viewing area. Still-hunters repeat this technique over and over again, not with the idea of covering as much ground as possible but rather to surprise and ambush a nonalerted deer within their view. Still-hunters must always be ready to take a quick yet accurate shot. That is the payoff for all their still-hunting efforts and patience. Going one on one with your quarry in its own backyard is a rewarding satisfying experience.

The best still-hunting conditions are those that allow hunters to move through the woods quietly, without spooking deer. After all, you must see it before it sees you or the opportunity to shoot an animal is lost. A wet forest floor, after a steady rain or covered by several inches of snow, makes for ideal still-hunting conditions. Here, patience is still a virtue! Wearing soft, quiet clothing, such as fleece and footwear that allows you to feel the ground beneath your feet so that you can avoid snapping branches or dislodging loose rocks, is definitely to the still-hunter's advantage. As with every hunting condition, always be aware of the direction of the wind. Quartering into the wind is always the hunter's best option. When a hunter quarters into the wind, the wind is angling toward to hunter, not from the face or back and not from either shoulder but at an angle in between. **See Drives/Push/Stalking/Stand Hunting/ Techniques.**

STOMACHS The four-chambered digestive system of the white-tailed deer. Its first stomach, or rumen, lies on top of the intestines and serves as a collecting compartment for food hurriedly gulped down and stored. It holds about two gallons of unchewed food. The deer can then leave for its bed, staying out of view of predators, and regurgitate this cud, thoroughly chew it, and then pass it on through the other chambers to complete the digestion process. **See Abomasum/Bezoar Stone/ Cud/Omasum/Regurgitate/Reticulum/Rumen/Ruminant/Ruminate.**

STOMP See Foot Stomp.

STORMS Severe, stormy weather. Deer, like humans, will seek shelter from storms. Gullies or conifer cover allow deer to avoid high winds or heavy, driving rain. A storm front moving into an area will cause deer to feed heavily before it arrives. After a heavy storm front has passed through an area, deer will be anxious to feed but will usually wait till the evening hours to feed, not necessarily feeding right after the storm has passed. **See Air Currents/Barometer/Foul Weather/Front/Hypothermia/Inclement Weather/ Prevailing Wind/Thermal/Warm Weather/Weather/Wind Chill.**

STRAP-ON STAND A type of portable tree stand that hunters can quickly attach to a tree for use at the immediate time of hunting. Its easy-on, easy-off nature allow hunters to change locations as needed. **See Fall Restraining Device/Harness/ Ladderstand/Permanent Stand/Portable Stand.**

STRESS Additional pressure for survival put upon the deer in times of low food supply, reduced territory, overcrowding, or predation. Usually the youngest and oldest deer are affected first by these increased pressures. **See Die-off/Hierarchy/Pre-dators/Winterkill.**

STRING LOOP An arrow-nocking device on a bowstring composed of a braided loop of bowstring or other material that a mechanical release attaches to. **See Archery Equipment/Nocking Loop/Nocking Point/Release.**

SUBORDINATE/SUBMISSIVE Ranking lower in the hierarchy, pecking order, or social order than another deer; having less dominance. **See Dominance/Hierarchy.**

SUBSISTENCE The means of existing, that is, the minimum amounts of food, water, and shelter that allow an organism to survive. **See Food/Food Plot/Nutrition/ Overbrowse.**

SUBSPECIES (White-tailed Deer) Seventeen subdivisions of the white-tailed deer species (family *Cervidae*, species *Odocoileus virginianus*) located within the United States and Canada. Subspecies have a third name after *Odocoileus virginianus* that describes the unique locale in which they live or physical adaptations or characteristics unique to the deer in that locale. **See Grand Slam of Deer/*Odocoileus virginianus*.**

SUDORIFEROUS GLAND Located in the spongy tissue of the buck's forehead, a gland used to mark or identify his licking branch and thus his scrape and even more, his dominance level. **See Dominance/Hierarchy/Overhanging Branch/Rut/ Scrape.**

SUMMER COAT The hair covering of an animal in summer. A whitetail's body is covered with two types of hair: (a) guard hairs that are shorter and of a reddish color during the warm months of the year, and (b) a fuzzy, wool-like inner-coat that is very light and serves to help radiate heat away from the deer's body. **See Albino/Bed/ Deerskin/Guard Hair/Hair/Pelage/Radiation/Winter Coat.**

SUMMER SOLSTICE The longest day of the year (June 20) in terms of sunlight. It is the time when the most minutes of daylight or sunshine occur. **See Equinox/ Photoperiodism/Solstice/Winter Solstice.**

SUNRISE/SUNUP The time just before the sun is beginning to peak over the hill and the shadows have not started moving up from the valley floor. Deer are often still in the feeding areas. During the hour or two of first light, they will start to move to their bedding areas in order to rest and ruminate or chew their cud. Early morning is an excellent time to ambush deer moving from their feeding to their bedding areas. **See Dawn/Dusk/Morning.**

SUNSET The time of day when the sun sinks below the horizon and thus goes out of sight. This is a particularly good time to observe whitetail movement as they are often approaching feeding areas with an increased feeling of security. **See Crepuscular/ Dawn/Dusk/Evening/Time of Day.**

SUPPLEMENTAL FEEDING A controversial technique of providing extra food for deer during scarce times, such as winter, deep snow, or overbrowsed conditions. **See Carrying Capacity/Food/Food Plot/Overbrowsed.**

SURROGATE MOTHER Not the "real" mother of a young animal, but rather one that has accepted the duties of motherhood (nursing, protection, cleaning, teaching) for a newborn mammal. **See Imprinting/Nursing.**

SURVIVAL Staying alive. Accidents can happen at any time and frequently do, especially during adverse weather conditions. The hunter's backpack should always include a water bottle, high-energy food, waterproof matches, a shank of rope, a flashlight and extra batteries, a space blanket, and a first-aid kit. **See Blaze Orange/ Compass/Fall Restraining Device/First Aid/Flashlight/Global Positioning Satellite/Harness/Hypothermia/Maps/Navigation/Orienteering/Safety/ Topographical Maps.**

SWALE A thick, brushy, impenetrable area, often a grassy depression, that bucks might hide in when pressured or heavily hunted. Deer prefer these locations because of the increased visibility needed for evading predators especially when the wind is blowing heavily. Hunters often pass them by because the deer are so well hidden in the brush. **See Cover/Edge/Swamp/Terrain/Thicket.**

SWAMP A wet, marshy area that provides an excellent sanctuary for pressured bucks. Because human hunters do not often penetrate very far into a wet, swampy area, bucks tend to grow both big and old there. Any approaching predator makes a splashing noise, thus alerting the buck of its presence. Often islands or raised areas exist within the swamp where bucks can find dry land, oak trees (acorns), and their desired security. **See Aquatic Vegetation/Cover/Ecotone/Edge/Swale/Terrain/Thicket/ Topographical Maps.**

Strong Swimmers

SWIM/SWIMMING To be able to propel through water. White-tailed deer swim very well. They do not hesitate to cross large rivers or lakes if they wish to get to the other side or to seek safety on a particular island. The extremely long and hollow nature of their winter guardhairs assists in keeping deer afloat. **See Creek/Guard Hairs/Island/Water.**

SYMMETRY The even or balanced spread of antlers in width, number of tines, and so on. **See Boone and Crockett Club/Browtine/G-1/G-2/ Main Beam/Net Score/Nontypical/ Pope & Young/Scoring/Spread/ Sticker Point/Typical.**

SYNTHETIC ANTLERS Used to rattle for bucks, artificial antlers often made of plastic, or resin, and tuned to sound like real antlers clashing together. **See Attractants/ Calls/Chase Phase/Communication/Prerut/Rattling/Rut/Tending.**

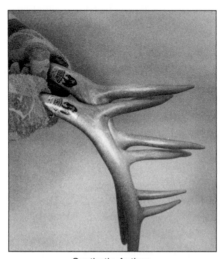

Synthetic Antlers

TAGGING/EAR TAG Placing coded metal, plastic, or fabric tags into the ear of a captured whitetail by placing a radio transmitter around its neck. Both allow biologists or deer researchers to relocate and identify that particular deer. State wildlife regulatory agencies often require successful hunters to place a "carcass tag" in the ear of their deceased quarry for regulation and transporting purposes. **See Doe Permit/Ethics/License/Sportsmanship.**

TAIL The distinctive feature that gives the whitetail its name. A whitetail's tail is approximately twelve inches long. When flared, it can be about ten inches wide and thus highly visible. **See Body Language/Communication/Flag/Flight/Tail Flicking.**

TAIL FLICKING A method deer use to communicate. Active deer trails are usually about a foot wide, places where many deer have traveled a route single file. By walking single file over these trails, deer communicate several messages to the other deer with them. Casual flicking of the tail lets other deer behind them know that all is well and no predators have been seen. However, when potential danger is spotted, the whitetail's body language changes. As the deer goes into an alert mode. Now, with head, ears and tail erect, the whitetail is communicating to all deer around it that something is potentially wrong. **See Body Language/Communication/Flag/Tail.**

TANNIC ACID Found in the bark of certain trees, a chemical useful for tanning deer hides. Tannic acid is also found in acorns. White oak acorns contain the smallest amount, thus making them the sweetest and most attractive to deer. **See Acorn/ Deerskin/Oak/Tanning.**

TANNING The preparing of an animal's hide and turning it into a useful leather. This process involves often removing the hair, then treating the hide with certain chemicals, e.g., deer brains, tannic acid, and urine. After treating and stretching to break down the stiff fibers within, the resultant buckskin becomes supple or softer and will not spoil as it would if not so treated. **See Deerskin/Tannic Acid.**

TAPETEUM LUCIDUM The back layer of a deer's eye. The glow or bright reflection one sees when shining a light into the eyes of deer is the reflection off this layer. **See Eyeshine/Jacklighting/Poaching/Retina/Vision.**

TARSAL GLANDS Glands located on the inside back legs of a white-tailed deer. The buck will urinate over these glands to deposit his unique scent into his scrape. Its odor is described as "pungent" and can often be smelled by hunters when a prerutting buck is near. When skinning your deer, be careful not to touch this gland. If this scent gets on the meat, the meat will taste like the gland smells. This is often one of the reasons

EXTERNAL WHITETAIL SCENT GLANDS

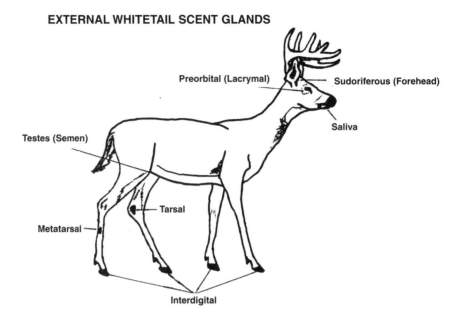

Preorbital (Lacrymal)

Sudoriferous (Forehead)

Saliva

Testes (Semen)

Tarsal

Metatarsal

Interdigital

nonvenison lovers describe the meat as having a gamey taste to it. **See Caping/Field Dressing/Follow-Up/Freshening/Glands/Musk/Nasal Gland/Scrape/Urine.**

TAXIDERMIST/TAXIDERMY One who makes a realistic mount of wildlife. Hunters sometimes take their trophy to a taxidermist to preserve the memory of the shot or a particular pose. **See Caping/Drying Period/Field Dressing/Mount/Scoring/Trophy.**

TEAR DUCT See Preorbital Glands.

TEATS The delivery portion of the udder of a nursing female that the newborn infant suckles from. **See Colostrum/Milk/Milk Teeth/Nursing/Singleton/Twins/Udder/Wean.**

TEETH Hard, bony structures used for chewing. An adult white-tailed deer has thirty teeth in its mouth. These teeth tend to wear down as deer age, because they eat sand and other abrasive materials as they forage. Deer biologists use the jaw bone and its teeth as a way to tentatively age a deer. The most accurate way is to take a tooth, slice it in half horizontally, and count the rings, just as in aging a tree. **See Age of Deer/Baby Teeth/Cementum/Incisors/Milk Teeth/Molars/Nursing.**

Teeth

TEMPERATURE The measurement in degrees of the outside air as measured by a thermometer. It should be noted that the best temperature for hanging and aging venison is between thirty-four to thirty-eight degrees fahrenheit. **See Aging Meat/Ambient Temperature/Barometer/Foul Weather/Hypothermia/ Inclement Weather/Layering/Weather.**

TENDERLOINS The most highly prized cut of venison meat. Tenderloins are located on the top and inside of the body cavity, running along the outside of the spine. Other venison cuts include roasts, chops, steaks, shanks, sausage, deer/hamburger, and stew meat. **See Back Straps/Field Dressing/Gamey Taste/Jerky/Recipes/Venison.**

TENDING/TENDING A DOE A buck staying with a doe until she accepts him. Just prior to the doe becoming receptive to breeding, she is emits estrous odors which the buck identifies through flehmen or lip-curling. He will defend his access to this doe, exercising his dominance and breeding rights, and chasing off and fighting if necessary any buck that attempts to breed her. **See Breeding/Chase Phase/Estrus/Late Rut/Prerut/ Primary Rut/Tending/Testosterone.**

TENDING GRUNT The unique guttural (piglike) sound a buck makes as he jealously guards the estrous doe that he is currently with. Other bucks, hearing these grunts, are attracted to the immediate area, with the idea of stealing the ready-to-breed doe. Hunters sometimes imitate this call as a means to attract bucks to their stand site. **See Body Language/Chase Phase/Communication/Grunt/Grunt Call/Prerut/ Rattling/Rut/Sounds in the Deer Woods/Vocalization.**

TENDON A tough cord or band of dense, cream-colored fibrous connective tissue that unites a muscle with some other part of the body and transmits the force the muscle exerts. It is sometimes referred to as sinew. **See Gambrel/Hanging Meat.**

TERRAIN Natural land formations. Deer are generally creatures of habit. They choose certain travel routes year after year, taking the easiest path and avoiding sheer embankments, deep ravines and so on.

Either an inside or outside corner, where fields intersect with fencerows or tree lines, are nearly always sure bets for finding a hub of intersecting trails. Deer naturally funnel around these natural and man-made obstacles when traveling from bedding areas to feeding areas and vice versa.

Thick, new growth is the cover that big bucks often seek out and need for security. They did not get to be a mature, breeding monarch of the woods by openly showing themselves and advertising their presence from easily seen vantage points.

Low saddles, often found near creek bottoms where ridges and gullies converge can be a nightmare of swirling air currents. They are difficult to effectively hunt.

Hunting a river or a major creek from a boat or a canoe can be a rewarding experience. The beauty of floating in a stream is that you are likely to observe serene and unalarmed deer at close range. Whitetails are not used to having danger approach by water. The best time to float hunt is during the first and last couple of hours of daylight, since these are the periods when the bucks are most likely to be moving. **See Bench/Draw/Edge/Fields/Funnel/Gully/Hollows/Ravine/Ridge/Saddle/ Topographical Maps.**

TERRITORY An area that a white-tailed deer has claimed as its home range. A doe giving birth to her fawns stakes a birthing area and will not let other deer intrude upon it. Bucks claim their own core area for breeding purposes and will challenge any intruder. Considerable overlap exists in territories of whitetails and no one area is absolutely exclusive. **See Core Area/Dispersal/Home Range.**

TERRITORIAL SCRAPE See Secondary Scrape.

TESTES/TESTICLES The male reproductive organs that produce the sperm needed for conception and testosterone, the male hormone that starts the whole reproductive or breeding sequence. Following the rut, the testosterone production in a buck's testes decreases and the buck goes through a drastic physiological, hormonal, and demeanor change. He becomes less aggressive toward other bucks. **See Adrenal Gland/ Castration/Cactus Buck/Hypogonadism/Hypogonadism/Impotence/Penis/ Pineal Gland/Scrotum/Testosterone.**

TESTOSTERONE The male sex hormone that is produced in the testes. This important hormone is produced prolifically during the late fall and early winter, peaking at the height of the rut. Immediately following the rut, the buck's testosterone level falls dramatically to its lowest annual level. The antler bases dissolve and are shed, but the pedicles will soon start a new growth period. So the relative lack of testosterone in late winter and early spring initiates antler formation in bucks, but its increased production in late summer and early fall increases Rutting activity after the antlers harden, stop growing and lose their velvet. **See Adrenal Glands/Agonistic Behavior/ Aggression/Alpha Buck/Breeding/Chase Phase/Prerut/Post-Rut/Rut/Rut Suppressants/Testes.**

THERMALS Rising or falling air currents that occur naturally in the morning, during the day, and at evening hours. They are generated by the difference in temperature between two areas of elevation. A hunter should always be conscious of the wind's direction, its strength, and any sudden changes, especially during mornings and evenings.

    A. Mornings. Wind in the predawn hours usually indicates a change in weather is coming through. Warm air rises, creating an uphill flow of air as the sun warms the hilltops, pulling up the open air from the valley below. Rising thermals can take your scent and keep it above a deer's nose. Thus, hunting at dawn means placing your stand above the area where you expect to see deer.

    B. Evenings. A noticeable lack of wind or wind dying off at sunset forewarns of a changing barometer. Evening air currents tend to flow downhill. As the

THERMAL AIR CURRENTS: Stand Placement & Scent Control

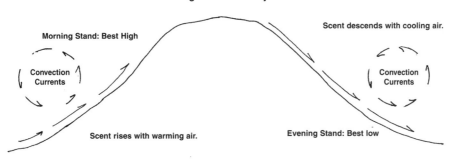

Air currents rise or fall as the temperature
changes on a calm day.

Morning Stand: Best High

Scent descends with cooling air.

Convection Currents

Convection Currents

Scent rises with warming air.

Evening Stand: Best low

Mornings: Warmed air rises, running uphill.

Evenings: Cooling air descends, moving downhill.

Thermal Air Currents

sun denies its heat to the valley below, cooler air sinks. Thermals tend to hug the ground and spread your scent to all below you. **See Air Currents/ Barometer/Convection Current/Downwind/Prevailing Winds/Scent/Storms/ Upwind/Wind.**

THERMOREGULATION Meeting the needs for body heat by adjusting (e.g., slowing down) the metabolic rate through lessening internal energy consumption, that is, burning fat reserves previously built up during the summer and early fall. The more fat reserves a whitetail has going into the winter months, the better its chances of surviving against cold and lean food resources. **See Basal Metabolic Rate/ Beds/Conduction/Hair/Radiation/Winterkill.**

THICKET Heavy cover, overgrown areas that provide security to whitetails. **See Cover/Edge/Habitat/Security/Swale/Terrain.**

THINSULATE Windproof, insulating material used in gloves, boots, and clothing for warmth with low bulk. This insulation material is claimed to be twice as warm as down and other polyester insulations of equal thickness. It is soft, extremely breathable, and comfortable. Unlike other insulating materials that lose heat-retaining efficiency when wet, Thinsulate is claimed to absorb less than one percent of its weight in water, which translates to retaining more body heat under soggy conditions. **See Camouflage/Clothing/Foul Weather/Inclement Weather/Gore-tex/Layering/Weather.**

THROAT The front part of the neck. In the white-tailed deer, it is generally covered by a white patch under the head. Internally, it harbors the windpipe or trachea, the esophagus, and the larynx. **See Caping/Esophagus/Field Dressing/Wind Pipe.**

TICKS/DEER TICK/DOG TICK/WOOD TICK Six-legged, blood-sucking insect that attaches itself to deer as a parasite. The black-legged or deer tick is difficult to see as it is no bigger than a poppy seed. It is this tick that transmits Lyme disease to its host. The wood tick is much larger than the deer tick, with white markings near its head. Ticks feed from April to October. It is strongly recommended that you tuck your pant legs into your socks and wear a long-sleeved, but light-colored shirt while in the woods at this time of year. Upon leaving the woods, a thorough examination of your body is also strongly recommended.

Once discovered, ticks can be removed with tweezers, a commercial tick removal instrument, or as a last resort, with your fingers by grasping the tick as close to its mouth parts (as close to the skin as possible) and pulling steadily and firmly until the tick lets go. Breaking its body off and leaving its head imbedded still makes you vulnerable to Lyme disease. Wash the bite area and apply an antiseptic. **See Arthropod/Hunting Maladies/Hygiene/Lyme Disease/Parasites.**

TIMBERLINE The upper limit of tree growth on mountains or at high elevations beyond which only shrubs and ground cover grows. Whitetails are usually not found above the timberline at high elevations. **See Cover/Security/Terrain/Travel Corridor.**

TINES The points on a whitetail buck's antlers, rising off of its main beam. Usually tines over an inch long are counted when measuring antler mass and/or length. **See Antlers/Beam/Bifurcate/Boone and Crockett Club/Brow Tine/Cheater Points/Drop Tine/Main Beam/Points/Pope & Young/Rack.**

TOES The four chitinous, hard projections coming out of a deer's lower leg. Usually only the bottom two touch the ground. **See Artiodactyla/Dewclaws/Hooves/Splayed Track/Tracks.**

TOPOGRAPHICAL MAPS Also called "topo" maps. Maps that show hunters the elevation changes, streams, watering holes, contours, flats, mountains, and ravines on the land that they hunt. Hunters may order topographical maps of any area from:

> **United States Geological Service Map Sales**
> **Box 25286**
> **Denver, CO 80225**
> **(303) 236-7477**

See Aerial Photographs/Bureau of Land Management/Compass/Contour Lines/Funnel/Navigation/Orienteering/Orthophotoquad/Scouting/United States Geological Service.

TOWER BLIND An elevated deer stand, popular in the western states, that allows hunters to see and position themselves above the ground brush and thus be more able to see deer movement. **See Blind/Stands/Tree Stand/Tripod.**

TRACKS/TRACKING Deer footprints, perhaps the easiest and most abundant deer sign to find, particularly along the edge of plowed fields, sandy creek bottoms, or muddy logging roads. These heart-shaped tracks are usually two and one-half to three inches long for adults. The deer's hind hooves are generally smaller than its front hooves. When walking, the hind hooves usually cover up the front hooves marks. A whitetail's walking stride is eighteen to nineteen inches, while its trotting gait (ten to twelve miles per hour) can be thirty to thirty-six inches. Examining the tracks of a running deer shows that the back or rearward tracks are those of the front hooves. One can distinguish a relatively fresh or recently made track because it has sharp, defined edges while an old track has a vague outline, usually from having been rained on, wind eroded, or walked on.

JUDGING A FRESH TRACK

Frost crystals in track mean an old track

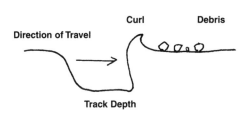

Track Depth

Clear, crisp edges means a fresh track

While it is extremely difficult for the average hunter to differentiate between a buck track or a doe print, there are usually some clues. For example, does and small bucks tend to lift their legs higher and leave tracks that point in a straight line. Should hunters be lucky enough to follow deer tracks in the snow long enough to come across a place where the deer urinated, they should be able to differentiate the sex of the trailed deer. Tracks of a doe will show where she hunched her legs together and urinated in a wide outward spray. Bucks do not hunch up but rather urinate straight downward, leaving a narrow pattern. Snow will also show the buck's drippings as he starts walking again. the rutting buck that urinates on his tarsal glands (located on the inside of his rear legs) also often leaves drippings of urine as he moves away from his scrape.

Large, deep tracks showing dewclaws are made by older, thus heavier deer. These may, but it is not guaranteed, have been made by a mature buck. With the advantage of a light coating of snow on the ground, the presence of long, narrow drag marks between tracks is a good indicator of a buck's having made those tracks. During the rut, mature bucks tend to walk with a stiff-legged gait, resulting in a track showing drag marks and outward arcing of their legs. This hoofprint pointed outward is caused by the increased width of the buck's neck and front body plus the greater amount of weight being placed onto his front legs. **See Backtracking/ Beds/Blood Trail/Dewclaws/Cloven Hoof/Deer Run/Doubling Back/Drag Marks/Follow-Up/ Splayed Track/Travel Route.**

TRAIL Narrow, defined lanes; usually devoid of vegetation, because of the frequency of their use by multiple deer. As deer move about their daily routines, particularly traveling from feeding to bedding areas, and vice versa, eluding danger, or checking scrapes, they feel more secure if they do so along a network of deer paths or trails. Any deer trail could change over the season as a particular food item becomes less available and another food source becomes the preferred choice.

Trail in Snow

Following a well-used trail backwards will often lead the hunter or off-season scouter to the current feeding areas (usually the trail leads downhill) or to the bedding areas (usually uphill). Along these trails will be evidence of other deer sign, such as rubs, scrapes, and droppings. Deer expend less energy by following established trails than when breaking in new ones, particularly in deep winter snow. **See Backtrail/Bench/Corridor/Deer Run/Doubling Back/Splayed Track/Tail-Flicking/Terrain/Tracking/Travel Corridor.**

TRAIL CAMERA A photographic device use to record on film animals that have used the trail or area being monitored. It can be tripped by a variety of means, such as infrared, motion or a tripwire. These devices take pictures at a set interval (e.g., every three seconds) as established by the owner. **See Night Vision/Trail/Travel Corridor.**

TRAJECTORY The pathway of a projectile, whether fired from a bow or firearm. It originates from the source, sometimes rising above that level, and then immediately begins dropping to its ultimate destination. **See Accuracy/Line of Sight/Shot Placement.**

TRANSITION ZONE Deer habitat areas that are edges where one type of vegetation or topography gives way to another (e.g., fencerows, power lines, funnels, fields, draws, thickets). **See Aerial Photographs/Cover/Ecotone/Edge/Escape Cover/Security (Deer)/Terrain/Topographical Maps/Travel Corridor.**

TRAP AND TRANSFER   A method used to reduce whitetail numbers that often involves nets, tranquilizer darts, and sometimes sterilization. Unless done by professionals who are trying to replenish a depleted resource (whitetails) in a new area, this method of herd reduction can result in stress-induced death of captured deer. **See Carrying Capacity/Contraception/Herd Size/Immunocontraception/Overbrowse.**

TRAUMA An injury or wound to living tissue that causes severe bleeding, shock, and excessive stress. leading to disorientation and ultimately death. **See Bleed/Hemorr-haging/Shot Placement/Wounded Game.**

TRAVEL CORRIDOR/TRAVEL ROUTE Paths between the bedding and feeding areas. Stands placed overlooking these routes provide the best opportunity to tag a buck traveling back to his bedding area in the morning or to the feeding area in the evening. Hunters can create travel corridors and funnel spots. For example, in thickly overgrown swamps, hunters can trim away narrow travel routes through the very thick cover between bodies of water or they can cut narrow pathways through thick cover on a hillside. If done in the off-season, deer quickly take over these paths, allowing the standhunter to get close to these deer. **See Bench/Core Area/Corridor/Cover/ Deer Run/Doubling Back/Security/Stand Placement/Terrain/Topographical Maps/Tracks/Trails.**

Tree Stand

TREE STANDS A device used for hunting whitetails from above. The golden rule of tree stand placement is to locate it in an area that is likely to attract bucks by providing something that they need, such as food, security, or sex (i.e., does). The tree stand should be fifteen to twenty feet in the air, in order to stay above the deer's line of sight (deer do look up), and to keep your scent flow above their noses. **See Fall Restraining Device/Harness/Ladder Stand/Permanent Stand/Portable Stand/ Safety/Stands/Tree Steps.**

TREE STEPS A variety of devices for hunters to place on or into a tree, which allow them to climb the tree, and/or get into a tree stand. They can be screw-ins, strap-ons, removables, hinged, or stiff. **See Equipment/Fall Restraining Device/Harness/Ladder Stand/Noise/Permanent Stand/Portable Stand/Safety/Stands.**

TRESPASSING The illegal act of being on someone else's property without permission. When the area is posted with warning signs, trespassing becomes a legal means of defending a property owner's rights of privacy and ownership. **See Ethics/Landown-ership/Poaching/Posted Signs/Sportsmanship.**

TRIMMING The selective cutting away of vegetation, saplings, or trees so that the hunter has a better shot placement area for approaching deer. **See Shooting Lanes.**

TRIPLETS Three infants born together. Triplets are rarer than twins and often stretches the maternal abilities of a doe. **See Fawn/Nursing/Twins/Udder/Umbilical Cord.**

TRIPOD A three-legged deer stand that provides hunters with an elevated view of the landscape. It is often used where trees are unavailable. **See Blind/Camouflage/ Ladderstand/Stand/Tower Blind/Tree Stand.**

TROPHY/TROPHY RACK An outstanding rack of antlers. Maturity of age, good genetics, and nutritious food all contribute to bringing the best rack out of a buck. The very best sets of antlers will be grown on bucks that are five and a half to seven and a half years old. Unfortunately, most bucks are shot as yearlings (one and a half years). Bucks with the genes for producing good antlers must become the dominant breeding buck in order to pass those trophy genes on to new offspring. In addition, food with a high protein content and lots of minerals (calcium, phosphorous, and so on) must be present in the soil in order for the antlers to produce their maximum growth. **See Alpha Buck/ Antlers/Boone and Crockett Club/Green Score/Hierarchy/Mass/Net Score/ Nontypical/Pope & Young/Typical/Wallhanger.**

TROPHY HUNT Specifically pursuing the largest and best specimens of game in a hunting area. **See Deer Fence/Ethics/Fair Chase/Grand Slam of Deer/Guided Hunt/Guides/High Fence Hunting/Managed Hunt/Outfitters/Poaching/ Quality Deer Management.**

Trophy Rack

TROT A gait in which a deer holds both its head and tail up, while waving its flag from side to side. **See Flag/Gait/Gallop/Walk.**

TUFT OF HAIR One of the first observed signs or indication of a "hit" on your deer, whether by an arrow or a bullet. This loose grouping of deer hair is usually found lying on the ground but could be found resting on a shrub or bush. Responsible hunters will not assume that this was just a close shave for the deer, but rather that they have mortally wounded the deer. They will follow-up, trailing their quarry. **See Follow-Up.**

TURKEY CALLS Sounds of the wild turkey mimicked by hunters. Whitetails live and share in the same environment as wild turkeys. They are accustomed to seeing them and hearing their sounds. The many alert eyes of a flock of turkeys help deer watch for disturbances in their world. Savvy hunters often take a diaphragm or mouth call with them so as to emit the calm, reassuring social calls of the wild turkey. They hope to convince any nearby deer that all is well for them too. **See Acorns/Leaves/ Pawings/Sounds in the Deer Woods.**

TWINS Two infants born together. Does giving birth for the first time generally have only one fawn. Thereafter, twins are the rule, and occasionally even triplets are produced. **See Afterbirth/Birth/Fawn/Gestation/Nursing/Singleton/Triplets/ Udder/Wean.**

TWO-WAY RADIOS Usually small, hand-held Citizens Band radios of limited range that outdoor enthusiasts use to keep in touch with each other while afield. Hunters use them to warn their partners of approaching deer, ask for assistance in trailing a wounded deer, and so on. **See Accessories/Communication/Equipment/Radios.**

TYPICAL (ANTLERS) A scoring category for antler spread, tine lengths, and score evaluation, as opposed to nontypical. Symmetry and near-even distribution of points is expected for this category for ranking purposes. **See Antlers/Boone and Crockett Club/Browtine/G-1/G-2/Genetics/Mass/Net Score/Nontypical/Pope & Young/Scoring.**

Typical Rack

UDDER The milk bag or female mammary gland of a nursing mother that the newborn mammal suckles from. As with dairy cattle, the udder of a whitetail doe is located on the underside of her body, between her hind legs. **See Colostrum/Fawn/ Milk/Nursing/Teats/Twins/Wean.**

ULTRAVIOLET LIGHT (UV) The range of light beyond a human's visible spectrum, comprised of wave lengths shorter than visible light and longer than x-rays. Biologists contend that many animals, including the whitetail deer, see ultraviolet radiation and are thus able to pick out human movement and/or clothing as "glowing" objects. This has sparked hunters to buy non-ultraviolet clothing and reduce usage of ultraviolet-enhanced dyes in laundry detergents. **See Eyes/Vision.**

UMBILICAL CORD An organ connecting the developing fetus to the mother's uterus that supplies needed nutrients from her bloodstream and passes back to the mother the fetus's waste components. It is expelled after the fetus is born and often eaten by the doe so it won't draw attention to the newborn. **See Afterbirth/Placenta/Uterus.**

UNDERSTORY/UNDERGROWTH The area beneath the branches and leaves of a wood lot, at ground level. After an area has been cleared, the early succession of forbs, grasses, and brush provide lush forage for whitetails as they wander through their wooded domain. As the forest canopy begins to completely shade the forest floor, a succession of shade-loving plants takes over, such as ferns, and mushrooms. **See Canopy/Nutrition/Overbrowse.**

UNGULATES Any hoofed mammals, such as swine, horses, and ruminants, including the white-tailed deer, that walk on their hard, chitinous toenails. **See Artiodactyla/ Dewclaws/Hoof/Splayed Hoof/Tracks.**

UNITED STATES FOREST SERVICE (USFS) The US government bureau that has dominion over vast amounts of public-owned lands, mostly in the western states. Its maps are of first rate quality and are available to hunters. **See Aerial Photographs/Bureau of Land Management/Maps/Navigation/Orienteering/Scouting/Survival/Topographical Maps/United States Geological Service.**

UNITED STATES GEOLOGICAL SERVICE (USGS) The US agency responsible for highly accurate topographical maps offered in two styles: (a) 7.5 minute scale or (b) 15 minute scale, which shows the same general area, only four times larger. **See Aerial Photographs/Bureau of Land Management/Contour Lines/Maps/Navigation/Orthophotoquad/Scouting/Topographical Maps/United States Forest Service.**

UPWIND An ideal hunting condition when the wind is blowing from the deer toward the hunter. Any hunter scent that is on the air currents will travel away from the deer. Since deer try to always travel with the wind in their noses, they will not smell the hunter. Hunters have actually reported being able to smell the musky odor of deer that are upwind of them. In essence, the hunter is "downwind" of the deer. **See Air Currents/Crosswind/Downwind/Prevailing Wind/Thermals/Wind.**

Urination

URINE The liquid waste from an animal's digestive processes. For white-tailed deer it is useful in identifying its owner, leaving an estrus trail for a buck to follow a doe or checking the breeding status of a doe. Urine if often found near a deer's bed. Urine directly in the bed is from a buck; a doe will spray it off to the side or back, out of her bedding area. Bucks will dribble urine over their hocks or tarsal glands and deposit their individual scents into a scrape, thus advertising their dominance for breeding purposes. Likewise, a buck will follow a doe in estrus, stop where she urinates, inhale some of this urine into a chamber located in his nose and determine if she is ready to be bred. **See Breeding Status/Estrus/ Flehmen/Freshening/Hocks/Nasal Gland/Nose/Prerut/Rub Urination/Scent Checking/Scrape.**

ULTRAVIOLET LIGHT(UV) Deer have more cone receptors in their eyes than humans do so they are able to see better during low-light conditions. Deer's eyes also do not have a UV filter, which blocks out ultraviolet light, as human eyes do. Ultraviolet light helps deer to see better at dusk and before dawn. Ultraviolet light is the glow we observe when a black light is shone on our clothing. Most laundry detergents brag about their ability to "brighten clothes." Hunters in a tree stand or ground blind do not want to stand out as a bright blue glow to deer. Be sure to wash all your clothing in "UV-free" detergent. **See Blaze Orange/Clothing/Color Blind/Eyes/Fluorescent Orange/Light Patterns/Retina/Rod Cells/Vision.**

USFS See United States Forest Service.

USGS See United States Geological Service.

UTERUS The female reproductive organ that holds the fetus after fertilization by the male's sperm. The umbilical cord connects the fetus to the mother's uterus so that nutrients can be passed to the fetus and waste products removed. **See Afterbirth/ Breeding/Gestation Period/Placenta.**

UV LIGHT See Ultraviolet Light.

VANES See Feathers.

VANTAGE POINT An elevated position or a concealed point where hunters can observe wildlife and not be seen by them. Wearing camouflage and sitting in an elevated tree stand or ladder stand gives hunters an advantage over their quarry. **See Ladder Stand/Shooting Lane/Tree Stand/Trimming.**

VELOCITY/MUZZLE VELOCITY The speed at which a bullet leaves the barrel of a firearm. **See Ammunition/Bore/Caliber/Firearm/Foot Pounds of Energy/Knock Down Power.**

VELVET The soft, fuzzy, "velvety" covering on growing antlers, which is made up of many nerves and blood vessels and feels warm to the touch because of the many blood vessels flowing through it near its surface. Velvet is the only self-regenerating skin found among mammals. The cartilage-like antlers growing under this capillary-rich outerskin are some of the fastest growing tissue in the animal world. Full hardening (i.e., filling in with calcium and other minerals) of a buck's antlers is followed by the shedding of this velvety covering.

Shedding Velvet

By fall, nerve impulses and blood supply to the velvet are gradually cut off. The velvet starts to crack and feels itchy to the buck. The buck will feel an impulse to rake its antlers against brush and small saplings. This helps peel the velvet off. The buck will often eat strips of velvet for their nutritional value. A buck can breed soon after he sheds his velvet. However, it is generally several weeks before the does come into estrus. This becomes a sexually frustrating time for bucks. The doe population determines the onset and timing of the rut, and, to some degree, its intensity. **See Adrenal Gland/Antlers/Buck/Fawn/Forehead Gland/Ossification/Pedicle/Rub/ Testes/Testosterone.**

VENISON The meat of a white-tailed deer consumed as human food. When prepared properly, venison is "fit for a king" and was often claimed and valued as the king's personal property in olden times. Care must be taken to properly handle and prepare venison from the initial field dressing through butchering and packaging to actual preparation for consumption. Venison cuts include roasts, chops, steaks, shanks, sausage, deer hamburger, and stew meat. **See Aging Meat/Back Straps/Fat/Field Dressing/ Gamey Taste/Hanging Meat/Jerky/Recipes/Tenderloins.**

VENTED PORTS Cuts made into a gun barrel by an experienced gunsmith that allow for the side emission of projective gases when shooting a cartridge. The positioning of the vents helps keep the barrel from rising and/or recoiling in an excessive manner, thus reducing inaccuracy. **See Barrel/Guns/Handguns/Rifle/Shotgun.**

VERNAL EQUINOX The spring equinox, falling about March 21 of every year, when the equal number of daylight hours and nighttime hours is equal. **See Autumn Equinox/ Equinox/Lunar Influence/Solstice.**

VIBRISSAE The collective name for the long whiskers or hairs that members of the deer family have around their eyes, chin, and mouth. Being nocturnal, deer often feed at night and these whiskers tell the deer just how close they are to the ground when feeding on a moonless (new moon) night. **See Cervidae/Nocturnal.**

VISCERA The internal organs of an animal that relate directly to its survival, such as the heart, lungs, stomach, kidneys, liver, intestines, and all interconnecting tissues and supporting components. **See Field Dress/Guts/Organs.**

VISION An animal's sight. A deer is an animal of prey. A deer's eyes do not face directly forward as a predator's do. Its eyes are located on the side of its head in order to see any possible rush of movement by a predator toward it. A deer's eyes have evolved to be extremely attuned to the slightest movement that would betray a predator's presence. To shoot a nonalerted animal, hunters should wait until the deer is looking the other way or has its head behind a tree before reaching for their bow or gun to get into shooting position.

A whitetail's eyes are large compared to the size of its body. This means that it has a large surface area for its retina. This inside, light-sensitive area of the eye is composed mostly of rods, which detect motion and work best in dim light. Deer do not see a wide range of color because they have a lower number of cones in their eyes' retina. It is believed that deer do see some color, specifically in the yellow-blue ranges. We know that they do not see reds and oranges as distinct colors but rather as hues of gray. Deer are also very sensitive to ultraviolet (UV) light. Hunters should not clean their hunting clothes in "UV-enhanced" detergents, as these brighteners, which humans like to see, are a red flag of danger to deer. **See Binocular Vision/Blaze Orange/Color Blind/Eye Contact/Light Pattern/Movement/Outline/Rod Cells/Silhouette/Skylined.**

VISUAL CLOSURE A physiological and psychological phenomenon that causes a hunter, because of excitement and extreme desire, to see a deer where none really exists. Also known as "early blur," it can account for hunters mistaking bird hunters or other deer hunters for deer and then shooting at them. There is no excuse for this type of behavior because one of the cardinal rules for a hunter is, always be sure of your target! **See Early Blur/Hunting Maladies.**

VITAL AREA A zone just behind a buck's shoulder that encircles his most important organs: his heart and lungs. A well-placed shot here usually brings the buck down within a short distance. **See Accuracy/One Shot Kill/Shot Placement/Wounded Game.**

VITAL ORGAN AREA

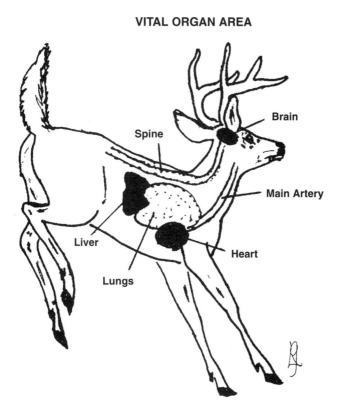

VOCALIZATION Vocal communications. Although deer cannot talk like humans can, deer do send out vocal communications. Their communications usually revolve around the search for food, signaling danger, doe-fawn affection, peer group play, dominance display and the sexual drive between a dominant buck and estrous doe. Some biologists and hunters have affirmed that deer possess about a dozen different sounds. Deer biologists compartmentalize these twelve calls into the following categories.

Alarm or Distress Calls

A. Snort. Emitted singly or in a series mainly by does when they detect danger. It is the most widely heard and recognized sound of a white-tailed deer.

B. Bawl. Produced when deer are extremely distressed or traumatized. Deer bawl generally only when grasped or injured. Other than nursing does, most deer flee in response to hearing a bawl.

Agonistic or Combative Calls

A. Low Grunt. Low guttural sound used when dominant animals of either sex attempt to displace or move a subordinate. If the subordinate deer does not respond appropriately, the dominant deer escalates the situation with a foreleg kick for emphasis.

B. Grunt-Snort. Emitted during intense dominance interactions by bucks during the breeding season. This call consists of the grunt, plus one to four rapid snorts.

C. Grunt-Snort-Wheeze. Emitted during intense combat. This call is a strong, drawn-out exhalation added to the grunt-snort. It is the most forceful combative vocalization issued by the buck.

Maternal-Neonatal Sounds

A. Maternal Grunt. Used by does as they enter the fawn's bedding area and when she searches for her hidden fawn.

B. Mew. High-pitched, low-intensity sound emitted by a fawn indicating its need for some maternal care.

C. Bleat. Constant and demanding care call emitted by a fawn for the doe's attention. Bleats are often heard when a fawn is disturbed. The nursing doe rushes in to investigate the source of the disturbance.

D. Nursing Whine. Repeated nursing or suckling sound given off by a fawn as it nurses or searches for the doe's nipple.

Mating Calls

A. Tending Grunt. Emitted by bucks during courtship of an estrous doe. This call is attractive to other males who would rather breed her themselves.

B. Flehmen-Sniff. Sound made infrequently when a buck is performing flehmen or "lip curl," while checking a estrous doe's urine for her readiness to breed.

Contact Call. Also called a "social call" and used by does when separated from their group. It apparently enables the does to maintain contact with one another when visual contact is lost.

See Alarm Posture/Alarm Snort/Body Language/Calls/Communication/ Contact Call/Ears/Grunts/Sounds in the Deer Woods/Tending Grunt.

VULVA The exposed female genitalia, or sexual parts, used for breeding. The doe usually raises her tail when she is ready to accept a buck to mate with her. This action exposes her vulva to the buck for penetration by his penis. **See Breeding/ Copulation/Ejaculation/Estrus/Penis/Rut.**

WALK/WALKING A gait. A whitetail's walk can range from slowly taking a step and nibbling the next morsel to taking determined multisteps in one direction. Its tail flicks back and forth to shoo flies or to signal its position to whichever deer is following it. When walking, white-tailed deer generally place their hind hooves into the track of the front hoof. Thus, a hoof print that you see is usually the imprint of a hind hoof stepping on top of and covering up the track of a front hoof. **See Cloven Hooves/Flag/Gait/Gallop/Hooves/Sounds/Tracks/Trot.**

Walking Doe

WALK 'N' STALK A hunting technique when hunters take two or three silent steps, then spend three times as long standing still and looking for deer before taking the next few steps. Felt overboots are ideal to muffle your steps.

Wallhanger

WALLHANGER An antler or head mount. It could be a hunter's first buck deer or one with antlers of considerable size or unusual spread. What is an average rack to one hunter may be trophy size to another. As the old adage goes, "Beauty is in the eye of the beholder!" **See Alpha Buck/Boone and Crockett Club/Dominance/Mount/Net Score/Nontypical/Pope & Young/Rack/Scoring/Shed/Trophy/Typical.**

WANING MOON After the full moon, any decreasing phase, but particularly the third quarter, until the new moon. **See Full Moon/Lunar Cycles/Lunar Influence/Harvest Moon/Hunter's Moon/Moon/New Moon/Rut/Waxing Moon.**

WARDEN **See Game Warden.**

WARINESS Being on guard, cautious, looking for danger. **See Eyes/Sixth Sense/Vision.**

WARM WEATHER Any temperature higher than the ideal comfort level for the whitetail or the hunter. In the Northern Hemisphere, if the temperature gets too warm when the whitetails have growth their winter coats, deer will move as little as possible, stay in the shade, and travel only at night in an effort to stay comfortable. **See Air Currents/Ambient Temperature/Barometer/Fronts/Guard Hairs/Hypothermia/Temperature/Thermal/Wind.**

WATCHER/STANDER/POSTER In a deer drive, one or more members placed at strategic points to intercept the deer being pushed ahead of the drivers. The job of the watcher is to be quiet, remain vigilant, and shoot the deer that are flushed out to them. **See Drive/Push/Stand/Stander.**

WATER A vital element for deer, like any mammal. Deer need to drink water, and usually do so at least once a day. Knowing their source of water could play to the hunter's advantage. Whitetails are excellent swimmers. They do not hesitate to jump into a river, lake, or pond to avoid a predator, including a hunter. All too often, hunters think of water as an obstacle to deer when, in fact, deer will often utilize a ditch, stream, river, pond or lake as an escape route. Deer traveling in water can also be a warning device of moving deer to the hunter. Likewise, savvy hunters can use water to cover their trail, that is, not leave a scent trail as they approach their stand. **See Aquatic Vegetation/Creek Bottom/Island/Noise/Swamp.**

WATERPROOF/WATER-RESISTANT Terms with two distinct meanings. "Waterproof" means that something does not let any water pass through it, whereas "water resistant" means the material will shed or repel water for a while, but persistent or hard-driving rain will cause the wearer to get wet. Needless to say, waterproof material is better than material that is only water- or moisture-resistant. **See Equipment/Pacs/Poncho/Rain Gear.**

WAXING MOON After the new moon, any increasing phase of the Moon's face, until the full moon phase is reached. **See Full Moon/Harvest Moon/Hunter's Moon/Lunar Cycles/Lunar Influence/Moon/New Moon/Waning Moon.**

WEAN/WEANING The act of removing a young mammal from dependency upon its mother's milk for sustenance. In whitetails, this process typically begins at two months of age and is usually complete after four months, when the fawn can subsist on vegetation alone. The doe is then free to begin the accumulation of fat for winter survival. **See Colostrum/Fawn/Food/Nursing/Nutrition/Singleton/Teats/Twins/Udder.**

WEATHER Conditions that are one of the prime factors that affect deer movement and hunter success. Uncomfortable weather patterns make deer behave in predictable ways. Really bothersome weather makes them congregate in specific places. The wise hunter takes advantage of being able to read the weather and how it affects whitetails. The following is a general summary of weather conditions, whitetails' reactions, and how hunters should adjust their tactics:

    A. Fog. Both fog and rain represent one hundred percent humidity in the air. Fog appears as visible, low-hanging, ground-hugging clouds, whereas rain is condensing water vapor that has begun to fall. These conditions often encourage deer to eat because the increase in moisture seems to enhance the smell and taste of their natural foods. Just as a buck can more easily scent a doe in heat or discover a hunter's scent when there is increased moisture in the air, deer are able to more easily smell food under these conditions.

B. Light Rain. Periods of drizzles and sprinkles are excellent times to hang stands, stalk or still-hunt, or even just sit in your favorite tree stand. The rain tends to wash away any scent that you left or are emitting.

C. Heavy Rain. Deer often react to downpours just as humans do. Coupled with wind or cold temperatures, deer tend to seek places of protection—usually thick, canopied cover such as pine forests.

D. Low Temperatures. When the first real cold temperatures hit, whitetails move to seek relief from that sudden change. Although their winter coats allow them to sleep while well insulated in the snow, they often gravitate to thick stands of pine, cedar, spruce, hemlock, or balsam, where the closed forest canopy can provide some retained warmth and resistance to the wind. In hilly country, whitetails often head for hilltops or ridges where they can bed down at night under north-facing timber. They will move along that ridge or bench during the daytime toward the south-facing slope, where the sun provides radiant warmth. This energy-saving tactic is often used by the whitetail. **See Ambient Temperature.**

E. Snow. Snow can be a blessing or a problem for hunters. All of us wish for a light snow during deer season. New-fallen snow muffles movement, and deer leave tracks showing where they have traveled. During a severe snowstorm, deer usually stay in the same heavy cover that they seek out for heavy rains. If a storm lasts a long time, deer will often be on the move for food as soon as the storm appears to be letting up. A heavy build up of snow seems to hinder deer movement. This is a good time to discover the trails that whitetails are using, because these trails will be packed down by regular use. Deer also tend to use travel corridors, particularly under forest canopies where the snow accumulation has not amounted to much. In particularly heavy snow country, deer will actually "yard up," staying in one special area, depleting the food supply, creating a highly noticeable browse line, and often not leaving the safety of that deer yard, even if other food sources are nearby. This behavior is still a mystery to deer biologists. **See Snow/Yard.**

F. Wind. Moving air is always a source of concern for whitetails, and they seem to let it govern their daily routines. Because cold air is heavy and falls and warm air is lighter and thus rises, deer tend to move to higher ground in the morning in order to bed down because the thermals are still flowing downhill. Likewise, in the evenings, deer will move to lower elevations because the wind is moving uphill. Deer seem to always try to face into the wind so that they can scent any danger ahead of them. On particularly warm days, deer will even seek out a shady tree or bush on a hillside or ridge, just to take advantage of any cooling effects of the wind.

On stormy days, when the prevailing winds are blowing strong and steady, deer will spend most of their time bedded on the leeward (away from the wind) side of a slope or behind an uprooted tree root or even in a ravine. Gusty, shifting winds are irritating and nerve-wracking for deer. These ever-changing breezes make it impossible for deer to get a true picture of the scents and sounds surrounding them. Hence, they will not stay put for long. In high wind, deer get nervous and without the benefit of two of their senses, smell and hearing, they will move to new cover, stay for a while, and then seek out a newer haven. They are relying mostly on their sense of vision for safety. It seems that they must move around just to check on the security of the area. These conditions are a golden opportunity, if the hunter realizes just how nervous the deer get and that they will be on the move. Here is the time to take a stand and wait for skittish deer to move by you. **See Air Currents/Movement/Prevailing Wind/Thermals/Wind Chill.**

G. Clouds. Visibly lowering cloud cover is usually a sign of impending precipitation. Distant sounds will also appear louder because the sound actually reflects off the low-hanging clouds, dispersing outward, not upward.

H. Before a Storm. Whitetails increase their activity when barometer levels are low or falling. They easily detect changes in atmospheric pressure, and associate them with approaching storm fronts. Deer often feed heavily during approaching storms, because they do not know when they will be able to eat next. Nasty weather or an approaching storm front will often prompt deer to start feeding earlier than usual (e.g., late afternoon). Really nasty weather will usually keep deer in the heaviest cover that they can find for the entire day. Under these conditions, a group of hunters may have to resort to a drive just to locate deer. **See Barometer/Cross Wind/Foul Weather/Fronts/Frost/Hypothermia/Inclement Weather/Nocturnal/Pressure/Temperature/Thermals/Wind.**

WEB SITE See Whitetail Web Sites.

WEIGHT OF DEER A deer's size. The average white-tailed deer weighs about 120 pounds. Bucks generally grow bigger and weigh more than does. Mature, breeding bucks will often experience extensive weight loss because of their rutting activities of chasing estrous does, chasing away interloper bucks, and actual fighting. Some published scientific reports have stated that an actively breeding buck will lose up to twenty percent of his body weight during the rut. **See Bergmann's Rule/Body Weight/Dressed Weight/Field Dressed/Trophy.**

WESTERN COUNT A method for counting antler points used west of the Mississippi River. Points are counted on only one side of a buck's antlers (usually the highest side). **See Boone and Crockett Club/Eastern Count/Points/Pope & Young/Rack/Spread.**

WHEELS Part of a compound bow. Wheels are usually slower than cams; however, they are also less noisy. The choice of wheels over cams is strictly up to the bowhunter. **See Archery/Equipment.**

WHISTLES/WHISTLING Sounds made to contact other hunters, often during a deer drive. **See Calls/Communication/Radios/Sounds in the Deer Woods.**

White-tailed Buck

WHITE-TAILED DEER *Odocoileus virginianus,* a species of deer. In North and Central America, there are thirty subspecies of white-tailed deer. North America alone has seventeen subspecies. In the Northern Hemisphere, whitetails range from the equator to sixty degrees north latitude (the southern Canadian provinces) and from the East Coast through Kansas, Oklahoma, and Texas. The white-tailed deer appears to be continuing its expansion to the west, once the separate domain of the mule deer. **See** *Odocoileus virginianus/*Subspecies.

WHITETAIL INSTITUTE OF NORTH AMERICA Publishers of *Whitetail News.* a magazine for the field testers of certain whitetail food plot seeds, such as Imperial Whitetail Clover and Alpha Rack. Once you purchase seeds from the institute, you become a "field tester" and receive the magazine and reminders to purchase your food plot seed from them.

WHITETAIL MAGAZINES Publications dedicated to deer hunting. Most serious hunters subscribe to one or more magazines, enabling them to stay current with some of the latest techniques and equipment for deer hunting. The following are strictly my personal choices for reading, listed in order of preference:

Deer & Deer Hunting
Krause Publications, Inc.
700 E. State Street
Iola, WI 54990-0001

Whitetail Hunting Strategies
Harris Publications, Inc.
1115 Broadway
New York, NY 10010

North American Whitetail
Primedia Enthusiast Group
2250 Newmarket Parkway, Suite 110
Marietta, GA 30067

Buckmasters Whitetail Magazine
Circulation Department
P.O. Box 244022
Montgomery, AL 36124

Rack Magazine
Circulation Department
P.O. Box 244022
Montgomery, AL 36124

Whitetail Magazine

Whitetail Journal
Vulcan Press
2100 Riverchase Center, Suite 118
Birmingham, AL 35244

Petersen's Bowhunting
Circulation Department
P.O. Box 54217
Boulder, CO 80322-4217

See White-tailed Deer Organizations/Whitetail Web Sites.

WHITE-TAILED DEER ORGANIZATIONS Organizations that focus on the white-tailed deer. The effective deer hunter should at least be aware of, if not a member of, one or more of the following:

Boone and Crockett Club
250 Station Drive
Missoula, MT 59801
406-542-1888

Pope & Young Club
P.O. Box 548
Chatfield, MN 55924
507-867-4144

Quality Deer Management Association
P.O. Box 227
Watkinsville, CA 30677

Safari Club International
501 2nd Street NE
Washington, DC 20002
202-543-8733

Whitetails Unlimited
1715 Rhode Island Street
Sturgeon Bay, WI 54235
800-274-5471

W

Whitetail Institute of North America
239 Whitetail Trail
Pintala, AL 36043
800-688-3030

WHITETAILS UNLIMITED   An organization founded to instruct the public on the importance of the study and sound management of white-tailed deer. It publishes a member magazine entitled *Deer Stand*.

WHITETAIL WEB SITES   The following are interesting computer Web sites that deer hunters may wish to explore:

Boone and Crockett Club	www.boone-crockett.org
Buckmasters magazine	www.buckmasters.com
Deer and Deer Hunting magazine	www.deeranddeerhunting.com
Department of Natural Resources	www.dnrlistings.com
Federal Wildlife Service	www.fws.gov
Hunting Net, Inc.	www.huntingnet.com
Hunting Links	www.huntinglinks.com
Orbimage: High Resolution Imaging	www.terraserver.com
Pope and Young Club	www.pope-young.org
Quality Deer Management Association	www.qdma.com
Rack magazine	www.rackmag.com
United States Geographic Service	www.usgs.gov
Whitetails Unlimited	www.whitetailsunlimited.org
Wildlife Research Center	www.wildlife.com

Wild Turkey

WILD TURKEY The largest bird in North America. The wild turkey easily co-exists with the white-tailed deer in woodlands and agricultural fields. Deer are not threatened by the presence of turkeys and even seem to appreciate or rely upon their separate and most often many sets of eyes as a hedge against predators. A hunter duplicating the sounds of turkeys in the woods, such as clucks, yelps, sounds of leaf scratching for acorns, will often put a wary whitetail at ease. **See Sounds in the Deer Woods/ Turkey.**

WIND Air movement. Wind can be hunters' friend or their worst enemy. Although it has betrayed many hunters, the wind, if paid attention to and utilized properly, can be hunters' ally. A high, steady wind can conceal hunters' scent, cover any noise they make while moving through the woods, and even mask some movement when objects are being blown around in the woods.

Always place your stand downwind from where you expect deer to appear. You can do everything right in terms of suppressing your own scent, but if you do not take account of the wind, all your efforts can easily be destroyed. Generally, the more moisture is airborne in the morning hours than in the late afternoon (the wind and sun help dry the air during the daytime). Scent lingers longer in the morning because of the morning dampness. A slight wind is advantageous because it helps carry away any lingering scent from hunters, so it doesn't congregate around their stands and potentially spook nearby deer. To see wind direction and plan for scent control, many hunters tie a short piece of string onto their bow stabilizer; some attach a light, wispy feather to the string; others use milkweed seeds cast to the wind; still others puff scent-free talcum powder. Use these techniques to check for any swirling convection currents that could betray your presence. **See Air Currents/Barometer/ Convection Current/Cross Wind/Downwind/Nor'easter/Prevailing Winds/ Thermals/Upwind/Wind Chill/Zephyr.**

WIND CHILL (FACTOR) The effect of wind as it compounds cold temperatures. In essence, the wind is pulling more heat away from the body and making hunters feel colder. Wind chill makes it more difficult to stay on stand as the temperature seems lower than it really is. Prudent hunters should always be aware of the wind chill factor and be prepared to address it by layering their clothing with fleece, wool, quality thermal underwear, and a wind-blocking jacket. **See Air Currents/Clothes/Foul Weather/Hypothermia/Inclement Weather/Layers/Nor'easter/Survival/ Weather/Wind.**

WINDPIPE The ribbed tube inside a whitetail's throat that runs down into the lungs. This internal part is one of the first to spoil and possibly taint the venison. It is recommended to remove this windpipe as far up into the throat as possible. **See Esophagus/Field Dressing/Internal Organs/Throat.**

WINTER COAT Special hair types grown for cold temperatures. Mammals that live in the great outdoors, such as the white-tailed deer, generally have two types of hair for covering their skin during the coldest time of the year: (a) the long and usually hollow guard hairs that give their winter coats a somewhat shaggy look, and (b) a soft, fuzzy layer of insulating undercoat. It is estimated by biologists that a whitetail's winter coat possesses over 2500 guard hairs per square inch, thus giving it a great insulating potential. In fact, whitetails have been observed sleeping in the dead of winter with snow piled up on their backs. Likewise, a whitetail's winter bed will have very little snow melted underneath it. It will be compressed due to the deer's weight, but not melted. **See Conduction/Guard Hair/Pelage/Radiation/Summer Coat/ Undercoat.**

WINTER FEEDING/SUPPLEMENTAL FEEDING Food provided by humans during winter. A debate arises every winter as to whether supplemental feeding of whitetails is a good idea. "Do-gooders" who begin to feed whitetails corn, alfalfa, or hay but do not keep it up through the whole winter and even past green up have naively caused many a deer to later starve to death. Likewise, whitetails have been found dead with stomachs full of the wrong type of supplemental food. Researchers tell us that this occurs when normal digestive bacteria are no longer in the deer's stomach but have been replaced because they have switched to browse (e.g., buds, sapling tips), which requires a different set of bacteria for digestion. **See Basal Metabolic Rate/ Browseline/Die-Off/Food/Forage/Habitat/Metabolism/Overbrowse/Stress/ Winterkill.**

WINTER HOME RANGE Usually about one tenth of a deer's summer range. Deer also yard up during times of deep snow and severe cold, often depleting the available food supply in that area. It has been observed that once in a yarding situation, deer will not leave it, even if adequate food is only a short distance away. **See Habitat/Home Range/Winterkill/Yard.**

Buck in its winter home range

WINTERKILL/WINTER DIE-OFF A sharp population decline in winter. Deer are highly dependent upon the amount of food that they can find—the carrying capacity of the land. If too many deer are concentrated in an area that exceeds its carrying capacity, and thus food is scarce, a hard winter with deep snow can produce a massive die-off that will cut the herd back severely. **See Balance of Nature/Balanced Herd/Carrying Capacity/Die-Off/Habitat/Overbrowse/Predators/Yard.**

WINTER SOLSTICE The shortest day (hours of daylight) of the year, usually December 23. Its shortness is due to the Earth being tilted away from the Sun, thus receiving less direct sunlight. Once the solstice is past, the minutes of daylight once again grow longer as the Earth begins turning back toward the Sun's direct rays. **See Equinox/Solstice/Summer Solstice.**

WOLF A member of the canine family, often referred to as a gray wolf or timber wolf. The wolf is one of the major predators of the white-tailed deer, usually working in packs of related family members to surround, overwhelm, and bring down an adult deer, even a buck. **See Canine/Carrion/Coyote/Die-Off/Dogs/Feral Dogs/Fox/ Predator/Prey/Winterkill.**

WOOD LOT Any heavily treed area, which can vary widely in size. It is often a favored hiding spot for the white-tailed deer **See Blowdown/Browse Line/Core Area/Cover/Edge/Security/Staging Area/Travel Corridor.**

WOODSMANSHIP Those specific skills needed and used by the outdoorsperson (deer hunter) to read signs, track game, actually locate and observe deer, field dress their quarry, and the whole host of other skills that complement the shooting of a whitetail. **See Deer Sign/Ethics/Sportsmanship/Tracking/Wounded Game.**

Wool Clothing

WOOL/WOOL CLOTHING As hunters have known for centuries, the quietest and warmest fabric (even when wet) to protect the hunter against adverse weather. **See Clothing/Foul Weather/Inclement Weather/Layers.**

WORKING A SCRAPE A buck's pawing the ground, usually under an overhanging branch, as he clears the forest floor debris away and then urinates over his tarsal glands into the scrape, thus freshening his scent in the scrape. He will rework this scrape again, as often as it needs it, in order to keep his scent and breeding status advertised to any receptive doe and to warn away any subordinate buck. That last goal is seldom achieved as several bucks have been known to work the same scrape. **See Freshen/ Hock/Overhanging Branch/Scrape/Tarsal Gland.**

Working a Scrape

WOUNDED GAME Game that has been shot but not mortally shot. Wounded deer will bolt out of the immediate area, then slow down, and head for an area of thick cover. If they can still move, after a while their loss of blood will drive them to seek water, to replenish their body fluid loss.

If you shoot at a deer and it immediately falls down dead, you are doing everything right! However, be cautioned that a supposedly "dead" deer may only be stunned or wounded and could get up at any time and run away. It may also suddenly flail its sharp hooves or antlers and attack you as you approach it. Remember, it has been suddenly hurt and is now fearful. Its survival instincts are now being activated. Fight or flight is the only question on its mind.

Approach any downed deer from behind, out of the way of its hooves or antlers. Prodding the deer on its buttocks with an arrow, the barrel of your gun, or a stick and then touching its open eyeball—again from some distance with a long object—will either cause the deer to react or prove to you that it is really dead. A floundering deer should be immediately and humanely dispatched with a second or, if necessary, a third shot. Do not to let the animal suffer. Wounded deer are typically sick and unwilling to flee as a healthy animal would. You often can get very close to this animal.

When trailing a wounded deer, always assume that you will need to deliver a fatal shot. Never leave your gun or bow back at the stand site. Always take it with you. Do not ever think about trying to dispatch a wounded deer with just your knife. That is a good way for you to get hurt, or even killed.

Listed below are the various body areas often hit on a deer and the deer's likely reaction:

A. Heart Shot. Usually bursts into frantic, headlong dash, sometimes preceded by a high leap. (A word of caution: A high leap could also indicate a creased chest shot.)

B. Lung Shot. Usually induces a slight haunch just before a burst of panicked sprinting. However, it is possible, especially with a sharp, cut-upon-impact broadhead slicing through this area, that the deer will not react at all, not even realizing that it has been hit. If you see no reaction, do not assume that you missed, especially if all other signs tell you that the hit was a good one.

C. Paunch Shot. Commonly referred to as a "gut shot" because the deer has been hit in the stomach or intestinal area. The deer may not run at all or may run only a short distance and then start walking painfully again. The deer is mortally wounded and will die, although it may take days as it sickens, weakens, and finally painfully succumbs to death. A paunch shot should never be purposely taken by the hunter. If it does accidentally occur, the hunter should wait at least three hours before he/she takes up the gut-shot deer's trail, rather than continue to push it mercilessly. When field dressing the gut or paunch shot deer, hunters will often find green, slimy stomach contents, and digestive juices in the body cavity of the deer. A paunch or gut shot deer should have its body cavity rinsed out with clean water as soon as possible so that the meat is not tainted or contaminated.

D. Head Shot. May cause an animal to go down immediately and appear dead. Although it is not common with archery equipment, such animals have been known to suddenly "recover their senses" and jump up to escape. The flailing hooves and/or antlers could inflict injury upon the unwary hunter. Never, never assume a deer is dead after the first shot. Rather, approach it from behind. Use an arrow, a stick, or even your gun barrel, and prod the deer, in order to see if it is genuinely dead.

E. High-Spine Shot. Usually causes the deer to go down immediately. Often, though with its back broken, the deer will try to crawl away using its front legs. This is accompanied by bawling or what sounds like vocal agonies. A merciful, fatal follow-up shot to the chest is most appropriate.

F. Chest Shot. Usually produces a solid, meaty "thump" on impact, like a ripe pumpkin being whacked by a stick. Once heard, you will never forget the sound.

G. Leg Shot. Usually sends a deer fleeing at breakneck speed, with little or no indication of a hit. Most deer can get along well on three legs and show little or no limp.

H. Bone Hits. Usually leg, shoulder, or hip shots sound like a loud "crack," rather like a home run being hit in baseball. The bow hunter may also hear the shattering of the aluminum arrow upon impact.

Wounded animals generally do not have any idea of your presence, or you would not have gotten an opportunity to shoot at them. Hard-hunted animals will run harder and farther, but most will not associate the sound or pain of your shot with humans. By keeping calm and not immediately showing yourself, a wounded deer will probably not travel past its initial run. **See After the Shot/Blood Trail/Downed Deer/ Ethics/Exit Wound/Follow-Up/Going Away Shot/Hair/One Shot Kill/Shot Placement/Tracking.**

X,Y,Z

YARD/YARDING Protective dense conifer cover where deer seek shelter in winter in order to minimize body heat loss and to reduce the threat from predators. Yarding occurs when mounting snow depths cover nutritious foods, impair travel and temperatures plummet. This shelter-seeking tendency by whitetails throughout their northern range is an evolutionary technique designed for survival. **See Browseline/Carrying Capacity/Die-Off/Food/Foul Weather/Home Range/ Predation/Security/Survival/Wind/Winterkill.**

Yarding Up

YEARLING BUCK A one-and-a-half-year-old (eighteen months) male deer, usually experiencing his first set of antlers. A yearling spike buck, if he is genetically inferior or if food is limited in quality or quantity, is limited in the size of rack that he will produce. The yearling buck will move (in the dispersal) about five miles from his family's core area, establishing a new home range but often one that overlaps another buck's home range. He may have to be subservient until he has gained enough strength to challenge the "Boss Buck" for breeding rights. **See Age of Deer/Antlers/Buck/Button Buck/Core Area/Dispersal/Dominance/Hierarchy/Home Range/Spike.**

YOUNG, ART An early archer, who, along with his partner, Saxton Pope, helped establish many of the standards we use today in bowhunting the white-tailed deer. His name, along with Pope's, is used in the title of the Pope & Young Club, which keeps bowhunting records of annual trophy kills. **See Fred Bear/Boone and Crockett Club/Saxton Pope/Pope & Young Club.**

ZEPHYR A breeze from the west, a west wind. This gentle breeze is often noticed while sitting in the quiet zone of a deer hunting stand. **See Air Currents/ Barometer/Convection Current/Cross Wind/Downwind/Prevailing Winds/ Thermals/Upwind/Wind/Wind Chill.**

ZEROING IN/ZERO POINT The precise adjustment of a firearm's scope or sights so that the firearm is extremely accurate and consistent in its shot placement. **See Accuracy/Benchrest/Bipod/Grouping/Shooting Sticks/Shot Placement/ Sighting In.**

ZOONOSIS The scientific term for any disease that humans can get from exposure to animals. **See Anthrax/Lyme Disease/Rabies/Rocky Mountain Spotted Fever/ Scavenger/Ticks.**

ZOOPHAGOUS The act of feeding on animals, whether from finding carrion, road-kill, or winterkill or through predation. **See Bears/Carnivore/Carrion/Cougar/ Coyote/Predator/Prey/Roadkill/Winterkill/Wolf.**